MY USUAL TABLE

MY USUAL TABLE

A Life in Restaurants

COLMAN ANDREWS

ecco

An Imprint of HarperCollinsPublishers

HarperCollins books may be purchased for educational, business, or sales promotional use. For information please e-mail the Special Markets Department at SPsales@harpercollins.com.

FIRST EDITION

Designed by Suet Yee Chong
Title page photography by Andrey Bayda/Shutterstock, Inc.

Library of Congress Cataloging-in-Publication Data has been applied for.

ISBN 978-0-06-213647-3

14 15 16 17 18   OV/RRD   10 9 8 7 6 5 4 3 2 1

For Joan Luther (1928–2011),
who knew restaurants better than anyone

La tavola è mezza confessione.

—Tuscan proverb

CONTENTS

THE BOOK THAT FOLLOWS IS FULL OF DETAILS ABOUT what I ate and drank, how restaurants and other places looked, and what people said and did at various points in my life, even when I'm recounting events that took place more than half a century ago. In summoning up these particulars, I've relied in part, of course, on that seductive trickster, memory, but memory has been greatly aided by the fact that, at least since my latter teens, I've taken notes. I have thousands of pages—on lined school paper, yellow legal tablets, sheets of "bloc-notes" bound in Rhodia orange; in typescripts banged out on my old Adler manual or my Selectric II—full of observations, descriptions, bits of conversation, menus, and more, and then, of course, thousands of computer files, holding everything from e-mails to interview notes to assorted recollections, published and unpublished. For one stretch in the 1970s, I even kept extensive journals of my own, eventually filling half a dozen hardbound notebooks with something close to 250,000 words about every aspect of my life over that period. A big box of deliberately unorganized photographs, some dating back almost three-quarters of a century, and a basement shelf of cartons containing four or five decades' worth of restaurant menus from both coasts of America and six or eight European countries helped me fill in some of the blanks.

I referred to a handful of books, as well, to verify facts or refresh recollections, among them *A Corner of Chicago*, a memoir by my late father, Robert Hardy Andrews; *A Taste of Hollywood* by Patrick Terrail; *Chasen's: Where Hollywood Dined* and *Hollywood du Jour: Lost Recipes of Hollywood Haunts* by Betty Goodwin; *Burgundy* by Eunice Fried; and several editions of the *Guide GaultMillau*, the *Los Angeles Restaurant Guide* by Lois Dwan, and my own Southern California restaurant guides under several titles. Of course, I also depended heavily, as one does these days, on our indispensable if sometimes vexing friend Mr. Internet—more than once discovering that the cited source for something I was looking up was one of my own old articles. Among the friends and acquaintances who answered questions of various kinds were Karen Miller, Gordana Sipovac, Julie Stone, Barbara Berg, Eunice Fried, Kerry Heffernan, Jean-Pierre Silva, Judith Sonntag, and Becky Wasserman. (My agent, Michael Psaltis, offered sound editorial advice, as always. Dan Halpern saw merit in the idea for this memoir and commissioned me to write it; Libby Edelson fine-tuned the manuscript.)

Any factual errors, misinterpretations, unfair characterizations, concatenations of events, and other deviations from the way things really were is, of course, my own doing, deliberately or not. In any case, as John Ruskin once proposed in a different context, "The errors of affection are better than the accuracies of apathy."

Introduction

I'm walking down the street in an unfamiliar city. It's dark, a little chilly, a little past most people's dinnertime. The stores are closed. A few cars prowl by, and a delivery van idles at the curb, but there's almost no one on the sidewalks—just a woman in gym clothes walking a dog, say, and maybe a couple of late workers crossing from their office building to the parking garage. I round a corner, heading vaguely back to my hotel, and catch the faint scent of grilled meat in the air. I haven't eaten, and it draws me like the aroma of an apple pie cooling on a windowsill used to draw young miscreants in old cartoons. I keep walking, following my nose, until I see, at the end of the next block, an inviting low-slung building with a big red door and a row of half-curtained windows through which a warm glow seeps. As I get closer, a smiling couple comes out of the place, and for a few seconds, before the door eases shut, I hear from inside a familiar din—the clatter of plates and glasses, the hum of conversation. I walk straight to the door and step inside. A willowy young woman in her twenties—or maybe it's a stocky, well-dressed gentleman thirty years her senior—greets me, reassures me that the kitchen is still open, and shows me into the dining room. I sit down, unfurl the napkin, order a Hendrick's martini—very cold, please, with a twist—and pick up the menu with as much agreeable anticipation as a crime-novel buff opening the latest Michael Connelly. I'm perfectly content, and for a very good reason: Even though I've never been here before, I'm at home.

I GREW UP IN RESTAURANTS. I don't mean that my parents owned or ran them—my father was a Hollywood screenwriter, my mother a onetime ingenue turned housewife and society dame—but they practically lived in restaurants themselves, and when they went out to eat, they often took me with them. Some of my earliest memories are of perching on a booster seat in a red or green leather booth at a table covered in thick white napery and crowded with silverware and glasses, and being waited on and fed and plied with Shirley Temples and told to sit up straight. I can still summon up a sensory impression of those evenings, romanticized, of course, and with the particulars of each occasion blurred hopelessly together, but vivid nonetheless: the ceaseless motion all around me, a choreography of waiters and busboys, arriving and departing guests; the reassuring clamor that suggested room-wide concord and contentment; the aromas intertwining in the air—cigarette smoke, Sterno, sizzling meat, coffee, the iodine-scented whisky in my father's glass, the floral sweetness of my mother's best perfume. It all washed over me, and never really went away.

At far too young an age, I'm sure, I fell in love with restaurants, and it was that love that ultimately led me to where I am today. My entrée, if you'll pardon the expression, into the world of what I later would call gastronomy came through the dining room, not the kitchen. I liked the food, certainly, but I also liked the ritual, the folderol, the whole experience—the way a place looked and felt, the friendliness and efficiency of the staff, the variety of choice, even the little sensory accents: the heft of the water glass, the dancing light of the table candle, the luxurious sensation of wiping greasy fingers on soft linen.

Eventually, almost accidentally, I found a way to turn my love for restaurants into a career—into, really, a way of life. When I first started to think seriously about that way of life and where it had taken me, it occurred to me not just that restaurants have been a constant for me but also that at virtually every stage of my existence, there has been at least one restaurant at the center of things for me, both literally and symbolically. This is a book about those restaurants, and about my life in and around them. They're a diverse bunch—some, world-famous temples of haute cuisine; others, more notable for their character or their clientele than for their cooking. All too many of them have vanished. I've picked them out for present purposes because they have been touchstones for me, personally and professionally, but also because they represent something, different in every case, about the history and culture of food in America and Western Europe. They are places that in some way help define who and what I was and have become, but that are also, for the most part, emblematic of the revolutions great and small, over the past half century or so, that have changed the way we eat and cook and think and feel about food.

Chapter One

CHASEN'S,
West Hollywood (1936–1995)

M Y PARENTS WERE THE PERFECT RESTAURANT
goers: Dad made good money writing screenplays and
Mom couldn't cook. They loved dining out, loved dressing up and
hobnobbing, loved getting their names in what were then called
the "society pages," and they went to all the best and smartest
places in Los Angeles. They had courted at one of the most famous
local restaurants of them all, the legendary Romanoff's in Beverly
Hills. Romanoff's was a glamorous movie-business boîte presided
over by a onetime Lithuanian pants presser who had reinvented
himself as a Russian prince; the menu offered beluga caviar, frogs'
legs, calf's brains, and the slightly naughty-sounding Devilled
Turkey Casanova for Two, and everyone who mattered in Hollywood ate there.

I never got taken to Romanoff's, for whatever reasons, but I
went along almost everywhere else: the always bustling Hollywood
Brown Derby, hung with charcoal caricatures of the same stars who
were frequently sitting at various booths around the room; the cool
and clubby Tail o' the Cock on La Cienega Boulevard's "Restaurant
Row," where I discovered swordfish and sand dabs and drank fruit

punch (and much later French 75s) out of tall frosted glasses; the handsomely appointed Beverly Hills Hotel dining room, where I ate prime rib au jus (pronounced "o juice"), carved from a silver-domed gueridon by a white-haired chef named Henry; the stylish King's in West Hollywood, where I saw my first live lobsters, languishing in big glass tanks against one wall—and found, probably to my parents' surprise, that the notion of picking out my dinner while it was still moving didn't bother me at all.

Not everything was fancy. Dad took me to lunch at the commissary at whichever studio was employing him, and to film-business haunts like Oblatt's, a few feet from the Paramount Studios gates, where I'd delight to see cowboys and Indians and Romans and medieval dukes in full costume and makeup slurping spaghetti at the counter, and Lucey's, a sprawling mock-adobe place across the street from Paramount, where I appreciated the Monte Cristo sandwiches (and where, Dad once told me, "more careers have been made and ended than on any movie lot in town").

Mom fed me at department store tearooms—Waldorf salad or cream cheese sandwiches on walnut-raisin bread, while I perched on wrought-iron chairs with pastel cushions—and at drugstore lunch counters, institutions that today have all but vanished, where I'd spin my stool from side to side and order a cheeseburger or a breaded veal cutlet and a milk shake made before my eyes in one of those splendid chrome-and-pistachio-green Hamilton Beach contraptions. If I was good, I'd get taken to Blum's in Beverly Hills, an outpost of the San Francisco original, where the main attraction was a kind of devil's salad bar—a do-it-yourself sundae cart wheeled around to every table, loaded with six or eight different kinds of ice cream and with toppings of every sort, from hot fudge and butterscotch to nuts, whipped cream, and nonpareils, to be assembled and combined and gloriously overdone at will. I loved it all.

The restaurant that made the most indelible impression on me, though, was Chasen's. I'm pretty sure it was the first restaurant I ever set foot in, though "set foot" is not the right term—there is photographic evidence somewhere of my early appearance there when I was still literally a babe in arms—and it is definitely the first restaurant that I remember specifically. It was also almost certainly the restaurant I went to the most often in my first fifteen years or so of life, and the one that shaped most strongly my admittedly idyllic image of what a restaurant should be.

Chasen's was originally Chasen's Southern Pit, opened as a chili parlor and barbecue joint in 1936 by an ex-vaudeville comedian named Dave Chasen. Chasen had been the stooge, or comic foil, to a celebrated headliner named Joe Cook. Cook could juggle, sing, dance, and tell jokes, and built elaborate Rube Goldberg–like constructions onstage; Chasen's job was to play the fool (he typically sported a red fright wig and blacked-out teeth), the bumbler, dropping things, tripping, goofing up Cook's supposedly serious endeavors. The duo had considerable success on the New York stage, and even appeared together in an early Frank Capra opus, *Rain or Shine*—but the closing of many theaters during the Depression and the ascendancy of the movies as popular entertainment had killed vaudeville by 1932 or '33, and the act broke up.

As an itinerant performer, Chasen had started cooking chili backstage for his fellow vaudevillians, and he became the designated chef at weekend parties at Cook's estate on Lake Hopatcong, New Jersey, turning out not just chili but barbecued spareribs and steaks. One of the regulars at these affairs was Harold Ross, founder and editor of *The New Yorker*, and at some point, questioning the future of his show business career, Chasen approached Ross with the idea of opening a restaurant. Ross agreed to invest thirty-five hundred dollars in the project—on the condition that Chasen set up shop in Stamford, Connecticut, where Ross lived. Happily for Hollywood, the location Ross had in mind burned down before a deal could be made, and around the same time another vaudevillian, returning from the West Coast, reported that you couldn't get a decent steak out there. Chasen knew all about decent steaks, and with Frank Capra's encouragement and Ross's blessing, he moved west, bought a stucco shack on the edge of a cornfield where Beverly Boulevard met Doheny Drive, and opened for business. Capra and James Cagney were among the first-nighters.

The Southern Pit was a small place—a cramped kitchen, six tables, an eight-stool counter, and a six-stool bar, with a few Ping-Pong tables out back—and business was spotty at first, but Chasen was well liked and had good Hollywood connections and word got around. Less than a year after he opened, he was again playing to packed houses and was able to enlarge the place. He eventually added a second story to the original shack and installed a sauna and a barbershop behind the dining room. In 1940, Chasen dropped the "Southern Pit" portion of his restaurant's name.

At first, the menu at his restaurant was minimal: chili, ribs, and a dish Chasen christened "hobo steak," based on a recipe he'd gotten from a fellow vaudevillian. This was a thick New York strip steak wrapped in leaf lard and encased in a crust of salt, roasted very rare at a high temperature, then finished at the table: a captain would crack open the crust with a mallet, slice the steak on a wooden cutting board, then season the slices and cook them to order in foaming butter in a copper chafing dish. The meat was served atop croutons of sourdough bread fried in butter and was (at least as I knew it in the sixties and seventies) about the most delicious thing imaginable.

The barbershop and sauna didn't last very long, but the building continued to grow over the years (together with its parking lot, it occupied most of the former cornfield by the time it closed), and as the restaurant grew, the food evolved. The ribs were phased out except by special order, and the chili and the hobo steak vanished (though both were always available to anyone who knew enough to ask for them). By the time I was old enough to read the menu, the choices included thirty or so appetizers, soups, and salads and forty or fifty main dishes—a veritable catalog of mid-twentieth-century "continental" and upscale American cooking, from shrimp cocktail, Caesar salad, and jellied consommé to lobster Newburg, chicken tetrazzini, and saddle of lamb with sauce béarnaise, and all the way on to strawberry shortcake and crêpes Suzette.

The clientele grew, too. A New York contingent—James Thurber, Dorothy Parker, Robert Benchley, Alexander Woollcott, and other friends of Harold Ross—made it their clubhouse. "They all pretended that they hadn't unpacked their suitcases because they weren't planning on staying very long in California," Dad once told me, "but the truth is they loved it here." The stars of Hollywood loved it, too. W. C. Fields played Ping-Pong with a drink in one hand, Ray Bolger was known to soft-shoe through the dining room, and Frank Morgan (whose best-known role was as the Wizard of Oz) used to perform stripteases on the bar. Jimmy Stewart had his bachelor party there in 1949, complete with two midgets (as they were then called) garbed in diapers jumping out of a cake. A pint-size Shirley Temple threw a tantrum at the restaurant one night because she couldn't have a cocktail like her parents, so Chasen improvised an alcohol-free concoction that he named for her—ginger ale with a splash of grenadine, garnished with a maraschino cherry—quite possibly the first-ever "mocktail."

Howard Hughes was a Chasen's regular in his movie-producer days, and hired Chasen to cater in-flight meals when he took over TWA. A list of other stalwarts reads like a checklist of Old Hollywood luminaries: Orson Welles, Cary Grant, Lana Turner, Charlie Chaplin, Paulette Goddard, Spencer Tracy, Katharine Hepburn, Peter Lorre, Gregory Peck, Bob Hope, George Burns, Marilyn Monroe, Elizabeth Taylor (who liked the chili so much that she had it air-freighted to her in Rome when she was filming *Cleopatra*), Errol Flynn, Humphrey Bogart, Groucho Marx, Clark Gable, Jack Lemmon, Frank Sinatra . . . And it wasn't just Hollywood: J. Edgar Hoover came in when he was in town, as did, it was said, "every U.S. president since 1936 except Roosevelt."

I remember seeing Lana Turner at Chasen's myself (though never, alas, Marilyn Monroe). I also remember meeting an actor friend of my parents' named Ronnie Reagan, who would probably have been dining with his then-wife, Jane Wyman, when he stopped by our table to say hello (he later proposed to his second wife, Nancy Davis, in a booth at Chasen's). I remember Alfred and Alma Hitchcock, who sat at the same table, to the left of the front door as you entered, every Sunday night, and who did *not* say hello. I remember being introduced to George Burns, complete with cigar, and, on another evening, to Jerry Lewis (he was something of a hero to me at the time, and I turned red when I knocked over my chair standing up to shake his hand).

One thing famous people seemed to like about Chasen's was that reporters and photographers were barred, and autograph seekers who had somehow gotten seated were quickly and politely requested to put away their pads. It was understood that Chasen's was more a refuge than a stage set. It was a clubhouse, open to anyone who had the means, but mostly meant for members, who wanted about as much privacy as they could expect in a public place. You went to Café Trocadero or the Vendôme if you were looking for publicity; you came to Chasen's to relax and maybe to misbehave a little, in a harmless way.

Chasen's was hardly the only Hollywood hangout of the era, but places like the Brown Derby or Musso's (officially the Musso & Frank Grill)—particularly known as a writers' refuge, though Charlie Chaplin once had a regular table there—were casual establishments, the kinds of places you'd go for a working (and drinking) lunch or a quick dinner on the way home after a long day at the studio. The more serious dress-up places in town, like LaRue or Victor Hugo's, were starchier and less hospitable to high jinks. Chasen's struck the perfect balance: It was a special-occasion kind of place, but one where celebrities could feel comfortable among their own kind, playing more than posing. In that regard, it was sort of the original Spago.

My parents weren't celebrities themselves, but they were not unknown in Hollywood, and they were good friends of the Chasens, often entertaining them at home or socializing with them away from the restaurant. I don't think we had a regular table at Chasen's, but we almost always sat facing the door in the front dining room, with its booths of firm, high-gloss, tuck-and-roll green leather. The room in back, where the bar was, had a more rakish and tentative feel to it (the booths were red), which of course appealed to me increasingly as I grew older. (I later learned that habitués of the place, always seated up front, called the back room "Fresno"—a Californian version of Siberia.)

I loved wandering around the restaurant. The walls were crowded with framed photographs—signed portraits, party shots, vacation scenes, family stuff, contributed by regulars—and there always seemed to be new ones to see. Above a booth on the right side of the front room as you entered, for some years, there was a "candid" snapped by my mother, showing two diaper-swaddled baby boys, myself and Peter Ford (son of the actor Glenn Ford and the dancer Eleanor Powell), lying on a towel in the sun, apparently having an intense conversation. (It somehow found its way onto the wire services and was widely published around the world, with a caption suggesting that young Master Ford and I were discussing the atomic bomb.) By the time I was six or seven, the photo had become an embarrassment to me—Mom never failed to point it out when I was introduced to someone at the restaurant—and I was happy when it migrated, one year, to the wall in Dave's office.

The men's room at Chasen's, past the rakish bar, was hung with racy cartoons, one of them by James Thurber; these confused me at first, but I eventually figured them out. I liked lingering around the bar itself, at a respectful distance, watching the bartenders mix drinks. I was also fascinated by a small two-person booth at one end of the bar, over which hung a brass plaque identifying it as the property of Billy "Square Deal" Grady. I had no idea who Grady was—I learned many years later that he was a legendary MGM casting director, and as such had probably helped many of the restaurant's famous customers get where they were—but the idea of a table "belonging" to somebody was a novelty to me, and I was attracted to the notion. Someday, when I was older, I always told myself, I'd sit at that table myself, if Mr. Grady didn't mind.

I MAY HAVE GROWN UP in restaurants, but we *lived* in a big house on Beverly Glen Boulevard, in a ritzy neighborhood in West Los Angeles called Holmby Hills. Our place was what my mother called "Cape Cod Colonial" in style, set on two acres of graded, planted hillside. At the top of our driveway were two sixty-foot deodar cedars, which my parents paid crews of UCLA frat boys to garland with colored lights every Christmastime. We had a shuffle-board court, a tennis court, and a long, narrow swimming pool enclosed by a high box hedge on one side and a thicket of oleander bushes on the other. Vincent Price lived next door; Claudette Colbert's house was just up the hill behind the pool, as was Westlake School, where young ladies went to learn the liberal arts and social graces—among them my sister, Merry, two years my junior (her second-grade classmates included a pretty little blond girl named Candy Bergen, who was the daughter of a famous ventriloquist, and whose real first name was Candice).

Counting the maid's quarters, our house had ten bedrooms—Mom and Dad had separate ones, behind a common door—and nine bathrooms; a large but cozy living room lined with book-shelves; and a ninety-foot-long linoleum-tiled grown-ups' "play-room" equipped with a fireplace, his-and-hers powder rooms, and a full-size semicircular wet bar, behind which rose a mirrored wall hatched with glass shelves filled with a shop's worth of fancy drink-ing vessels. In front of the bar were six high, sturdy chrome bar-stools with round leather seats. I used to love climbing onto one of them, leaning on the bar, and sipping 7Up or root beer while I gazed up at the infinitely varied array of glasses, their numbers doubled by reflection—cobalt blue and ruby red tumblers, hand-painted floral-pattern mugs with scroll handles, mile-high pink-ish collins glasses with my father's monogram frosted onto them, jaunty martini coupes whose stems were molded into the form of a top-hatted, monocled dandy's bust. I still love perching at bars, and infinitely prefer a good barstool to the armchair at that quiet little lounge table in the corner; I believe this is the result of something called "imprinting."

On one side of the playroom, behind a locked door, was a storeroom the size of a mogul's walk-in closet, with oilcloth-lined wooden shelves, floor to ceiling, on both sides. Unused small appliances and Christmas decorations and other seasonal accoutrements were kept here, but the room was primarily a storehouse for canned goods, which my parents bought, cases at a time, from fancy markets like Balzer's or Jurgensen's, and which formed a large part of our daily diet. Some of the cans, with dark burgundy-hued labels, contained clam chowder, baked beans, Indian pudding, and other New England specialties from S. S. Pierce, the famous old Boston food company; these seemed exotic to me, beyond my experience (I remember wondering if Indian pudding had anything to do with Indian summer). There were also more prosaic cans of corn, peas, carrots, new potatoes, hollowed-out black olives, button mushrooms, fruit cocktail, mandarin orange segments, pineapple and tomato juice, and such ready-to-eat staples of the family table as Andersen's pea soup, Mary Kitchen roast beef hash, Dinty Moore beef stew, Franco-American spaghetti with meatballs, and Chef Boyardee beef ravioli.

Our kitchen was a white, L-shaped room, larger than some apartments I later lived in, with the appliances clustered at one end of the L's longer leg and a kitchen table probably ten feet long occupying much of the shorter one. My first memory of food, as opposed to restaurants, comes from that kitchen, and it is an unpleasant one: I'm sitting in my high chair, wearing a terry-cloth bib rimmed in blue satin and embroidered with frolicking lambs—and spitting out my scrambled eggs. I have no idea why. Were they cold or oversalted? Did I have an incipient egg allergy? Or did I just plain not like their texture or the way they tasted? All I know is that I had no intention of swallowing them, that I wanted them out of my mouth—and that to this day I can't stand eggs in any recognizable form.

EGGS ASIDE, I was a pretty good eater as a youngster, graduating quickly from puréed Gerber's pears and carrots and whatever else they fed babies in those days to Cream of Wheat, grilled cheese sandwiches, fish sticks, and baked potatoes (skins and all). Food was always ample in our household, if not sophisticated, and I considered the refrigerator a repository of good things, much as I imagine most boys and girls my age would have viewed the toy chest or the cookie jar—not that I was immune to the charms of those containers, either.

When my parents went out for dinner and didn't take us with them, my sister and I would eat at the kitchen table, or on TV trays in the living room in front of our little DuMont while we watched *The Howdy Doody Show* or *Captain Midnight*. Our meals were often, appropriately enough, Swanson frozen TV dinners, in segmented aluminum trays, or chicken, turkey, or beef pot pies. We also had a lot of Spam. When everyone was home, we'd eat together in our formal dining room, sitting at a long table set with satiny linens, eating off Spode china with Royal Danish silverware and drinking from elaborate cut-glass goblets—usually filled with skim milk, even for my parents. For years, we had a live-in maid, who doubled as a cook. The food, as I recall it, was mostly pretty bland, but this wasn't the maid's fault. My mother had an almost primal aversion to onions, garlic, and their kin, and looked on herbs and spices with grave suspicion. My parents had some Lebanese-American friends, the Maloufs, and I remember that once when we visited them at their hillside home in Hollywood, the man of the house gifted us, as we were leaving, with a big clump of wild rosemary he'd been excited to find growing on his property. Mom tossed it out the car window as soon as we were safely down the driveway.

Our family meals were mostly meat or poultry (fish was a rarity, unless it was those fish sticks), canned or frozen vegetables of some sort, and potatoes—sometimes Tater Tots or frozen French fries (lightly charred under the broiler on a cookie sheet); sometimes mashed (either real or out of a box); sometimes baked, with butter (sour cream was beyond my mother's comprehension, and chives were considered virtually poisonous). Occasionally, canned sweet potatoes or Minute Rice made an appearance in their place. Once every few months, Mom would cook, preparing one of her culinary specialties—either spaghetti with ground beef and canned corn mixed together or "roast beef," which was a big hunk of round roast, put into an oval aluminum roasting pan atop a bed of small fresh carrots and canned new potatoes, then seasoned with salt and pepper, covered, and roasted for three or four hours, until the color of the meat resembled that of the vessel it had cooked in. Even then, I knew enough to realize that the beef was lifeless and dry, but the potatoes and carrots got all leathery and salty and meaty and were actually quite delicious.

An early and comparatively brief presence in our house was Deirdre, my father's daughter from one of his two earlier marriages, who must have been about a dozen years my senior. Deirdre taught Merry and me how to make cinnamon toast and what she called "hard sauce," which was just powdered sugar stirred into softened butter, to be spread on sweet rolls or eaten alongside mincemeat or raisin pie. I was already something of a wiseacre by then, and I remember Deirdre once telling me to finish my (frozen) French fries because there were children starving in Europe, to which I responded by getting an envelope, inserting a handful of fries, and saying, "Okay, what's their address?" On another occasion, I filled a small pot with water and put it on the stove over high heat and stared at it until the water started bubbling. "See?" I announced to Deirdre. "A watched pot *does* boil." My mother didn't like Deirdre much—maybe because she was a living reminder of Dad's younger life—and on one occasion I actually saw her chasing my half sister around the kitchen brandishing a black cast-iron frying pan. (Happily, she never connected.) I inherited that pan, and still cook in it almost nightly.

MY FATHER, Charles Robert Hardy Douglas Andrews (he went by Robert Douglas Andrews and later Robert Hardy Andrews professionally), was born in Effingham, Kansas—at the train station, he always said, while his mother was en route to St. Joseph, Missouri—and lived for several years on an Arapaho Indian reservation in southwestern Oklahoma, where his father was a doctor. He was naturally loquacious (the Arapaho kids on the reservation nicknamed him Little Big Mouth), and as a boy, he once told me, he fell in love with the rhythm and sound of words. Not surprisingly, he became a writer, early. When he was ten years old, he mailed a sheaf of poems off to *The Kansas City Star*. He heard no more about it until a year later, when he was sent to live in Hiawatha, Kansas, with his grandmother. "She had saved a full-page clipping from the paper," he wrote, "because the names were the same. It was headed IS THIS MAN THE NEW PRAIRIE POET LAUREATE?" He parlayed that success into a job melting hot type, cleaning presses, and correcting galleys for the *Brown County* [Kansas] *World,* then worked a series of other newspaper jobs around the Midwest, eventually becoming a reporter for *The Minneapolis Journal*. A story he wrote there— largely invented, he was quick to admit—caught the eye of his hero, the legendary editor Henry Justin Smith of the *Chicago Daily News,* and before he was twenty-one he found himself working for that great American newspaper, sharing an office with an older and more accomplished poet, Carl Sandburg.

My father became quite the young man-about-town in Chicago. He was something of a dandy, wearing a raccoon coat and a homburg and carrying a walking stick, and was well enough known to have been mentioned, as "Bob Andrews, the novelist," in John Drury's 1931-vintage restaurant guide, *Dining in Chicago,* as one of the celebrity customers at a place called Casa de Alex. He was a novelist by virtue of a book called *Three Girls Lost,* which he wrote in a week, on a bet, while still working for the *Daily News,* and which he promptly sold to Grosset & Dunlap. He liked to tell the story that Carl Sandburg, growing tired of his gloating about this accomplishment, took him down the street to a huge bookstore one day, led him inside, surveyed the shelves, and said "Turn around," and then "Keep turning." He finally got the point: All around him were thousands and thousands of books by other men and women, all of whom had doubtless thought they were pretty special, too. "Now suppose you start trying to learn how to be humble," said Sandburg, walking out and leaving my father standing there, having perhaps acquired a better sense of scale.

Three Girls Lost did two things for Bob Andrews the novelist: To begin with, it attracted the attention of the pioneering radio drama producers Frank and Anne Hummert, who hired him to develop some of the earliest radio soap operas, among them *Just Plain Bill* and *The Romance of Helen Trent.* His speed and fecundity as a soap writer were legendary. In his 1948 *New Yorker* series about the medium, James Thurber called my father "the granddaddy of the soap opera" and reported that he produced "a hundred thousand words a week over a period of years, without losing a pound or whitening a hair."

The novel also brought my father to Hollywood: *Three Girls Lost* was bought for "the pictures" by what was then called the Fox Film Corporation. The result starred Loretta Young and, in one of his earliest credited roles, a tall, young romantic lead named John Wayne. By the time I was born, at St. John's Hospital in Santa Monica, Dad had moved to the West Coast and become a contract screenwriter, which meant that he would be employed for various fixed periods of time at one of the major movie studios, where he was paid to adapt novels, expand synopses, rewrite other people's screenplays, and turn out original scripts of his own.

My mother, born Irene Charlotte Bressette into a French-Canadian family in Nashua, New Hampshire, but using the stage name of Irene Colman by the time she met my father, was a glamour girl. She'd won a beauty contest at Chicago's Century of Progress World's Fair in 1933 as "the girl with the most beautiful eyes" and soon found herself in Hollywood, first as a chorus girl (in *Gold Diggers of 1937*, one of her fellow chorines was a tall, sexy redhead named Lucille Ball) and then as an ingenue—dark-eyed, buxom window-dressing in films like *Anthony Adverse* with Fredric March (she played the Empress Josephine) and *At the Circus* with the Marx Brothers. (She was cut out of the last of these, but I have a production still of her, sitting in a courtroom witness box in a low-cut dress, while Groucho questions her with his trademark arched-eyebrow leer.) She always claimed that she had also had a part in *A Tale of Two Cities*, starring Ronald Colman, and that she had asked his permission to borrow his last name, later passed on to me, for herself—but there is no record of her having appeared in that film, and in any case, most of her early screen credits spell the name "Coleman." You never knew with Mom.

When she gave up her acting career, after marrying my father, the former Irene Colman became an attention-loving Hollywood wife: She wore floral prints, costume jewelry, Persian lamb, and Jungle Gardenia. She made entrances, and seemed to know everybody. She was loud and fearless (outwardly, at least), and always took charge, often to herd people into clusters so that she could take pictures of them with her thirty-five-millimeter Argus camera. She must have taken thousands and thousands of snapshots over the years, very few of them entirely in focus or coherently composed.

Besides going out to restaurants, Mom and Dad gave countless parties in our massive playroom. Almost every month throughout the late forties and early fifties, with almost any excuse—a friend's birthday, an out-of-towner visiting L.A., a holiday major or obscure—they'd fill the room with illustrious guests, pouring them good liquor and feeding them canapés. By the age of eight or so, I had become part of the action, greeting people, helping to pass the canapés, and, a bit later, taking cocktail orders from people like Dick Powell, Barbara Stanwyck, Rhonda Fleming, and the songwriter Jimmy McHugh, my sister's godfather, who was apt to be sitting at our Steinway grand playing "Don't Blame Me" or one of the other great songs he'd written. I loved the electricity in the room, and the inevitable attention; I loved the way people just sat down at the piano and started playing; I loved being part of the social whirl.

WHEN WE DINED OUT at Chasen's, we'd always dress up, Dad in a suit and tie, Mom in something bright and bold from Saks or Bullock's, accessorized with fake gold and rubies and possibly a hat adorned with millinery foliage, Merry and I in our Sunday church clothes. Pulling up to the restaurant in our Buick sedan, Mom at the wheel (my father never learned to drive), we'd be welcomed by name by the parking attendants, then ushered into the vestibule. I remember vividly the scent of the fur coats, sometimes damp from the evening mist, in the coat check just inside the door, and I remember the strange painting that hung over it: a portrait of W. C. Fields as a grumpy-looking Queen Victoria. Then we'd pass into the dining room—I loved that moment of entering the place, that quick, seamless transition from real life to what I had come to see as a kind of fantasy world, where nothing but good things would be served—to be greeted effusively by the maître d'hôtel or by Dave Chasen himself or his glamorous Kentucky-born wife, Maude.

Dave was short, about five-foot-six, with thick hair, big ears, and a prominent mole on his right cheek. He wore horn-rimmed glasses and smoked a pipe. I thought he looked like a garden gnome, but he was always animated and seemed warm and kind. He used to do magic tricks for me when we stopped by his office to say good-bye after our meal, sometimes making cards disappear or pulling nickels out of my ears. Maude was tall, slender, and dauntless, with a handsome face framed by golden hair, and she pretty much seemed to run the place. She doted on me. I recently came across a note from her, dated December 20, 1949—I would have been two months shy of my fifth birthday—reading, "This is a Christmas invitation. After the holidays, would you please be my guest for dinner at 'Chasen's'? You may bring your mother and father—as we will need them to chaperone us!"

My favorite dinner as a youngster at Chasen's was ground sirloin steak with a side of potatoes O'Brien, little cubes of fried potato tossed with minced onion and red and green bell pepper. If I was lucky, the meal concluded with a coupe snowball, which was simply a ball of vanilla ice cream coated in shredded toasted coconut, then generously anointed with Hershey's chocolate syrup. As I grew older, I came to appreciate the vichyssoise, the Caesar salad (made tableside with many flourishes), the Maude salad (shredded romaine, iceberg, and chicory with diced tomato with a Roquefort dressing; I always asked them to leave off the chopped hard-cooked egg with which it was usually finished), the Dover sole meunière, the boneless squab with wild rice, and certainly the hobo steak. And every meal had to begin with an order of Parmesan cheese toast.

In an L.A. restaurant guide that I wrote in 1982, I confessed that I had practically lived at Chasen's as a child and that "I could no more critically analyze [it] . . . than I could review the interior decoration of the house I grew up in." The truth is that as I gained experience of food and became an avid, and critical, restaurant goer on my own, I came to realize that Chasen's was not a paragon of the culinary arts. But I also came to realize that that didn't matter one bit—that a restaurant could please you, and even nourish you, in more ways than one.

DAVE CHASEN DIED of cancer in 1973, but Maude kept the place going. One evening in 1981, at Maude's invitation, I took my first wife to dinner there, the first time I'd been in probably a dozen years. We ate cheese toast, Maude salad, and hobo steak, with martinis first and red wine along the way, and Maude sat with us and reminisced. Afterward, by previous arrangement, she took us over to the house where I'd grown up, by then the property of one of her friends. My parents had sold off the roadside plot on which the tennis court stood just before we moved away, and another house now occupied the space. The deodar cedars were long gone. The playroom had been broken up into three or four smaller rooms. The kitchen had been moved. I couldn't find a single room, in fact, that looked like anything I remembered. The exterior of the house was no longer Cape Cod Colonial but Generic McMansion in style. After looking around for half an hour or so, we thanked the owners and went back to Chasen's for a nightcap, which I badly needed.

Maude died in 2001, at the age of ninety-seven, but the restaurant had predeceased her. With increased competition from trendier establishments like Ma Maison, Spago, and the Ivy, Chasen's lost business. The old-timers still went (Ronnie Reagan celebrated what was probably his last public birthday there), but it was considered too dressy by the younger crowd (jeans were frowned on), and the old-fashioned menu didn't appeal to diners looking for goat cheese pizza and tuna tartare. Maude could no longer run the place, either. In her later years, though she still liked to dress up and work the room, she was forgetful and would nonplus longtime customers by failing to recognize them or sitting down with them and saying things like "You know, I used to run a restaurant." Kay MacKay, Maude's daughter from her first marriage, kept things going as long as she could, but in 1995 closed the restaurant for good. A new Chasen's opened, with MacKay's son as a partner, on Cañon Drive in Beverly Hills in 1997, but it closed three years later. The original Chasen's building is now an upscale market called Bristol Farms; there are a few of the old Chasen's booths in the market café, and Chasen's chili is on the menu.

I went back to Chasen's a few times after my last dinner there with Maude, and had planned to have a farewell dinner there around Christmastime in 1994, just before I moved to the East Coast. We were short on time and money, though, and never made it. "We'll come back next year and go for sure," I told my wife. But by the time we made our next trip to L.A., Chasen's was gone. I never did get to have dinner at Billy "Square Deal" Grady's table.

Chapter Two

TRADER VIC'S,

Beverly Hills (1955–2007)

M Y FORMAL EDUCATION BEGAN IN SEPTEMBER 1950,
when Mom took me up a set of broad wooden steps into a
bungalow at St. Paul the Apostle School in West Los Angeles for
my first day of kindergarten. The teacher was Miss Clary, a bright-
faced laywoman, but the school was run by an order of nuns called
the Daughters of Mary and Joseph, and the mother superior who
wrangled them was standing just inside the classroom door to welcome the new students. I took one look at this tall, hooded specter
garbed in black and deep blue robes, her sharp face framed by a
blindingly white starched wimple, her chest covered by a blindingly white starched bib, and started screaming. I'd been to Mass
with my parents by that point and had seen priests and altar boys
aplenty, but I don't think I had ever seen a nun before, certainly
not close up, and frankly I was terrified—inconsolable, in fact, to
the extent that Mom apologized and turned around and took me
home.

I tried again the next day, and this time there was no nun
in sight, and by the time I started seeing the good sisters again,
crossing the playground, their veils flapping in the breeze, they no

longer scared me. I went on to acquit myself well as a fledgling student—so well, in fact, that at the end of the school year, I was invited to be the valedictorian at my kindergarten graduation ceremony, complete with pale blue cap and gown. I've been getting up in front of crowds and blabbering about one thing or another ever since.

I don't remember much about my first couple of years of grade school, except that Mom would drive me to St. Paul's each morning and pick me up each afternoon; that I'd find peanut-butter-and-jelly or American cheese sandwiches and raw carrots or an apple in my Hopalong Cassidy lunch box at noontime; and that I brought home good report cards. I got into trouble in third grade, though. I don't know whether I was showing off for one of the cute girls I liked or whether I was just bored, but for some reason—I was, remember, a precocious wiseacre—I became the class clown, keeping up a running stream of jokes and comments at the expense of the nice young Irish nun who was attempting to imbue us with some rudimentary knowledge. I have no recollection at all of what I said, but I know that almost every time she opened her mouth, I'd make a wisecrack. My classmates loved it, and I kept them laughing all day long. There were time-outs and detentions, of course, and visits to Mother Superior's office and conferences with my parents, but none of it did any good. I liked the attention too much. When school let out in June 1953, I was asked not to return to St. Paul's for fourth grade. In fact, Mother Superior suggested, a stint at one of the area's military schools might instill in me a little respect for authority.

For fourth grade and half of the fifth, then, I wore a flattop haircut and donned a gray flannel cadet's uniform every weekday morning, riding the school bus to St. John's Military Academy, on the fringes of downtown Los Angeles. I hated it—the drill-team exercises with make-believe carbines, the demerit system enforced with fearsome authority by the military washouts who patrolled our corridors and grounds, the Saturday detentions in which we were sadistically forced to do the very thing preadolescents are least capable of doing: sit still and be quiet for hours on end.

I also had egg trouble at St. John's: One day, when I was in fifth grade, we were served poached eggs for lunch, firm rubbery orbs that probably would have disgusted me even if I'd been an egg eater. I refused to touch them, and Major Scanlon, the squat martinet who ran the school, called me up in front of the entire cafeteria and forced me to choke them down. Needless to say, this did nothing to dispel my prejudice—but the incident did help convince my parents that it was time to send me back to a regular school. Fortunately, St. Paul's agreed to readmit me halfway through the year.

For the rest of my elementary school career, I think that I was probably more or less an average kid. There was no more acting up. I got okay grades, played catch during recess (not particularly well), got picked on by the class bully (Dave Wilson, where are you now?), read comic books surreptitiously in class, mooned over girls, played at friends' houses after school—cowboys and Indians at first, later "war" (some of my classmates had older brothers who had been to Korea).

At night, I did my homework, puzzling over math problems at our kitchen table, constructing 3-D maps for geography class on the playroom floor, writing book reports and diagramming sentences on lined binder paper at my little white desk. The only TV show Merry and I were allowed to watch on weeknights was *Disneyland*, on Wednesdays—the original Disney anthology series, which began before the first theme park of that name was built, and which launched the Davy Crockett craze (and, yes, I had a coonskin cap). I spent the rest of my spare time reading. I was particularly fond of the children's history books in the American Landmarks series, works with titles like *The Barbary Pirates, Kit Carson and the Wild Frontier, Gettysburg* (written by MacKinlay Kantor, one of my father's old colleagues at the *Chicago Daily News*), and *Ben Franklin of Old Philadelphia*. I would get lost in these, and daydream about finding myself at war (in a Confederate uniform; it seemed more romantic), or on a tall ship, or strolling through a Colonial-era city. I led a rich fantasy life. I had imaginary friends.

When I was eight or nine, it occurred to me to wonder if my father was a spy. He had a great romantic fascination with the Middle East and the Indian subcontinent—the lands "east of Suez," as he often said (he liked Somerset Maugham, whose line that was)—a fascination he ascribed to the fact that his own father had read Kipling's *Barrack-Room Ballads* to him when he was young and living with the Arapaho in Oklahoma. As the old Hollywood studio system began to fall apart in the early fifties and Dad's contract writing jobs became ever scarcer, he got his first chance to visit that part of the world: Somehow, improbably (I never did learn how it happened), he got hired by the United States Information Agency to write and produce three short documentaries about Pakistan's armed forces.

A man less military than my father would be difficult to imagine (he hadn't served in World War II, another story I never got), but, uncertain what his professional future held, and quite possibly disillusioned by a changing Hollywood anyway, he took to the assignment with unusual enthusiasm. I have a faint recollection of sitting in the backseat of the Buick as Mom drove him to the original Los Angeles International Airport, across Sepulveda Boulevard from where it stands today, to start his arduous prop-plane journey across the Pacific, and I remember him talking with great animation about the fabled Khyber Pass, where he was ultimately headed. Once he got to Pakistan, he wrote back long letters on his little green Hermes portable, recounting his adventures—flying over the Himalayas in a DC-3 with a missing door; buying American cigarettes in the bazaar in Peshawar from merchants squatting on the ground next to disassembled machine guns spread out on threadbare carpets that should probably be hanging in a museum somewhere; drinking scotch with husky, bearded Pathans swaddled in turbans and armed with long daggers that had to "taste blood" once they were drawn.

When he returned home, after a month or so, a man named Joe, wearing a conservative dark suit and big shoes whose soles extended far beyond their leather uppers, came over to our house and sat with him in our playroom for three or four hours, apparently asking him all manner of questions about what he'd witnessed on his trip. I say "apparently" because the doors were shut and my sister and I were warned sternly not to disturb the men—but I had no doubt that there was espionage afoot.

Dad's travels to Asia continued. He went back to Pakistan, and became a regular visitor to India, where he conceived the notion of writing a biographical film about Gautama Buddha—an ultimately fruitless project on which he was to expend enormous time and energy for the rest of his life. (I remember him meeting for hours one afternoon in the playroom with Marlon Brando and David Lean, pitching the film to them to no avail.) He traveled to Sri Lanka (then called Ceylon), Burma, and the Philippines, and even found his way to Egypt, where he wrote the screenplay for a historical epic called *Wa Islamah*, and to prerevolutionary Iran. And whenever he came home, Joe would drive over and sit with him for hours—debriefing him, I think it's safe to say. I hope his observations did the world some good, in some small way, though given the political climate in America in those days, I tend to doubt it.

ASIA DIDN'T INTEREST me much. My fantasies took me in a different direction. By the time I was in my early teens, I had gone mad for another part of the world: the South Pacific. I'd never been there, of course, but the whole idea of the place had hopelessly seduced me—thanks initially, I'm pretty sure, to a restaurant.

When I was eight, a handsome six-story fifties-modern hotel called the Beverly Hilton arose on the prow of land that stuck out into the X-shaped intersection of Wilshire and Santa Monica Boulevards in Beverly Hills. At the tip of the prow was a restaurant called The Traders. It was obvious to me even from the outside, when we first drove by, that this was no ordinary eating place. The windowless exterior walls were textured with stylized geometric patterns. Along the Wilshire Boulevard side stood a quartet of dark brown wooden tikis, probably fifteen feet high, set on concrete pedestals. Banana trees, their wrinkly fronds akimbo, sprouted along the walls. The most remarkable thing about The Traders, though, was the savory siren smell, meaty and woody and sweet, that wafted out from the place. Every time we passed, I was surprised by it anew, and drawn to it. Then one evening, dressed up as if we were going to Chasen's, we pulled into the parking lot and actually went inside. Half an hour later, I decided that I had found my new favorite restaurant—not just for the food, which I thought was wonderful, but for the world conjured up by the interior, an island world, floral, fragrant, foreign, beguiling.

The South Seas were big in America in the fifties. In 1947, the Norwegian ethnographer and zoologist Thor Heyerdahl had sailed a balsa-wood raft, the *Kon-Tiki*, from Peru to the Tuamotu Islands in French Polynesia, in an attempt to prove that ancient peoples could have traveled great distances and influenced faraway cultures, and his chronicle of the voyage became a best-seller. The musical *South Pacific*—based on James Michener's collection of war-in-the-Pacific stories, *Tales of the South Pacific*—had been a smash on Broadway and was made into a hit movie in 1958. Michener's epic novel *Hawaii* was published the following year, and at more or less the same time a Michener-inspired TV series, *Adventures in Paradise,* started airing, starring Gardner McKay as the dashing captain of the schooner *Tiki III,* who sailed from one Polynesian island to another in search of both paradise and adventures.

Then there was the musical genre called "exotica," a kind of light jazz involving unusual percussion instruments and birdcalls, apparently invented more or less by accident in Hawaii in 1954 and subsequently popularized nationwide by its creators, the pianist-bandleader Martin Denny and his vibraphonist, Arthur Lyman. Denny's hit record, *Quiet Village,* released in 1957, is sometimes credited with having ignited the tiki-bar craze and its adjuncts—backyard luaus illuminated by tiki torches, knockoff aloha shirts, tropical-style cocktails even at the local bar and grill.

I bought into it all. I read Michener and Heyerdahl, and any other book I could find about the South Pacific, from Robert Louis Stevenson's *In the South Seas* to a volume, whose title I've long since forgotten, by a man who had packed up his family and cruised off to Tahiti with them for a couple of years—my dream. I saved my allowance to buy every new Denny and Lyman album as it came out. I was too young for cocktails, but I drank tropical fruit juices almost exclusively for a while. I learned to wrap a beach towel sarong-style around my waist, and made leis out of oleander flowers from the bushes by our swimming pool. When I was twelve, my parents let me move out of my bedroom into an unused bedroom in the back of the house, and decorate it any way I wanted to. I painted the walls turquoise, laid down grass matting on the floor, and hung a piece of genuine tapa cloth on the wall. I also extracted a promise from Mom and Dad that if I got straight A's my first year in high school, they'd take me to Hawaii for summer vacation.

In the meantime, a trip to The Traders was the next best thing. The Traders was in fact an outpost of a Bay Area establishment called Trader Vic's, and after a few years it was renamed to reflect that connection. On my earliest visits, my favorite dish was "Chopped New York Steak Hawaiian Style," consisting of a thick, oval-shaped hamburger, a toasted English muffin, a fried banana, and a heap of crisp shoestring potatoes—just exotic enough for a boy who had been brought up on Spam and canned ravioli. I subsequently learned to love the "Cosmo Tidbits," an appetizer assortment that included crab Rangoon (crabmeat and cream cheese deep-fried in wonton skins), sweet barbecued spareribs, small oval slices of lacquered pork loin, and battered deep-fried shrimp. I also developed an affection for the mahimahi, which was scattered with shards of almonds (later macadamia nuts), and for the Javanese saté, which the menu called "Meat-on-a-Sword Skewered with Pineapple"—cubes of marinated lamb, roasted on wooden skewers, served with a thick peanut sauce that I couldn't stop eating.

Of course, part of the point, to me, was that this food was being served not in a clubby Chasen's-like dining room with photos on the walls, but in a South Seas fantasyland. The slightly fuzzy sounds of slack-key guitar purred from hidden speakers. The hostesses wore flowing hibiscus-print dresses, the captains jaunty crested blazers. The tables were bare polished tropical hardwood with brightwork fittings. Inflated blowfish turned into lanterns hung overhead. There was tapa cloth on some of the walls, and fishnets, with amber glass floats attached, were draped on others;

a carved Hawaiian war god glowered from one corner; a full-size outrigger canoe was suspended from the ceiling; the table lamps had squat tiki-figure bases, and the ceramic salt and pepper shakers were tikis, too. There were tikis everywhere.

The tiki thing had started not with Trader Vic's but with the onetime New Orleans bootlegger Ernest Raymond Beaumont Gantt, who had roamed the tropics before washing up in Holly-wood, in the early thirties, where he did odd jobs—parking cars, waiting tables, and occasionally consulting at the studios on mov-ies with a South Seas setting. When Prohibition was repealed, in 1933, he opened a bamboo-and-palm-frond watering hole just off Hollywood Boulevard called Don the Beachcomber, furnishing it with artifacts he had gathered on his travels and with pieces of wrecked boats he'd found along the California coast.

Theme restaurants were already popular in Los Angeles. Back in 1928, the travel writer Katherine Ames Taylor had reported, in *The Los Angeles Tripbook*, that "At 533 South Grand Avenue is the Bull Pen Inn, where you dine in stalls. There is the Zulu Hut on Ventura Boulevard, near Universal City, where knives and forks are dispensed with, and you dine most informally, in native fash-ion, eating fried chicken with your fingers." Gantt's vision of is-land life in the middle of Hollywood fit right in. And he knew just how to fuel the fantasy: Rum was cheap and readily available at the time, so he devised a number of rum-based cocktails, among them the Sumatra Kula (light rum with honey and grapefruit, orange, and lime juice) and the Zombie—so named, it was said, because more than a couple would turn you into one—which involved three kinds of rum, Pernod, and Angostura bitters, among other ingredi-ents. In 1934, Gantt, who later changed his name legally to Donn [*sic*] Beach, started serving Cantonese-American food, and in the process quite possibly invented the assortment of snacks known to posterity as the pupu platter (the term is apparently a Hawaiian word for a kind of relish). He'd made friends working in Hollywood, some of them famous, and the place quickly became a popular hangout for people like Humphrey Bogart, Joan Crawford, and Marlene Dietrich. (Celebrated regulars had their own personalized ivory chopsticks.) When Beach was drafted into the navy during World War II, he left his ex-wife in charge of the business, and when he returned he found that she had expanded his original establishment into a sixteen-unit chain. He signed the business over to her, maintaining a role as a consultant, and went off to Waikiki to open a new place of his own.

In the next two decades, imitations and elaborations of Don the Beachcomber appeared all over America. None was to prove more successful or ultimately influential than Trader Vic's. In 1934, Victor J. Bergeron, a young entrepreneur with a wooden leg (the original lost to tuberculosis of the bone at the age of six), opened a bar and restaurant called Hinky Dinks in Oakland, across the street from his father's grocery store. Besides beer and cocktails, Bergeron served all-American fare—roast chicken, steak sandwiches, and the like. The most exotic thing on the menu was a dish of ham and eggs with fried pineapple and bananas on the side, which he dubbed "ham and eggs Hawaiian."

After a trip to New Orleans and Havana, Bergeron added daiquiris, planter's punch, and other tropical-themed drinks to the Hinky Dinks repertoire. Then, in 1937, after a visit to Don the Beachcomber, he remade the place into a "Polynesian" restaurant, with an exotic-drinks menu supplemented by a Cantonese bill of fare. Bergeron's wife suggested that he rename the place Trader Vic's because he loved making deals. The father of his Chinese-American bartender built a barbecue pit behind the restaurant, and this evolved into the huge, tandoor-like cylindrical wood-burning ovens that Trader Vic—as he quickly started to call himself—designed and later installed in all his restaurants, calling them Chinese ovens and claiming that they dated from the Han Dynasty.

Trader Vic's developed a loyal following—in 1941, the beloved San Francisco columnist Herb Caen wrote of it that "the best restaurant in San Francisco is in Oakland"—but when Bergeron invented the mai tai there, in 1944, the drink became an international sensation, and the fame of his restaurant redoubled. (Donn Beach always claimed to have invented the drink himself, years earlier, at his own establishment, but Bergeron cited chapter and verse: He mixed up the first mai tai, he said, for a friend of his named Carrie Guild, who lived in Tahiti. Tasting it, she apparently exclaimed, *"Maita'i roa ae!"* Tahitian for "very good," thus giving the drink its name. Beach's recipe was, in any case, much more complicated than Bergeron's.)

Trader Vic's began evolving into a chain in 1940, when Bergeron opened his first outpost, in Seattle. San Francisco and then Beverly Hills later followed. Bergeron turned out to be an innovative restaurateur. He admittedly had some funny ideas about food—he thought gazpacho was Mexican, and that Indonesia's saté was "a powder from India," best defined as "a mixture of screwball spices"—and he liked to make up food and gave it imaginative provenances (as much as I loved his crab Rangoon, I sincerely doubt that any Burmese cook ever wrapped crabmeat and cream cheese in a wonton skin and deep-fried it). But he could boast some real gastronomic accomplishments, too. He traveled widely once his restaurant empire started to grow, and he seemed to constantly discover new ingredients and new ways of preparing them. He was the first restaurateur to popularize mahimahi, limestone lettuce, kiwifruit (which he called "Chinese gooseberries" and served cut into pieces on a bed of shaved ice), morel mushrooms (in a cream sauce, on toast), and green (or, as he called them, Malagasy) peppercorns. He was also one of the first to use fresh cilantro, tofu, and snow peas outside strictly ethnic restaurants. He was serving thin disks of fried parmigiano years before anybody outside Friuli had heard of frico. His were almost certainly the only upscale restaurants of the time anywhere in America that cooked much of their food with wood fires. He flirted with the idea of Asian fusion cooking long before the idea had become commonplace (and then quickly a cliché). Bergeron was also, incidentally, an early and enthusiastic supporter of California wines, featuring extensive selections of the best available examples, at least in his Northern California restaurants, long before the wine boom of the latter twentieth century.

I NEVER MET Trader Vic himself (he died in 1984), but we did correspond briefly when I wrote to him, in the seventies, complaining about the inadequate wine list at his Beverly Hills restaurant. He wrote back to explain that the matter was out of his hands, that the Hilton hotel management chose the list—but he arranged for me to have access, whenever I dined at the restaurant, to the considerably more extensive list offered at the Hilton's pricey rooftop French restaurant, L'Escoffier. I enjoyed more than one bottle of 1949 Clos des Lambrays with my Indonesian lamb roast as a result. That, of course, was long after my childhood visits, when I had rediscovered Trader Vic's on my own terms.

By that time, as I aged into my twenties, I was being drawn to the place by its good food and strong drink as much as its exoticism—but it was the whole experience that I enjoyed most, and that I can still summon up most vividly: I walk through the heavy varnished wooden front door, maybe alone, maybe with a friend, maybe even with a date. The aromas envelop me as I step inside—the faint hint of smoldering wood from the Chinese ovens; the pleasantly sour smell of heady rum and other liquors from the bar. I have cascading long black hair and what my mother likes to call, with distaste, a Fu Manchu mustache, but I am wearing a jacket (albeit corduroy) and tie, and anyway, they're used to me here. The host, Laurence Abbott, always tan, greets me at the podium and hands me over to some vision of serenity in a flowered dress who leads me to my table. On the way, I stop to exchange pleasantries with Alex Kaluzny, the wise and genial Russian-born manager of the place. The moment I sit down, my favorite captain, Jack Chew, appears, greeting me like some long-lost relative. Depending on my mood (or my date's mood, if that's an issue), I order a serious rum drink—a tortuga or a sufferin' bastard or even maybe a mai tai—or ask for the wine list and choose something red and good. It almost seems as if I don't have to order, as if the food appears magically, but probably I do glance at the menu before the array of riches begins to appear: Cosmo Tidbits, possibly, or at least one or two of the assortment's constituent parts; maybe some cheese bings, little crêpe packets of ham and melted cheese. Or if I'm feeling more grown-up, perhaps some bongo bongo soup (a silky purée of spinach and oysters) or morels on toast or just a limestone lettuce salad. Next, maybe an intermediate course of messy, garlicky pake crab, one of those dishes whose delicious residue lingers on your fingers for a day. Then almost certainly meat: Indonesian lamb roast or Javanese saté or a triple-thick lamb chop, or possibly a dish of veal fillets in tarragon sauce, something long vanished from the menu but still available to those who know enough to ask. And on the side, pake noodles scattered with bread crumbs and sesame seeds or perfect golden-brown cottage-fried potatoes, snow peas with water chestnuts, still-crunchy stir-fried asparagus. . . . Alex comes by to ask how I like the wine. Jack asks if I'd like some more peanut sauce for the saté. The room is glowing. I'm glowing. I smell the meat, the wood, a gardenia garnishing a nearby cocktail. I'm in paradise.

I NEVER MADE IT TO HAWAII—I did get straight A's as a high school freshman, but times were tough financially for my parents that year, and my island vacation was indefinitely postponed (coincidentally or not, I never got straight A's again)—and I've long since stopped having South Seas fantasies. I haven't been to a Trader Vic's in years. There are about thirty of them around the world today, most of them in Europe, Asia, and the Middle East. The one that meant so much to me at the Beverly Hilton was shuttered in 2007. It has been replaced by a poolside Trader Vic's Lounge, and there is also a full-scale version of the restaurant in the L.A. Live entertainment complex in downtown Los Angeles. They're not the same. But then, of course, I'm not, either.

Chapter Three

THE RANCH HOUSE,

Meiners Oaks, California (1958–)

THE RANCH HOUSE, IN A HAMLET CALLED MEINERS Oaks, next door to the town of Ojai, is a rustic, idiosyncratic restaurant with a faint aura of Eastern mysticism, and roots in mid-twentieth-century vegetarianism. It didn't invent the fresh, Mediterranean-influenced, ingredient-focused idiom that came to be known as "California cuisine," but it was certainly among its spiritual progenitors. It was also the place where I had some of my earliest real culinary adventures and, I suppose, first really noticed that identical or similar raw materials could be manipulated in the kitchen into myriad forms. (I'm not counting my mother's ways with canned corn.)

We came to live in Ojai, an agriculture-and-tourism town about sixty miles northwest of Los Angeles, more or less by default. Ours was a family that took vacations, over Easter and Thanksgiving breaks, when Merry and I were out of school, several times each summer, and sometimes on long weekends, just because. Our vacations weren't cross-country road trips or flights abroad, but two- or three-hour drives to resorts in various Southern California communities—the Inn at Rancho Santa Fe or the La Jolla Beach and Tennis Club near San Diego; the Smoke Tree Ranch or La Quinta in Palm Springs; the San Ysidro Ranch in Montecito or its distant neighbor, twenty miles or so across the Santa Ynez Mountains, the Ojai Valley Inn and Country Club.

The Inn, which was slightly closer than our other destinations, became a particular family favorite. I'm not sure what my parents did there all day—they didn't play golf or tennis—but my sister and I loved rollicking in the pool, bouncing on the trampoline, knocking brightly colored golf balls around the putting green, and moseying through the woods and underbrush on trail rides, clutching our saddlehorns, on big, shambling steeds with names like Tumbleweed and Lady B.

On the road to Ojai, about a mile before the Inn, was a sprawling complex of pink stucco buildings called Villanova Preparatory School, run by priests of the Order of Saint Augustine, and on one of our visits to the Inn, when I was seven or eight, my parents noticed that they had a summer camp for boys. I was promptly enrolled. My monthlong stay there, beginning in mid-June, was the first time I'd been away from home, and in the best going-to-summer-camp tradition, I was lonely and homesick for the first week or so, and then started having fun—fishing in shallow streams clogged with mossy rocks, camping out overnight under towering trees, learning how to use a bow and arrow, taking field trips to the beach at Ventura or the Natural History Museum in Santa Barbara, playing endless games of Old Maid and War, or watching cowboy movies in the rec room when it rained. When my parents came to pick me up at the end of the session, they told me that they'd decided I should come back to Villanova for high school.

I graduated from the eighth grade at St. Paul the Apostle in 1958—this time I was not asked to be the valedictorian—and in the fall of that year was packed off to Ojai. I found school difficult—

elementary chemistry and physics were impenetrable to me, and I never heard the music or felt the rhythm of Latin, though I ended up studying it for four years—but I worked hard, and managed good grades (I was trying to get to Hawaii, remember). My friends were the outsiders—the gawky kids who were *good* at chemistry and physics, the aristocratic Mexican boys sent up to Alta California by wealthy families—not the jocks or the haloed scholarship geniuses. I went out for junior varsity football, but, though I had the bulk, I lacked the hand-eye coordination and didn't make the team. I did better with the photography club, and found myself shooting gridiron games for the school paper instead of playing in them. (I did shooting of another kind, too: I joined the rifle club and proved reasonably adept at putting holes in targets.) And, as I had been at summer camp, I was lonely and homesick, though this time the feelings didn't go away.

One of the worst things about being a boarder at Villanova was the diet, which was institutional in the humorless, bulk-grocery sense. For breakfast, we ate cereal from little boxes and gummy oatmeal and doughnuts that tasted of onions (because, I eventually figured out, they'd sat next to onions in the refrigerator overnight); lunch and dinner were spaghetti with generic red sauce, bready meat loaf glazed with ketchup, Salisbury steak, chicken à la king served over dense "patty shells." Desserts included dried-out, unfrosted brownies, unglazed rectangles of spice cake, and damp apple pie. There were always extra servings of these treats put out, and students who had finished dinner and their original dessert were allowed to have another, on a first-come, first-served basis. This, of course, encouraged the bolting, and sometimes hiding, of food. One evening, one of my tablemates secreted a brownie on an unused chair so that he could rush back for another. I got the idea of anointing the brownie with the Tabasco sauce that was always on the table (a concession to the Mexican and Central American students at the school). I still recall, not without a certain satisfaction, my tablemate's remarkable delayed reaction when he took his first bite of the doctored confection. I was still a wiseacre.

BACK IN WEST LOS ANGELES, meanwhile, my father's professional life was falling apart. The old studio system under which he'd thrived had disintegrated. It was no longer economically viable for studios to keep writers (or directors or actors) under contract; the industry was changing, decentralizing, and industry veterans who'd had more or less dependable jobs now had to scramble for work. My father was by then in his early fifties, not exactly a young man, and he had never been an aggressive player in the movie business, a studio politician or a deal maker. The young hustlers with the right friends were getting the three-picture deals, and he was left to play catch-up.

My parents' attitude toward money had always been that it was meant to be earned and then spent, a misguided notion (apparently) that I seem to have inherited. Their mortgage payments must have been negligible (they'd bought our Beverly Glen mansion in 1944 for around twenty thousand dollars) and, with the exception of my father's trips to Asia, which were usually subsidized, they didn't travel, other than to resorts within driving distance. But they had an extravagant lifestyle, full of nice clothes, generous parties, good booze, and, of course, all those dinners out, and they had only token savings accounts and no real investments; I'd be surprised if they even knew what stocks and bonds were.

They had, in other words, nothing to fall back on, and in 1959, worried that they wouldn't be able to continue paying the property taxes and upkeep on our house, they put it on the market. Away at Villanova and already missing the place, I was devastated. This was home. How could we be leaving it? I'd just automatically assumed that, well, we'd always live there. It was a given, a constant in my life. I cried and railed, I got sick, I prayed—literally—that somehow it wouldn't sell. It did, of course, fairly quickly, for what was then a decent if hardly excessive price of eighty-five thousand dollars. I've hated moving ever since. Counting Beverly Glen, I've lived in probably twenty or more houses and apartments in my life, and every act of packing up has hurt.

MY PARENTS NEVER OWNED a home again. We relocated first to a rented ranch house in Encino with orange trees in the yard, cottage-cheese insulation on the ceiling, and Jack "Sgt. Friday" Webb next door. After a year there, we moved to a place we all knew well, where nice houses could be rented for reasonable prices: Ojai. It was, my mother explained to me one day, a matter of "saving face." If they had downsized in Los Angeles, their friends would have known that they were in financial difficulties and—horrors!—they might be drummed out of the society pages. By moving to a resort community, ostensibly so my father could concentrate more on his writing projects, they were able to maintain the fiction that they were still doing well.

The first house we rented in Ojai was an architectural monument of sorts, a soaring steel-frame, glass-walled structure on the brow of a hill. It was fun for a while, but there were gaps in the corners that allowed birds to fly through the place and tarantulas to creep in, and moisture from a wall of tropical houseplants set into sphagnum moss by the front door, which had to be soaked with water daily, made the interior permanently humid. After a year, we moved to another rental, a sprawling ranch house on the grounds of the Ojai Valley Inn, owned by Loretta Young (who had, remember, starred in the first movie made from one of my father's books). It was a comfortable place with a big rose garden, a one-of-everything orchard between the house and the street, and an immense hedge of night-blooming jasmine, a ghost of whose aroma sometimes still haunts me on summer evenings.

Ojai is said to take its name from a Chumash Indian word meaning "the nest," and the town is inevitably described as being "nestled" in its little valley. Ringed by purple mountains and green with orange and avocado groves—the tarry odor of the smudge pots lit to protect the fruit on frosty evenings competes in my memory with the scent of jasmine—Ojai had a population of about five thousand in those days (it's only around seventy-five hundred now) and was famous for its annual tennis tournament and music festival. It is also home to the Krotona Institute of Theosophy—a system of esoteric philosophy—and to the Indian religious teacher Jiddu Krishnamurti, who was one of the valley's best-known celebrities, along with Young, Irene Dunne, Anthony Quinn, and the artist and ceramicist Beatrice Wood, known to her friends as Beato.

Once my parents moved to Ojai, and I became a "dayhop" at Villanova, I found myself eating considerably better food than I'd choked down as a boarder. Vegetarianism was rife in the community, but I was definitely a carnivore, and unapologetically so. I loved the steaks at a restaurant in town called the Firebird, and had at least as many hamburgers and Cokes every week as any normal red-blooded American kid of the era did, either at the Foster's Freeze in town or on the Inn's oak-shaded terrace.

We ate dinner at the Inn once or twice a week. It was an all-American affair: Meals started with an iced relish tray and finished with cheesecake, cherry cream pie, or a slab of Neapolitan ice cream; in between were things like crabmeat cocktail, New

England clam chowder, broiled lobster tails with butter, Cornish game hens with wild rice, broiled ground round steak with mushroom sauce, roast prime rib with creamed horseradish, and roast rack of lamb. The Inn was also famous for its big weekend luncheon buffets, complete with ice sculptures. From these, I'd eat roast beef carved to order and fruit salad and green beans with slivered almonds. It was all good, but I remember eventually starting to think that the food was a little monotonous. Some part of me must have craved more salt and sourness and spice, I suspect, whether I realized it yet or not. That's probably why my first experience at the Ranch House was so electrifying.

The Ranch House was just that, a rambling one-story fifties-era California bungalow shaded by live oak and eucalyptus trees set amidst open fields, little plots of vegetables, and makeshift paddocks in which a scattering of horses stood, licking big pink salt blocks or rubbing their necks on splintery rails. There was a small dining room, bohemian in a ranchy sort of way, with louvered windows and unfinished wood paneling covered with drawings and ceramic plaques by Beatrice Wood. Most of the tables were outside, on a redwood deck under an awning, overlooking a fantasyland garden full of latticework arbors, ferns, wisteria, and tall thickets of bamboo, through which ran both a brick pathway lined with clumps of herbs and a gurgling stream in which diners used to cool their bottles of white wine back when this was a bring-your-own establishment.

I don't remember exactly when I had my first Ranch House meal—it might have been while I was still a freshman boarder at Villanova—but I do remember the first bite of food I had there: At home, pea soup had always come in cans. Made from dried split peas, it was pale green and as thick and murky as hot cereal, with little bits of ham lurking here and there. I liked it pretty well, and when I ordered pea soup as my appetizer at my first meal at the

Ranch House, that's what I thought I'd be getting. Instead, what was set in front of me was as thin as vichyssoise (the only "fancy" soup I'd tasted up till then) and bright electric green in color. There wasn't a speck of ham in it, but it tasted unmistakably of sweet, faintly earthy peas—not dried but fresh ones, real vegetables instead of some mysterious substance in a can. It was like nothing I'd ever tasted before, and I thought it was delicious. I don't remember what I had for a main course that evening, but the out-of-nowhere gustatory surprise of my first taste of that Ranch House pea soup is something I'll never forget. We ended up going to the Ranch House often over the years we lived in Ojai, and I discovered many new flavors and ingredients there. It was at the Ranch House that I had my first chicken liver pâté, creamy and laced with cognac; my first spinach salad; my first beef stroganoff (there was the sourness I'd been craving). One evening I ordered meat loaf, and found to my surprise that it was inset with pieces of a buttery green something I'd never seen before—which was how I first came to taste avocado. I also discovered the flavors of fresh herbs at the Ranch House. I'd encountered basil, oregano, and rosemary before, but only as brownish green flecks in glass jars on the spice rack. Suddenly, I was tasting not only those herbs in their fresh glory but such exotica as lemon verbena, chervil, summer savory, and salad burnet. At the Ranch House, my palate almost literally blossomed.

THE RANCH HOUSE was the domain of Alan and Helen Hooker, a quiet, white-haired couple who had never quite intended to become restaurateurs. Someone once called Alan "the grandfather of California cuisine." In reality, he was more like an intuitive but vaguely eccentric uncle. The Ranch House certainly anticipated some aspects of the California culinary revolution, but it was not in any sense a direct antecedent of Chez Panisse or Spago. The *Los Angeles Times*, in its obituary of Hooker, described him as a man "who helped introduce the lighter fare that came to represent California cuisine." That was closer to the mark.

The Ranch House menus have always been more "continental" than regional American. Hooker's recipes, set down in his self-published *Alan Hooker's New Approach to Cooking* (1966) and in other cookbooks, sometimes called for MSG, onion and garlic salts, canned vegetables, and meat substitutes (including something called Choplets; don't ask). Even that pea soup, I later learned, was often made with frozen peas. But Hooker was undeniably ahead of his time in many ways. In an age of margarine and bottled salad dressings, he baked with real butter and dressed his herb-strewn salads with extra-virgin olive oil when that compound adjective still drew titters. In a society that still equated fine food with French food, he served, with pride but also with a sense of fun and of experiment, elaborate Indian curries and dishes inspired by recipes from Puerto Rico, Indonesia, Hungary, and Japan. In what was still largely a meat-and-potatoes dining culture, he cooked his salmon medium-rare and elevated a myriad of fresh fruits and vegetables to a place of honor on the plate. And decades before restaurants hired foragers and contracted for baby lettuces from boutique farms, Hooker was buying Swiss chard, raspberries, and avocados from neighbors with tiny kitchen gardens or mini-orchards and plucking mushrooms from the Ojai woods.

The Hookers came to Ojai from Ohio, as followers of Jiddu Krishnamurti. To support themselves, they rented an old ranch house in Meiners Oaks and converted it into a boardinghouse, offering rooms and vegetarian meals to fellow Krishnamurti followers for fourteen dollars a week. In 1950 they opened their "Ranch House" to the public. Four years later, the house was sold, and the boardinghouse and restaurant closed. In 1956 the Hookers bought an abandoned apple orchard down the hill from the original place and built the structure that is still the heart of the Ranch House, this time serving Alan's vegetarian specialties but not taking in boarders. Business was slow, however, and this new enterprise closed, too, after a few months. Trying one more time in 1958, the Hookers decided to make a significant change to the menu: They added meat and poultry—specifically, at first, beef stroganoff, veal scaloppine, and chicken cacciatore. As Hooker recalled in his *New Approach to Cooking*, "As I began to investigate meat dishes, I came upon names which held a certain fascination for me but had no meaning as far as personal experience went. . . . I had no way of knowing how things should taste . . . so I had to depend upon my own palate and sensitivities." He always said that this was perhaps the secret of his success as a cook of nonvegetarian dishes: that he had created them as he imagined they should taste, not as they had been made in the past. He was an original.

The Hookers retired from the Ranch House in 1969, leaving David Skaggs, who had joined the staff as a busboy in 1963 and worked his way up, in charge as manager. Alan died in 1993. When Helen followed him, seven years later, Skaggs and his wife, Edie, another veteran of the restaurant staff, inherited the place. In 2012, the Skaggses divorced and put the Ranch House up for sale, for a reported one million dollars. At this writing, they both still work there, apparently amicably, and there have been no takers for the place.

I WAS NOT AT MY BEST in high school. After my freshman year of straight A's, I slid steadily down to a comfortable berth somewhere between B and C. I liked to read but found rote study boring. Fortunately (or perhaps not) I was already facile enough as a writer to be able to "snow" at least some of my teachers, filling those pallid little "blue books" with fine-sounding verbiage that probably ultimately meant very little but was well crafted enough to earn me at least a passing grade.

I had a tough time socially at school. I wasn't particularly athletic, I didn't have a driver's license (and didn't get one until a couple of years after I graduated), and my mother was entirely too visible a presence, loud and intrusive, at school functions or when picking me up after school. I got mocked regularly and occasionally "pounded" by the red-blooded local boys who drove up to school from Oxnard or Ventura in their pickup trucks or muscle cars. I had a few friends among my classmates, but none that I particularly cared to keep in touch with after my senior year.

My political leanings didn't help my popularity. My parents were hardly radicals—they'd voted for Eisenhower—but my father had been on the ground in some of the Asian battlegrounds of the Cold War and I think considered communism more as a deeply flawed ideology than a poisonous plague. He had also had Hollywood friends and colleagues blacklisted during the McCarthy era, and despised the climate that made that kind of career wrecking possible.

Father Glynn, the headmaster at Villanova, was a rabid anticommunist. A stern-faced man even when he was in a good mood, he conducted obligatory seminars in which he'd harangue us, spittle occasionally spraying from his sneering lips, about the satanic godlessness of the Soviets and the Red Chinese and their plans to conquer America. He'd load us into buses and take us off to hear professional rabble-rousers or to screenings of propaganda films endorsed by the maleficent House Committee on Un-American Activities. On one occasion, he assembled the entire student body to listen to a right-wing activist from Mexico who assured us that her country was about to "go communist" and that we'd be next. As it happened, I'd recently been reading an article about that very subject, probably in some pinko journal, and when our speaker asked for questions, I asked how a political party that had been active in Mexico for at least fifty years without significant impact and whose membership currently amounted to about one-fifth of one percent of the total population was going to take over the country. Father Glynn shut me down quickly, saying something like "You're not as smart as you think you are, young man"—and I got mildly pushed around and goaded ("Commie lover!") by a few of my classmates after the assembly let out.

Away from Villanova, I was a pretentious little squirt, arty and supercilious (a word that my mother once assured me, over my father's vigorous objections, meant "very silly"). I listened to folk music and read Camus, Dos Passos, *The Great Gatsby*, Paul Tillich, and Huxley on LSD (both books), without understanding much of any of them. I also took to writing letters to the editor of the local newspapers denouncing what I saw as various political or cultural stupidities (Father Glynn just *loved* those). I played the guitar, a few chords' worth at least, and sang songs like "Where Have All the Flowers Gone" and "The Inebriated Pig," sometimes by myself and sometimes with my friend Dave Shepherd, who was a far better guitarist. (I think we won a talent contest one night at the Ojai Bowl.) On trips to L.A. with my parents, I'd visit my oldest friend, Gary Lund, who was several years my senior, and go off with him to coffeehouses and clubs to see anyone from Reverend Gary Davis to Barney Kessel to Lenny Bruce. For a while, I wore dark glasses day and night.

On Saturdays in Ojai, I hung out at the workshop of a Polish-born sculptor named Leon Saulter, who welded dramatic abstract sculptures of jagged metal and loved to talk to me—to everyone—about the nature of art and the dynamics of the creative process.

Beatrice Wood, who had also come to Ojai originally to be near Krishnamurti, was a friend and frequent dinner guest of my parents—she taught me how to twist a bottle of wine slightly after filling a glass to avoid dribbling any on the table—and I also spent time at her studio, watching her work wet clay on her potter's wheel or listening to her stories over cups of herbal tea. These were unfailingly colorful: Wood had been an associate of Marcel Duchamp and Man Ray in Paris—someone dubbed her "the Mama of Dada"—and may have been the model for the woman in her onetime lover Henri-Pierre Roché's novel *Jules et Jim*, made into a famous film by François Truffaut. She was definitely an inspiration for the character of Rose in Ojai resident James Cameron's film *Titanic*.

In the fall of 1961, the Villanova senior class took a "preference test," and to nobody's surprise, I scored high in the literary, musical, "persuasive," and artistic categories; average in social service and clerical; and low in computational, outdoor, scientific, and mechanical. The same year, I talked myself into a freelance gig at the *Ojai Valley News*, and for the next twelve months or so wrote church news, synopses (rather than reviews) of movies that were opening at the little Ojai bijou, and other local miscellany. This was my first writing job; I got paid thirty-five cents per published column inch (I had to measure my copy in the paper every week and submit an invoice). I think I have probably subconsciously tended to embellish my prose ever since, in hopes of earning just a little more.

I never sat down and made a conscious decision to become a writer, but it seemed like a natural thing to do. When my father wasn't working in an office on a studio lot, he'd be in his office at home, sitting on a big custom-made white leather chair with an oval back, probably suspect ergonomically but very comfortable in the short term, pounding away without cease on his big black

Royal standard typewriter, its end-of-line bell ringing every second or two. He typed something like 125 words a minute, and would sit there for hours and hours, hammering the keys, sometimes muttering dialogue to himself, rarely getting up, even for a bathroom break, and stopping only long enough to pour himself another cup of inky coffee from the percolator at his elbow (his cup was huge, and emblazoned with the legend "I Am Not Greedy but I Want Enough") or light another cigarette. (He went through three or four packs of unfiltered Lucky Strikes or Camels a day, letting most of each one smolder out in the ashtray after he'd had a drag or two. He died of lung cancer.) I had a pint-size kids' typewriter myself, one that actually worked, and I remember writing a short story on it (very short, less than a page double-spaced)—something about a mad scientist in a box canyon—when I was seven or eight. I guess I just grew up thinking that writing was what guys did. I've always suspected that if Dad had been out in the yard in overalls working on the Buick every day, I'd probably be an auto mechanic by now.

Chapter Four

El Coyote Cafe,

Los Angeles (1931–)

O NE LUNCHTIME AT THE SCHOOL CAFETERIA, WHEN I was in the fifth grade, I watched Mr. Reed, who ran the place, spooning foreign-looking reddish brown glop into round, white, waxed cartons, a thin rim of orange grease beading around its edges. As I tentatively placed one of the cartons on my tray, a sweet, slightly sharp aroma filled my nostrils, strange and compelling. When I raised a plastic spoon full of the stuff, not without apprehension, to my mouth, it tasted salty, faintly sweet, a little earthy, a little fiery. "What is this?" I asked my buddy Charlie, who had recently moved to Los Angeles from Texas. He looked at me as if I'd just asked what apple pie was. "It's chili con carne," he said.

My first taste of what I eventually figured out was an emblematic Texas specialty introduced me to flavors I had never imagined—cumin, chili powder, *garlic*—and I was smitten. Back home that afternoon, I told my mother, with considerable excitement, that I'd tried this great new dish called chili and that I couldn't wait to try it again. She scrunched up her nose and informed me, with unimpeachable maternal authority, "Oh, you don't like *that*."

When I started spending time down in Charlie's home state

about forty years later—for reasons having to do more with music and romance than with gastronomy—I would always establish my bona fides as an aficionado of Tex-Mex food by telling people "Hey, I'm from L.A.; I grew up eating all the same stuff." Unfortunately, that wasn't really true. Mexican food had no place in our house—no place in our family consciousness. Chili powder and exotic spices were banned from our kitchen as surely as were garlic and onions. We wouldn't have recognized a fresh chile, let alone known what to do with one. Tortillas would simply have made no sense; you couldn't put them in the toaster like the English muffins or Wonder bread we ate every day. Shortly before my father's death, in 1976, he asked me in all seriousness, after noticing a sign at a Mexican fast-food place we were passing, "Just what *is* a taco, anyway?" At that point, he had lived in Southern California for more than thirty-five years.

What finally made me fall in love with the flavors and textures and perfumes of Mexican food (and I include Cal-Mex, Tex-Mex, and New Mexican in that category, as well as what it is now trendy to call "interior Mexican")—which today I regularly tell people, honestly this time, is my favorite food of all—was a noisy, friendly, colorful, Americanized Mexican place on Beverly Boulevard, a couple of miles and a world away from Chasen's, called El Coyote. It took me a while to get there, though.

My dining experiences at the Ranch House undeniably broadened my culinary horizons (and probably my waistline as well), but it wasn't until I went off to college, in the fall of 1962, that I really began discovering the variety and surprise of international cuisines. Having finished four years at Villanova with credible grades, I was pretty much a shoo-in for a berth at Southern

California's major Catholic college, Loyola University (it's now Loyola Marymount), near L.A. International Airport. At Loyola, I fell in briefly with a loose clique of foreign students—mostly Latin American and French-speaking African—and regularly dined with them in the cafeteria. I have no recollection of what we ate, but it was from them that I picked up my lifelong habit of using my knife and fork "foreign" style, holding the fork upside down in my left hand for eating instead of shifting it to my right hand after cutting my food like everybody else seemed to do.

On one of my earliest excursions off campus for dinner, my roommate introduced me to the Lebanese food of his childhood at a wonderful, now long-defunct place called Hatton's, which billed itself as the first Middle Eastern restaurant in Hollywood. I fell immediately in love with this strangely flavored fare, even farther than chili con carne from anything I'd known at home: creamy, garlicky hummus, with its faintly chalky sesame-paste flavor; tabouleh, so bright and sharp and lemony; kibbee, both cooked and raw (this was the first raw meat I'd ever eaten), which revealed lamb, which I'd formerly known only as chops, to me in a whole new form; pine-nut-studded, sumac-dusted ground-lamb flatbread. . . . This was heady stuff for me.

I loved music, and that affection, in a roundabout way, led to my further culinary education. My parents weren't musical themselves, but Dad had racks of 78 rpm albums lined up underneath our old blond-wood Capehart music console, everything from Ambrose (an English dance band leader) to the gospel-singing Blind Boys of Alabama, from the jazz pianist Hazel Scott to the leftist folksinger-actor Tony Kraber, and I put these on the turntable constantly as a kid. Famous composers of the era—not just Jimmy McHugh, but also Gene Austin, Ralph Blane, and Frank Loesser, among others—used to play piano at our parties. I was a faithful fan of *Your Hit Parade* on radio, and then on TV, and remember vividly the first time I heard "Rock Around the Clock." I used to listen to Hunter Hancock playing R & B on KGFJ, concealing the radio under my covers at night when I was supposed to be asleep. Probably inevitably, then, I was drawn to Loyola's campus radio station, KXLU-FM, and wanted to be a part of it. I already had a fairly deep, resonant voice, so I auditioned to become a college DJ, and got the job. My show was called *Soul Meeting,* after an LP by the great R & B and soul-jazz tenor player King Curtis, and I featured, as I would intone in what I imagined was a hepcat voice at the beginning of every broadcast, "the finest in blues and jazz and the blues *in* jazz."

At KXLU I fell in with an older crowd, former students who still hung out around campus and helped run the broadcasts. They all lived off-campus, of course, and before long, I was sneaking into Hollywood to meet them, going to hear Lou Rawls and Ernie Andrews and Richard "Groove" Holmes at places like the It Club and Memory Lane in central Los Angeles, where we'd fantasize about the pretty waitresses and drink Cutty Sark on the rocks (nobody ever asked us for ID). Then I'd hitchhike back to campus along Manchester Boulevard at two or three in the morning, dodging the sprinklers that would sometimes suddenly spring to life along the grass strips separating the sidewalk from the street, and accepting rides from drunken businessmen and sleepy restaurant workers and jumpy kids out doing things their parents would probably kill them for. Just like me.

After a few months of this, I began extending my off-campus stays to whole weekends, sleeping on a cot in an enclosed porch off the kitchen at a house in Hollywood owned by one of my new friends, a recording engineer named John Stachowiak (he later mastered the Beatles' White Album, among many other classics).

John introduced me to my first fresh mushrooms, and to a weird vegetable I'd only vaguely heard of, called eggplant, which he ate for breakfast. I didn't like the sound of it, considering my aversion to eggs, and I watched with skepticism bordering on mild fright as he sliced one of these shiny, purple-black ovoids thin, salted the slices, let them sit for a few minutes, wiped them off, dipped them into a bath of, yes, beaten egg, dredged them in flour, and browned them in bubbling Wesson oil. He pretty much shamed me into trying a piece, and of course it was delicious—and before long I was making fried eggplant myself.

John's house was a gathering place for an oddball group of ex-Loyola students, fledgling artistic types, and stereo-music lovers (John had a knockout sound system and a record collection that went on for miles), among them a young photographer and television-history buff named Allen Daviau, who became one of my best friends. (He grew into an award-winning cinematographer, shooting *E.T. the Extra-Terrestrial* and other classic films.) John's house was on Serrano Avenue, and we took to calling the place the Serrano Gay Bar, in recognition of the fact that women were rarely seen on the premises (though we were all straight, at least as far as anyone knew at the time). Throughout these weekends, various configurations of regulars would sit around and talk and drink supermarket gin and Squirt and listen to Nina Simone and Muddy Waters, the Dukes of Dixieland and *Candide*. (None of us had started smoking pot yet, much less ingesting LSD-soaked bits of fuzzy paper.)

We ate sandwiches and I think must have ordered in pizza; we'd go pick up ribs from Carl's Hickory Pit on Pico or, when somebody felt brave enough, from Mr. Jim's ("You need no teef to eat Mr. Jim's beef"), a few miles to the south in what we called Soultown. When John or Allen had some money, they'd buy aged rib eyes or pork chops at Larsen's Meat Market on Western and John would pan-fry them. But it was also at John's house, one weekend in the spring of 1963, that I first really cooked dinner myself—not just assembling a salad or a sandwich or opening a can but following a recipe and producing something good enough for us all to eat. The dish was carbonnade, a Belgian beef stew made with dark beer. I'd clipped the recipe out of some magazine or newspaper just because I liked the sound of it—I vaguely knew that chefs cooked with wine, but I'd never heard of anybody cooking with beer—and I followed the directions precisely. I remember standing at John's old gas range and browning the meat and onions and pouring in the beer and simmering it for however long I was told to simmer it as the aromas gathered and blended and grew. If it garnered any effusive praise from my companions, I don't remember it, but I'm pretty sure that there wasn't any left a half an hour later.

I started cooking for the group at least once a weekend. Our typical Sunday evening dinner, which didn't cost much more than a dollar—for all four or five of us—was pasta of a sort, though I don't think anybody used that term back then: a Franco-American spaghetti-in-a-box kit (a pound of noodles, a little can of tomato sauce, and a metallic envelope of powdery so-called Parmesan cheese), a pound of ground beef, and—thanks for the idea, Mom—a small can of corn. I'd cook the ground beef loose, toss in the corn, moisten it all with the tomato sauce, then toss it all with the doubtless long-overcooked noodles before dusting the whole thing with the "Parmesan." Filled out with a loaf of what passed for French bread in those days in L.A. that somebody had contributed, it made a fairly satisfying meal.

Sometimes, we'd go out to eat, to the definitive Googie-style coffee shop Norms, on La Cienega; to Nickodell, next door to KHJ-TV on Melrose, where we'd eat roast chicken and watch the local celebrity news anchor Jerry Dunphy drinking at the bar; sometimes to the Balalaika, farther east on Melrose, where I was introduced to borscht, piroshki, and Pojarski cutlets. One night, John suggested that we go to a place called El Cholo Spanish Cafe, on Western Avenue south of Wilshire Boulevard. For decades, Mexican restaurants around Southern California, and probably beyond, called themselves "Spanish." El Cholo was one of the older such establishments in town, growing out of a café that had first opened in downtown L.A. in 1923 and had occupied its present location since 1931. (It is probably the second-oldest Mexican restaurant in America, after the 1922-vintage El Charro in Tucson.)

El Cholo was my first Mexican restaurant, by a long shot, and I was full of anxiety as we walked into the cluttered, warmly furnished, pleasant-smelling dining room and sat down. I doubt that I admitted this to my friends, but when I opened my menu, I recognized almost nothing—tamale, enchilada, tostada, chile relleno. . . . These were another language to me, literally and otherwise. I did see my old friend chili con carne, but I ended up ordering what looked like the safest thing (and I quote): HAMBURGER STEAK, with Chile Beans, Spaghetti and French Fried Potatoes. I think my friends must have ribbed me for my pedestrian (and non-Mexican) selection, but I enjoyed my dinner, and I had the same thing the next couple of times we went. Then one night I tried the albóndigas soup and eventually the enchiladas and even the chile relleno. I started liking the food, though I remained intimidated for some time by the leaf-wrapped lumps of damp dough called tamales. There's no question, though, that El Cholo introduced me to Mexican food. It also got me ready for El Coyote.

MY FRESHMAN YEAR at Loyola was not a success. I spent too much time at KXLU and listening to jazz and drinking scotch in

Hollywood, and I was not invited back for my sophomore year. I stayed out of school for the next eighteen months or so. Through an old film business associate, my father got me a summer job that turned into a yearlong post as an "apprentice film editor" at ABC-TV. In those days, the network sent out sixteen-millimeter prints of its various series—*Wagon Train, General Hospital, Hootenanny,* and so on—to affiliates around the country; my job involved inspecting the returned prints, making minor repairs as needed, and helping keep track of them in our film vault. While I was at ABC, I rented a studio apartment in Beverly Hills. I also auditioned for a part in a theatrical presentation, an evening of excerpts from García Lorca plays, at the women's college Mount St. Mary's, on a hill high above West Los Angeles, where my sister had enrolled. I ended up playing the bridegroom in a scene from *Blood Wedding* (with the poet Michael C. Ford as my valet) and the husband in a fragment of *Yerma*. A few months later, I got on a Greyhound bus to follow my Lorca costar, a tall senior with dark hair and Cherokee cheekbones named Vickie, to Atlanta, where she had gone to live and work for the summer.

We set up housekeeping in a little efficiency apartment on Thirteenth Street between Peachtree and West Peachtree. Vickie went off to Kelly Girls every morning, ending up in some office or another, usually answering phones; I went to the Manpower office and stood in line with an assortment of young white boys and older black men (never, for some reason, the other way around), waiting for whatever came up. I worked at the Ford Motor Company tractor parts warehouse in Decatur for a week or so, wheeling an overgrown shopping cart around and filling orders for bale counters and fan belts from the huge metal shelves; I helped dismantle an Arrow Shirt Company warehouse; I unloaded a boxcar full of office furniture for Cole, the big office products distributor. My worst job was laying tennis courts in a public park, which involved load-ing wheelbarrows full of molten paving goop from the machine that mixed it up, wheeling it up a slope to the courts through the hot, damp Atlanta summer air, dumping it out, then returning for more. The words "fire and brimstone" occurred to me more than once, and I'd come home at night with my skin and hair flecked with bits of sticky black tar.

We ate Sugar Pops cereal or Sara Lee coffee cake for breakfast. Lunch was mostly sandwiches on the job. At night, Vickie made sloppy joes, spaghetti with meat sauce, or tuna à la king on toast with frozen peas and jarred pimiento strips. Occasionally we'd splurge and go out. One night we ended up at Aunt Fanny's Cabin, a sort of Old South theme restaurant with murals of pleasant plan-tation life on the walls, complete with frolicking little black girls in pigtails and gingham dresses. "Dixie" played loudly on the sound system every half hour or so, at which point half the customers stood up proudly, as if it were the national anthem. We ate there only once.

In the fall, I followed Vickie to Cambridge, Massachusetts, where her father was working for an outfit called the Academy of Applied Science, dedicated to "promoting creativity, invention and scientific achievement" (one of the academy's projects was a long-running search for the Loch Ness Monster, using the most advanced sonar equipment). The director was a polymath named Robert H. Rines, who put me to work on various writing proj-ects, and allowed me to bunk in a room adjacent to the AAS of-fice. I spent a lot of time walking around Cambridge, stopping in shops, and reading restaurant menus. I remember in particular a spice shop on Massachusetts Avenue with big wooden barrels of olives in half a dozen colors and shapes by the door; nearby was a neon-lit Greek restaurant where, for ninety-nine cents, I could eat my fill of white rice with meat sauce spooned on top. I used to say, and honestly felt, that I experienced a New England boyhood, greatly compressed, that fall in Cambridge, and I conceived a real affection for Boston and, by extension, for New England—but as the holidays approached, I wanted to go home. Vickie stayed on in Cambridge for a few months, then came back to L.A. We broke up soon afterward.

Meanwhile, I had reclaimed my apartment in Beverly Hills, gotten a Christmas job at Campbell's Book Store, a Westwood Village institution across the street from the UCLA campus, and enrolled at L.A. City College, trying to get my higher education back on track. I declared my major as philosophy—partly, I'm sure, because I was putting on airs, but also because I'd come across a Bertrand Russell line in which he said something to the effect of "There'd be no reason to study philosophy if it weren't so much fun," and I thought I'd find out for myself if that was true. As long as I was putting on airs, I also thought, for some reason, that it might be a good idea to study Arabic, which I did for two years with an eccentric Sardinian named Dr. Curti, who'd taught himself the language. I never learned to speak more than a couple of words, but could read a little and can still transliterate the script. One of my fellow students around the language department was a young Sicilian named Piero Selvaggio, who went on to become the city's most distinguished and successful Italian restaurateur with his Valentino in Santa Monica. Another was an Armenian-American named Misha Markarian, whose family owned a restaurant called Kavkaz, in the old house above the Sunset Strip that later became the home of the original Spago.

After about a year at Campbell's, I talked myself into a position as a stockboy and sales clerk in the bookshop at the Los Angeles County Museum of Art, starting there a few months before the institution opened. I also found a new apartment, closer to the museum, a studio overlooking a little fountain in the courtyard of a red-brick Gothic Revival castle—actually an office building with a few apartments attached, built by the company responsible for many of L.A.'s classic art deco theater interiors. It was quiet, romantic, convenient to my new workplace, and reasonably cheap. And El Coyote was two blocks away.

EL COYOTE BEGAN LIFE as a little Cal-Mex café, opened by Blanche and George March on La Brea Avenue in 1931. Their intention was to feed their friends and neighbors the kind of fare Blanche had grown up with in Thatcher, Arizona, northeast of Tucson. George was in the kitchen, and Blanche ran the dining room. The restaurant got off to a slow start, but John Wayne and some of his fellow actors discovered it, and business slowly built. In 1951, when their original lease was up, the Marches moved El Coyote to a much larger building nearby, on Beverly Boulevard a few blocks west of La Brea.

By the time I arrived in the neighborhood, the restaurant had become something of a local institution, and I had become an experienced consumer of tacos, enchiladas, and the rest—even tamales. The sign the Marches installed outside their place—"El Coyote Mexican Food" in white neon against a bright red background, "Mexican" in block letters, the rest in script—usually dramatically silhouetted against a vivid blue or inky blue-black L.A. sky, was like a beacon to me. Almost as soon as I had unpacked my boxes, I headed over for a meal.

El Coyote was a hive of color, sound, and animation, a nonstop party in a series of lively dining rooms more festooned than merely decorated. Walking in that first time, I hardly knew where to look. Autographed photos of Hollywood luminaries, John Wayne and otherwise, lined the entryway. (The place remained popular with celebrities; its macabre claim to fame is that Sharon Tate and her friends had their last meal at El Coyote the night they were murdered by the Manson Family.) Christmas lights drooped everywhere, year-round, and clusters of plastic grape leaves hung from latticework; ornate sombreros, portraits of señoritas on black velvet, and mirrors framed in seashells hung on every stretch of brightly painted wall; in every corner stood huge sprays of plastic flowers, and papier-mâché birds perched here and there. The waitresses, rustling around the place in flouncy embroidered eyelet bodices and petticoated peasant skirts, seemed dedicated to keeping the festivities alive, beaming broad smiles and chattering with customers as they dispensed pitchers of margaritas and beer and big plates full of food. Somebody once described the place as a Chuck E. Cheese for adults.

I'd heard that those margaritas were famous, so of course I had to try one on my first visit. I'd never had a margarita before, so I had no basis for comparison, but I loved it. It was sweet and foamy, with no discernible tequila flavor (not that I could have discerned tequila flavor back then), and it sure went down easy. For years, that was my ideal of what a margarita should be, even after I learned that the El Cholo margarita's sweetness was due partly to a "secret ingredient," pineapple juice, and that the drink was foamy because it was mixed up in huge batches and dispensed through a bar gun. (Today I rarely drink any margaritas but my own; few bartenders get the proportions of tequila, Cointreau, and fresh lime juice—the only acceptable ingredients, in my view—right.)

My first time at El Coyote, I ordered what was to become my

standard meal there: a No. 1 combination plate, which included a shredded beef taco, a ground beef enchilada, and rice and beans. Though I eventually figured out that the platter, with its soggy meat-stuffed rolled tortilla resting in a soupy lake of melted cheese and mildly spicy brown sauce, its crisp-shelled taco overflowing with shredded yellow cheddar and iceberg lettuce that obscured its meaty filling, its pasty refried beans and tomato-flecked soft rice, didn't have much to do with what people actually ate in Mexico, it quickly became for me an emblem of what I loved about Mexican food: It was friendly, accessible fare; it was reasonably complex in flavor (even if the blend of spices that made it so probably came powdered out of 128-ounce Smart & Final canisters); best of all, it was foreign, but foreign in a way over which I could claim partial ownership as a native and longtime resident of a city whose original name was El Pueblo de Nuestra Señora de la Reina de los Angeles del Río de Porciúncula.

I tried other things in the years that I was an El Coyote regular, of course.

There was the really quite remarkable tostada, which was in fact a kind of lunch-counter salad: shredded iceberg, frozen peas, frozen green beans, canned three-bean salad, canned shredded beets, and tomatoes, anointed with something I suspect was Thousand Island dressing, heaped atop a crisp-fried corn tortilla, with beans on the side. There were nachos, of course, made with sharp cheddar and pickled jalapeño rings, and "El Coyote Pizza," which was the same thing, but with beans and salsa added. There was a respectable albóndigas soup, bready, parsley-flecked meatballs in a meaty broth with a polite kick, served in big bowls. There was something the menu listed as chili con carne, but it was far from Mr. Reed's version; it was cubes of pork in a medium-spicy brown sauce—really good—that probably should have been called chile colorado con puerco. There was even a ground round steak with French fries, though I'd gotten far beyond that by this time.

THE LOS ANGELES County Museum of Art opened in April 1965, endowed by some of the richest men and women in the city—*Life* called them "the instant Medicis"—and hordes started streaming through the galleries, and the bookshop, too. I worked hard, unpacking and putting out books, straightening and restocking the shelves, watching for shoplifters, eventually helping to do the accounts and order both books and art (we sold original lithographs and etchings, and I took a night class in graphic arts sales at artist June Wayne's esteemed Tamarind Workshop). I also hung out in the bowels of the place, with the preparators and conservators, watching as they unpacked and readied for exhibition what must have been many, many millions of dollars' worth of art and artifacts, even then. I got to know a number of the best young L.A. artists of the time—George Herms, Peter Alexander, De Wain Valentine, Eric Orr—and renewed my acquaintance with another of them, Ron Cooper, who'd lived in Ojai and whom I'd last seen when he used to bag our groceries at the Bayless supermarket, before going off to hitchhike around Europe for the summer. (I renewed our friendship yet again, thirty years later, when he started importing artisanal mescal into the United States, and we'd end up at the same food-and-wine events together, usually in Texas.)

It was a great time to be at the museum. The energy and imagination of the curators, above all the contemporary art wunderkind (as he was frequently described) Maurice Tuchman, were amazing. They mounted one dazzling show after another—an immense array of etchings, lithographs, woodcuts, and other graphic works by Picasso; a major retrospective of seductively luminous paintings by Pierre Bonnard; a show of paintings, objects, photographs, and "Rayographs" by Man Ray (who signed one of the exhibition posters for me and took me to coffee at the museum cafeteria one afternoon; I wish I could remember what we talked about); and a big collection of New York School abstract expressionists, which afforded me the chance to linger in empty galleries, before opening hours, looking at huge canvases by such artists as Jackson Pollock, Barnett Newman, Ad Reinhardt, and Mark Rothko (talk about luminous; I'd swear that the temperature in the Rothko room was five degrees warmer than anywhere else in the building). Then there was the scandalous Ed Kienholz retrospective, which an L.A. County supervisor named Warren Dorn tried to close down for obscenity—mostly defined, in his mind, by a chicken-wire couple locked in chicken-wire coitus in the artist's now iconic *Back Seat Dodge '38*. The museum couldn't have asked for better publicity, and for weeks lines of museumgoers streamed down the front steps and along the sidewalk on Wilshire Boulevard, waiting to get in.

Shortly after the museum opened, a young English girl, several years my senior, came to work at the bookshop. She was small, cute, raven-haired, smart, bitingly sarcastic, very English; she dressed in Mary Quant and Carnaby Street outfits, and carried a lethal-looking penknife. Without ever having been to England, I was already an Anglophile—this was the mid-sixties, after all, era of the Beatles and the Stones, of "swinging London"— and I was captivated by her.

I called her Martin, which was her last name, and she called me Andrews, and after a few weeks, I got up the nerve to ask her out to dinner. No doubt depleting my bank account—I knew the meal would probably cost at least twenty-five dollars—I took her to one of the classiest places in town: the Bistro, which was the Beverly Hills society restaurant of the time. Its name might suggest some modest family-owned French place, but in fact the Bistro was a fancy Continental eatery, with tableside service and flaming desserts, run by a haughty Austrian-born restaurant veteran named Kurt Niklas. The interior suggested some Hollywood set designer's vision of a Parisian brothel, complete with fringed table lamps, smoky mirrors, and black leather upholstery. It was the kind of place where ladies out of Jackie Collins novels lunched, and it was the site of the agent Swifty Lazar's famous annual Oscar Night party, later moved to Spago. (It was also the restaurant in whose upstairs banquet room Julie Christie serviced Warren Beatty under the table in *Shampoo*.)

Though I'd only been there once before, I liked the Bistro. Decor and clientele aside, it had pretty good food, and a cosmopolitan electricity that wasn't easy to find in L.A. back then, and I hoped it might impress Martin. I put on a tie for the occasion and donned my most fashionable sport coat, a sort of Italian variation on the Nehru jacket in gray tweed. Martin wore a short cotton dress banded in black and purple, and big silver hoop earrings. I have no idea what the habitués of the place, with their Don Loper dresses and London Shop blazers, must have thought of us, but we didn't much care. We sat down, ordered our dinner (the particulars elude me) and a couple of glasses of wine, and had a wonderful time. Our captain was a handsome Irishman named Jimmy Murphy (later a successful restaurateur himself), who was delighted when Martin chose fresh strawberries for dessert and then asked if there was any clotted cream to go along with them. Her question prompted an Anglo-Irish dialogue about the virtues of this opulent dairy product—for a minute or two they seemed to forget I was there—and then he went off to the kitchen, where he somehow found Martin exactly what she'd asked for. She was, she said, "chuffed."

This was our first of many meals together over the next couple of years. As we'd sit at one table or another, I'd pepper her with questions about music, fashion, theater, and politics back home, and drink in her answers. I loved her accent, her skeptical grin, her sophistication (she'd been to countries I'd barely heard of and spoke credible French and Italian as well as the fluent German of her Sudeten Czech parents)—and I loved the way she made me think before I spoke, made me sidestep constantly to avoid the clichés and cheap sentiment I knew she'd mock mercilessly. She must have liked things about me, too, as a few months after our first date, she moved into my castle on Beverly Boulevard.

Among the artifacts she brought with her was a book that opened up a whole new world to me: Len Deighton's *Action Cookbook,* a collection of brief cooking lessons in comic strip form that spy novelist Deighton had been producing for several years for *The Observer* in London. It was about as unintimidating as a cookbook could be, and, with Martin's approval, I decided that I'd teach myself to cook from its illustrated pages. There was plenty of no-nonsense culinary lore within, and I tried many of the recipes, with varying degrees of success. The single most illuminating sentence in the book, though, was Deighton's simple statement "When onions are cooked a chemical change takes place: they no longer make the eyes water, and they taste quite different." This was an absolute revelation to me—having grown up in a house where onions and their kin were anathema—and I suddenly understood what that faint appealing sweetness was in so many of the dishes I had grown to love, Mexican and Italian and down-home American alike. I also understood why Dad, who wouldn't have eaten a slice of raw onion to save his life, was mad for French onion soup, even if Mom rarely let him order it ("Oh, you don't like *that*").

Deighton was hardly my only source of culinary inspiration in those days. I started reading *Gourmet* and *Bon Appétit* and the *Los Angeles Times* food section and checking cookbooks out of the library. I clipped or transcribed recipes, putting them into a big red envelope and pulling them out more or less at random when I wanted to cook something. Among the dishes I remember making more than once are tuna steaks with onions and curry sauce (fresh tuna was a rarity in those days, and it took me a while to find it); a putatively Greek preparation of lamb baked in a foil packet with garlic, carrots, leeks, and two kinds of Greek cheese; pommes de terre Bretonne, which were thin-sliced potatoes baked with beef stock in a dish lined with bacon; ragout of pork with cider; and the Argentinean artist Lucio Fontana's puchero, the recipe for which I clipped from *Vogue*, whose celebrity cooking pages also gave me Federico Fellini's recipe for sangria, which I made to acclaim at parties for years afterward. (The secret ingredient was two table-spoons of Strega.)

I didn't cook every night, of course. Martin and I ate crisp-crusted rice and sweet, aromatic lamb stew at a little Persian place across La Brea from Hollywood High, and went to Musso's for the big pancakes they called flannel cakes, or Welsh rarebit. We went back to the Bistro when we could afford it. And I think we probably went to El Coyote at least once a week. I must have cel-ebrated three or four birthdays at the place. It was always crowded, full of film and record business types, quasi-hippies, old folks from the neighborhood, multigenerational families, big groups celebrat-ing special occasions. The food never changed, and the margaritas never stopped flowing from that bar gun.

It's hard to imagine this today, but in the sixties, sit-down Mexican restaurants were still something of a rarity around the country, especially outside the Southwest. El Coyote was hardly the first one, but the combination of its central location, its friendly spirit, and its easy-to-enjoy and reasonably priced food made it probably the most popular Mexican place in Southern California, at least in that era, and in a way one of the most influential. I wonder how many modern-day lovers of South-of-the-Border food—even aco-lytes of Diana Kennedy or Rick Bayless, or more-authentic-than-*usted* devotees of moles in Oaxaca, tamales in Pátzcuaro, or sea urchin tacos in Ensenada—were first introduced to basic Mexican forms and flavors, or really came to love them, at El Coyote. I'll bet I'm not the only one.

Chapter Five

THE ADRIATIC,

Los Angeles (1964–1974)

I've NEVER UNDERSTOOD WHY WE ARE DRAWN TO certain places, places that, at least when we're first attracted to them, we've never seen, places with which we have no familial or cultural connection. Why are we enthralled, sometimes seemingly out of nowhere, by what we know or imagine of the look and feel and sensibility of other cities, countries, corners of the world, or even by just their very names? As a young teenager, I was drawn to the notion of the South Pacific. This probably isn't hard to understand, considering the romantic image I had of Polynesia: sun, sea, sand, palm trees, warm breezes, and, yeah, okay, exotic cocktails and babes in bikinis. But why not, then, the Caribbean, Mexico, Rio de Janeiro? No idea. No logic. Generations of European intellectuals dreamed of Tibet or Timbuktu, for not much more reason than that their names sounded mysterious and impossibly far away. My father, for his part, had only a passing interest in Europe and none at all, as far as I know, in Africa or Latin America, but as a boy conceived a lifelong fascination with India.

By the time I turned twenty-one, having long since realized that I wasn't going to make it to Tahiti or Samoa in the foreseeable future (and frankly no longer caring whether I did or not), the region that was beginning to capture my imagination was Eastern Europe, meaning places like Bulgaria, Romania, and Yugoslavia— and in particular three cities whose names I'd come across in various contexts: Sarajevo, Dubrovnik, and Zagreb. I have absolutely no idea why I found the idea of these places so compelling. I had read no stirring adventure novels, seen no memorable films about that part of the world; I knew no Eastern Europeans. And Sarajevo, Dubrovnik, and Zagreb? I couldn't have found them on a map, and at first I didn't even realize that they were all in the same country (and later, of course, it turned out that they weren't)—but they sounded irresistibly romantic to me.

I was abetted in my Balkan daydreams by the Adriatic, a restaurant that opened in 1964 on Wilshire Boulevard in Beverly Hills. The proprietors were a genial couple named Bob and Gordana Sipovac, she a warmly pretty blond woman with a genuine smile, he an amiable, husky fellow with a broad Slavic face and an athlete's shoulders. The couple had moved to California from their homeland in 1959. They'd had only limited experience in the restaurant business—Gordana's family had run eating places in Serbia before World War II; Bob, who'd grown up in Sarajevo, in Bosnia, was tending bar at the Beverly Hills Italian restaurant and celebrity hangout La Scala—when they decided to open their place, but they were naturals, with a good sense of food and a talent for professional hospitality.

In decor, the Adriatic could have been mistaken for a more or less standard Italian restaurant of the time, with red-and-white-checked tablecloths, red leather booths, and wine bottles lined up on shelves and hanging from wooden archways—except that some of those wine bottles, interspersed with the usual Chianti fiaschi, bore names like Žilavka, Plavac, and Dingač, and there were paintings of Adriatic scenes, including that unmistakable walled mini-peninsula of a city, Dubrovnik, on the walls.

The menu was something else, though. Here I learned to eat—and to pronounce the names of—yet another whole new category of food: Bosnian-style bureks, which were damp but flaky snail-like coils of pastry filled with ground lamb or a sort of cottage cheese; ćevapčići and ražnjići (skinless sausages and flat veal kebabs, respectively, with chopped raw onions on the side); sarma (cabbage stuffed with ground pork and veal); the Serbian mixed rice-and-vegetable casserole called djuvec. . . . The food was always accompanied by slabs of the restaurant's extraordinary bread, a yeasty, crumbly, faintly lemony white loaf of a kind that I've never encountered anywhere else but can still almost taste. (It was made from a family recipe of Gordana's.) As a condiment for both the bread and the meat dishes, the restaurant served the Serbian relish called ajvar, made of roasted red peppers, garlic, and olive oil. I liked it so much, I practically ate it as a vegetable.

At the Adriatic, too, I developed a taste for šljivovica, or slivovitz, the throat-scorching, soul-stirring clear brandy, consumed under various names all over Eastern Europe, distilled from bright blue damson plums. Something about its flavor, tart, faintly metallic, fruity in a lean but rounded way, appealed to me immensely. I liked it so much that one evening Bob and Gordana invited me over to their apartment near the restaurant to sample a special bottle they'd brought from Yugoslavia. And I liked it so much that, in later years, I drank enough of it to provoke what were easily the worst hangovers of my life, more than a few times.

The Adriatic fed my gullet, but also my imagination, fueling my determination to actually visit Yugoslavia. In 1966, I managed to scrape together a little money, secured a two-month leave of absence from the art museum, and began to plan a summer trip to the places I had been dreaming about. This was a major undertaking for me. Apart from one visit to Vancouver with my parents when I was fourteen or fifteen, I'd never been out of the country. I was reasonably well educated and well read, but I wasn't at all what you'd call worldly. Fortunately, Martin—who actually *came* from the other side of the Atlantic—was an old hand at traveling around the continent. She'd even been to Yugoslavia.

We flew to London on a cheap charter flight (I think our tickets cost $150, round trip), then took a train to Manchester, where Martin's parents lived. I then went off to Paris on the boat-train by myself for three days. Martin met me there and we took the overnight train—the Orient Express!—to Trieste, traveling in second-class couchettes. Trieste was the Italian gateway to Yugoslavia, but that's not why we stopped there. I had unfocused aspirations to be a filmmaker in those days, and had invented an imaginary production company, given the dubious credibility of business cards and letterhead, called Serrano Films, Ltd. (a reference to my days at the Serrano Gay Bar). On this letterhead, at some point, solely out of idle curiosity, I had written for information to the organizers of Trieste's annual Science Fiction Film Festival, and received by return mail, to my considerable surprise, a letter offering me a free pass for two to the event, with complimentary hotel accommodations and meals for a week included. It would have seemed churlish not to accept.

The festival installed us at the Albergo Corso, a comfortable old hotel with creaky floors and warm wood paneling and bathrooms down the hall, and gave us meal vouchers good at several local trattorias. Our favorite became the Birreria Forst, where we had repeated meals of insalata mista, pasta with livery meat sauce, and Italian lager. Martin spoke some Italian, of course, and ordered for us. I sat there pretty much in a daze, at least for the first few days, not quite believing that I was in a real Italian restaurant, in Italy, surrounded by Italians. The festival screenings were alfresco affairs in a big courtyard at the Castello di San Giusto, on a hill overlooking the city. We saw Russian space epics, Belgian ghost stories, American monster movies, and a Czech fantasy called *Who Wants to Kill Jessie,* in which speech balloons appeared over the heads of live-action characters. In between screenings, we'd cool ourselves with ice cream bars sold by wandering vendors or order salami sandwiches and half liters of cheap wine from the castle caffè, sitting under a grape arbor that I was inordinately impressed to notice had bunches of real grapes on it, not the plastic ones that restaurants back in Los Angeles had.

When the festival was over, we backtracked to Venice, where my uncle Paul, who worked for an advertising agency in Manhattan handling travel accounts, had arranged to have us put up for free for a week at the Quattro Fontane, a rambling resort hotel on the Lido, which seemed part California guest ranch and part Alpine chalet. Venice stunned me. As much as I'd read about it, as many pictures as I'd seen, I couldn't quite completely grasp that most of the streets really were water, and that all that decorative sugar frosting on the buildings was stone, and very old. The Quattro Fontane was nice enough, but we spent most of our time in the city itself, taking the vaporetto from the Lido to the Piazza San Marco every morning and prowling around endlessly, getting intentionally lost down narrow alleyways smelling of cat urine and espresso, which sometimes ended abruptly at water's edge but sometimes opened into beautiful little squares where children kicked a soccer ball around and old men sat on benches in the sun playing cards. We ate in pizzerias or fixed-price student places, went to every museum and art gallery we could find, and allowed ourselves one coffee a day at one of the expensive caffès in the shadow of the Campanile. Back at our island hotel each night, we'd dine on cold antipasto and grilled fish or veal, sipping from a bottle of wine that, as inconceivable as this is to me now, we never quite finished at one sitting (they'd mark it and save it for our next meal).

Then, finally, Yugoslavia. After our week in Venice, we boarded a Jadrolinija steamer, with a big red star on its smokestack, rented a couple of wood-slat deck chairs, and settled back as we headed down the Dalmatian coast toward Dubrovnik, along the way passing towns of sand-colored stone buildings with red-tile roofs, isolated green-shuttered villas surrounded by tall trees, rocky coves and shrub-covered islets, and in the background endless barbicans of barren gray karst cliffs.

Our arrival in Dubrovnik was less than auspicious. A museum bookshop colleague of mine in L.A. knew a Croatian woman named Rose, who worked at the Bank of America in Beverly Hills. When he learned that I was going to Dubrovnik, he introduced us, and Rose told me that her grandmother had some vacation cottages for rent in an ideal location on the edge of the city. We gave her our dates, and she made reservations for us. I had visions of a charming little bungalow with whitewashed walls and a terrace looking out over the wine-dark Mediterranean. Disembarking from the boat, we found a taxi driver and gave him the address that Rose had given us—Kraljevića Marka Ulica, Prince Mark Street. He looked at us blankly. There was no such thoroughfare, he assured us. We asked to be taken to the local tourist office instead. They were as puzzled as the taxi driver had been. No, no such street existed, and no rooms were registered to rent under the grandmother's name. The tourism folks were very nice, though, and booked us a rental room in a big private house surrounded by palm trees between the walled town and the port.

It turned out that Rose's grandmother was real; after we'd

gotten settled, the tourist office helped us track her down. Not a little apprehensively, we knocked on her door. Fortunately, she spoke German in addition to Croatian, so Martin was able to communicate with her, and she invited us in for tea. She had never owned any cottages, she told us, and hadn't heard from Rose for years, and she certainly couldn't imagine why her granddaughter would mislead us. Neither could we. Did she dislike Americans and enjoy playing tricks on them? Was she simply a pathological liar? We never found out. When we got back to L.A., I was tempted to call her or just drop into the bank, but decided against it, and simply chalked it up to experience. (I am still sort of curious, though. . . .)

Our nonexistent cottage aside, Dubrovnik didn't disappoint me. It looked like a smaller Venice without the canals (no wonder: under its old name of Ragusa, the city was controlled by the Venetians for 150 years in the thirteenth and fourteenth centuries), but with an overlay of something Eastern, non-Mediterranean, doubly foreign. And, I had to keep reminding myself, something communist—though about the only signs we saw of the totalitarian dictatorship I'd been conditioned all my life to expect in "commie countries" were official portraits of Marshal Tito in every shop and restaurant.

We settled into a rhythm. We did some touristy things: We poked our heads into dark, chilly churches full of gilt-framed icons with Slavic features; visited the medieval pharmacy (still operating) with its shelves of old ceramic apothecary jars in the Franciscan monastery, and an exhibition of not very good local cityscapes in a city gallery; eavesdropped on an open-air concert of Vivaldi (we couldn't afford even the cheap tickets); climbed up on the city ramparts and walked the walls; joined hundreds of evening strollers walking back and forth along Dubrovnik's main street. I bought a phrase book and learned a few words of what was then called Serbo-Croatian, beyond the dish names I'd learned at the Adriatic. Mostly, though, we just lay in the sun on the seaside rocks outside the Pile Gate or took a motor launch to the pebbly beaches on the tiny island of Lokrum, just beyond the city's harbor, and swam in the sea, and took afternoon naps, and read three-day-old English newspapers in cafés with wobbly tables and rickety metal chairs.

After a few weeks in Dubrovnik, we got back on a ferry and went a bit farther south to the old sea captains' town of Orebić, not much more than a handful of quiet houses and a shop or two, and then across a narrow strait to another walled city, Korčula, on the island of the same name, which was like a smaller, less touristy Dubrovnik. We continued to rent rooms in private houses, and spent our days on rocky beaches framed in tamarisk and pine trees or wandering along old stone streets and through scraggly vineyards. One of the vineyards, near a bare-bones swimming cove we frequented, grew an ancient grape variety called grk, and the rich, yellowish, aromatic white wine it produced, under the same name, became my favorite.

I got very tan that summer and about as thin as I have ever been as an adult. What I remember most from my five or six weeks in Croatia, in fact, is being hungry. We didn't have a lot of money, for one thing, but it was something else, too: The restaurants we patronized, modest places above the beaches or in the warrens of narrow stone streets in the towns themselves, were universally understaffed and very busy. Once we got seated and ordered our meals—occasionally veal gulaš (goulash) but more typically ražnjići or ćevapčići or a kind of onion-specked hamburger patty called pljeskavica, made with pork, lamb, and beef—it would typically take an hour or more to get our food. We'd have to just sit there, sipping bubbly, salty mineral-rich water or nursing sour Croatian beer, our stomachs gurgling as other tables got served in order, painfully slowly, one by one. Sometimes instead of going to a restaurant, we'd buy food at a shop—grapes, tiny plums, or peaches; bread and butter, liquid yogurt, tangy cheese, maybe a chocolate bar to share—and eat in the shade by the beach. This wasn't exactly backpacking and sleeping under bridges, but it was no packaged tour, either, and in retrospect I felt glad that I hadn't been spoiled, in my first experience of Europe, by too much ease or comfort.

For practical reasons—time and money, most of all, but also a reluctance to leave our seaside life too soon—I'd taken Zagreb out of my fantasy visit to Yugoslavia, but I was determined to get to Sarajevo. Martin wanted to go back to England for a week to spend more time with her family and see some friends in London, and I decided to stay on and head inland to the Bosnian capital myself by bus. The day before she left, I got very sick—dizzy, with aching joints, a bad headache, and a high fever. Martin couldn't change her ticket home, so we took the ferry back to Dubrovnik together, I wishing for an early death as the boat sloshed through the water, jiggling my insides. She left me in Dubrovnik with a copy of the *Newsweek* international edition in whose margins she'd written a number of potentially useful phrases—"Call a doctor," "Where's the hospital?," "I have a fever," and so on—in German, and I bought a bus ticket and went off to follow my dream.

The bus was a rattletrap affair, a big old pale blue, mud-splattered coach with hard plastic-covered seats and tired shock absorbers. It was packed, but as we jostled up the coast and then turned right, up into the foothills of the Dinaric Mountains, the driver seemed to stop every twenty miles or so to pick up a few more passengers, who'd perch on the edges of already occupied seats or stand, holding on to the luggage racks and swaying with the bus. I was still feverish, and the jouncing of the bus made my sore joints and muscles throb—but looking out the windows as we idled at our first stop, Mostar, and then crawled through the town, I was enthralled. I'd never seen a minaret before, and Mostar's shot up from a bank of greenery like a rocket aimed at paradise. We passed the elegant Ottoman-built Stari Most, or Old Bridge, from which Mostar takes its name—a perfect humpbacked arch of luminous limestone spanning the Neretva River—which seemed to me one of the most graceful things I'd ever seen. (It was destroyed by Croatian Defence Council artillery in 1993, during the Bosnian War; a replica now stands in its place.) Most of all, I was amazed by the people I saw on the sidewalks or sitting on café terraces—men in black vests with nubby woolen caps, women in long embroidered skirts with scarves on their heads, children wearing necklaces of what looked like gold coins. Dubrovnik was more or less a Mediterranean tourist town, not dramatically different from one in Italy, but now I felt as if I were in the Middle East. I remember thinking that I was a very long way from a table at the Adriatic.

When I got to Sarajevo, I was so weak that I could hardly move. I found a clean, surprisingly attractive, vaguely Alpine-looking hotel near the bus station, bought two bottles of mineral water, and went to bed. I spent the next twenty-four hours in something approaching a delirium, sweating, sleeping, moaning to myself. A maid poked her head in the door at one point, took one look at me, and disappeared. It never occurred to me that there might be something seriously wrong with me, even something life-threatening. I suppose I was young enough to still feel more or less indestructible. By the evening of my second day in Sarajevo, in any case, I'd begun to feel a little better. I went down to the hotel dining room and managed to eat a meat-filled burek and a salad of tomatoes and raw onions. The next morning, still weak but no longer burning, I went out to see the city.

I went down to the Miljacka River, which flows through Sarajevo. Near the Ottoman bridge called the Latinska Ćuprija, I eased my feet into what were said to be the footprints, sunken into the concrete, of Gavrilo Princip, who had stood in that very spot when he shot the Archduke Franz Ferdinand of Austria in 1914, setting off World War I. I crept into the sixteenth-century Gazi Husrev-beg Mosque, with its turreted minaret, fatter than the one in Mostar, and gray-green domes—non-Muslim visitors were allowed in the afternoons—and gazed in wonderment at the expanse of warm-hued Turkish carpets covering the floor, the soaring whitewashed arches and tracery-etched wood doors, the icicle ornamentation descending from the edges of the dome.

What I remember most vividly, though, is wandering through the Sarajevo market. This was in a big square just beyond the Husrev-beg Mosque, which loomed over one end of it. The stands were closely packed together, shaded by identical umbrellas in yellow, red, green, and blue. The aisles were crowded with housewives in drab dresses, farm women in white tunics and bright scarves, men in black vests and black caps, boys in T-shirts. A big woman in a peasant skirt and dark blue hood sat behind a low table filled with broad earthenware dishes heaped with spices—paprika, cumin, cinnamon, peppercorns. An old man with a furrowed face and an embroidered fez sold ceramic-lined copper cezves, long-handled pots for making Turkish coffee. There were piles of green tomatoes, jumbles of large, twisted squashes, acres of long red and squat green peppers, braids of onions, braids of garlic, bowls of apricots and plums both blue and green, cartons of light brown eggs, mounds of fresh white cheese sitting in yellow plastic tubs, a glass case full of chickens with their heads and feet still on. . . . I had never seen food sold like that. Even the famous fish and vegetable markets near the Rialto Bridge in Venice, though they were filled with things I'd never seen, had seemed somehow accessible, understandable. This was another world. I could have been in Istanbul, I thought. I had certainly never been anywhere else remotely as exotic. This was why I'd come to Yugoslavia, even if I hadn't known that when I left Los Angeles.

BACK HOME, MARTIN AND I parted ways, and I transferred from L.A. City College to Cal State, L.A., where I continued studying philosophy. I kept dining at the Adriatic, though now, I felt, with more authority. A few years later, I got a magazine job a few blocks from the restaurant, and for a time used to walk over to have lunch, either alone or with coworkers, at least twice a week, dispatching a bottle of red wine myself, and sometimes a slivovitz or two, before returning to my desk. I took girlfriends to the place, hoping to impress them with my pronunciation of the dish names on the menu and, I suppose, with my worldliness at having been to Yugoslavia. One night I had a twilight dinner there with somebody I was seeing, then dropped her off at home and met a late date, with whom I went right back to the place to have another meal. Gordana just looked at me with a faint smile when I reappeared, and almost imperceptibly shook her head.

As the seventies unfolded, I went a little less often to the Adriatic, as I discovered other interesting restaurants and started spending more time at local music clubs in the evenings. In 1974, I came back from a two-week vacation to discover that the place had closed. The Sipovacs, it turned out, had decided that they didn't want their teenage sons to go to Beverly Hills High—"There were lots of drugs on campus," Gordana told me years later—and had moved to a town near Palm Springs, where they opened another version of the restaurant. It lasted until 1982, but I never got there. Bob and Gordana got divorced. The Socialist Federal Republic of Yugoslavia began falling apart in 1992, and after years of bloodshed splintered into seven independent states.

Chapter Six

AUX AMIS DU BEAUJOLAIS,

Paris (1921–2009)

I'M IN AN OLD-STYLE BISTRO DU QUARTIER—A NEIGH-borhood joint—in Paris, on the corner of the rue de Berri and the rue d'Artois, two blocks from the Champs-Élysées. In the front room, there's a long zinc bar, scratched and pitted. Behind it is a man of medium height, in his fifties, with shiny dark gray hair, an angular face glowing with bright red blotches, and a seen-it-all expression that is part grin, part grimace. With deliberate speed and a steady rhythm, he fills glass after glass with Sancerre or Beaujolais and serves up plates of shredded celeriac and carrots, pâté or Camembert sandwiches on hunks of baguette, and bowls of quivering crème caramel to waves of locals who stop in for a quick stand-up lunch. At small tables crowded against the windows, other customers take more time, eating, between cigarettes, their faux-fillet with frites, rabbit in mustard sauce, or blanquette de veau.

The back room, with its murky off-white walls and red leatherette banquettes, is crowded with more tables, lined up neatly, almost touching one another, draped with pink patterned cotton tablecloths covered with sheets of shiny, dimpled paper. Daylight floods the room, through gauzy half curtains, softening the metallic glow of the fluorescent tubes along the ceiling. The air rings with rapid-fire French, accented English, and the clink of tinny flatware on cheap china.

I'm sitting here with Claude. We've had glasses of Sancerre, icy and tart, at the bar, and now, elbow to elbow with our neighbors—a couple of tweed-suited businessmen on one side; two junior editors from *Newsweek,* whose Paris office is just down the street, on the other—we have finished lunch: pâté de campagne and a quarter of a roasted chicken for me, marinated herring and boeuf bourgignon for him, all irrigated with a bottle of pretty decent Beaujolais-Villages. We decide, as usual, to have another couple of glasses of red wine and some cheese. Claude leans back with an imperious scowl and booms "Jean-nine!" quite oblivious to the waitress's whereabouts. "Un Can-tal! Un Roque-fort! Jean-nine!"

I repeat moments like this, with Claude, at Aux Amis du Beaujolais, at least once or twice a year for almost thirty years, and it is at these moments—in this workaday establishment, devoted to nothing more than the consumption, in reasonable haste and marginal comfort, of ample quantities of dependably good food and wine in the pure French bistro style—that I feel most vividly and undeniably as if I am in Paris.

I do love dining in the city's temples of gastronomy—Robuchon, Guy Savoy, L'Ambroisie, even touristy old Maxim's and La Tour d'Argent—and I love sitting in cafés on the place Saint-Michel or the boulevard Saint-Germain or the rue de la Paix, nursing my double espresso or my cheap calvados and watching the city pass by. I get goose bumps when I come upon the place de la Concorde at night, or watch the multicolored lights flickering on the Seine from the pont des Arts. I can happily prowl the Louvre or the Centre Pompidou for hours, and I duck into every open church I see, just to look at the stained-glass windows and the paintings of Saint George, Saint Peter, and the Madonna barely visible in dark little chapels along the outer aisles. Merely walking the streets and boulevards here makes me happy. But lunch with Claude at Aux Amis du Beaujolais *is* Paris to me, and always will be, though both he and the bistro are now gone.

CLAUDE CASPAR-JORDAN. Where to begin? I met him in 1966, on my first night in Paris, when I'd left Martin behind in England and taken the boat-train down to the French capital. On the recommendation of a friend, I'd checked into a tiny Left Bank hotel called the Esmeralda, just across the river from Notre-Dame. It was the perfect place for a young romantic on his first trip to Paris. I liked the name, to begin with—Esmeralda was the ill-fated gypsy girl in *The Hunchback of Notre-Dame*—but the hotel's appeal was much more than literary: The building was ancient, with broad, rough-hewn ceiling beams and stone walls. A narrow, winding wooden garret staircase led up four stories, with three or four rooms on each floor, minuscule, furnished with flea-market antiques and dusty bedspreads. The only amenity was a small sauna off one of the landings, with a framed faded color photograph of a slender, naked, sauna-taking blonde on the door. Out the casement windows, you could see not only Notre-Dame but also, just across the street, the Gothic walls of the oldest church in Paris, Saint-Julien-le-Pauvre. It didn't hurt that there always seemed to be a couple of pretty, willowy young girls coming or going in the low-ceilinged lobby (French *Vogue* apparently liked to put up models there), and that there was a man staying in a room on the top floor who would practice his flute, sitting by the open window, several times a day. (I recognized him on the staircase one day: It was the English actor Terence Stamp, an Esmeralda regular.)

I remember perfectly my first day in Paris: I arrived midmorning from London, left my suitcase at the Esmeralda, then followed the sidewalk above the quais along the Seine, walking west past an endless line of bouquinistes, the used-book sellers hawking everything from old *Life* magazines to illuminated first editions of *Le petit prince* to reproductions of naughty nineteenth-century postcards out of their dark green wooden storage bins. It was June, and the girls were wearing light, clingy skirts; the faint breeze was perfumed with Gauloises smoke and the scent of damp stone; the plane trees were thick with luminous green leaves. Light bounced off the river, as long, slow tourist boats glided by and seagulls (I was surprised to see) swept past. I kept saying to myself, "I'm in Paris! I'm in Paris!"

By two in the afternoon, I was getting hungry. My ability to speak French didn't extend much beyond *bonjour, merci*, and *un* through *dix*. With no experience of Paris, and no idea of how much English the Parisians might speak, I seriously wondered whether I'd be able to communicate well enough to get anything to eat. Then I had a bright idea: Consulting my map, I crossed over the pont du Carrousel, then took the rue de Rivoli to the neighborhood of the U.S. Embassy—in those days a hospitable symbol of a proud country, not a fortified bunker. Surely the waiters in the cafés around there would speak English, I reasoned. I ducked into a little place beneath a black-and-white-striped awning on the rue Boissy d'Anglas. The place was nearly empty. A waiter greeted me with a none-too-friendly "Yes?" while looking at his watch, and then begrudgingly showed me to a rickety marble-top table, where I ordered my first meal in France: a thin, chewy T-bone steak with pommes frites, a bottle of dark Alsatian beer, and a sliver of strawberry tart.

After lunch, I trekked back the way I'd come, wandered around the streets of the Quartier Latin for an hour or so, then returned to the Esmeralda and took a nap. That night at half past seven, by previous arrangement, Claude and his wife, Pepita, came to pick me up and take me out to dinner. Claude was sixty at the time, and I was twenty-one. When he saw me standing on the sidewalk waiting for him, he told me much later, he recognized me at once. "I could have been looking at your father as he was the last time I saw him," he said. That had been in 1930, in Chicago.

IN THE TWENTIES, the *Daily News*'s Paris bureau sometimes shipped young French newspapermen to Chicago for an immersion course in American journalism. One of these was Claude, then a fledgling reporter for the left-wing Parisian daily *Le Quotidien*. "In practice," wrote my father in *A Corner of Chicago*, his memoir of his newspaper days in that midwestern capital, "this produced a passing parade of scapegrace sons whose prominent parents were being repaid for favors done to our correspondents overseas. Generally, they came with loud reluctance, and departed as soon as foolishly forgiving mothers sent return fare. But Claude Caspar-Jordan came because he wanted to come, and arrived prepared to scalp red Indians on State Street and spit in Al Capone's eye." The two became fast friends. My father liked Claude's devil-may-care attitude and his taste for the city's underbelly, and ended up, unexpectedly, being inspired by the young Frenchman. "After two weeks," he wrote, "[Claude] knew Chicago like a book. I hadn't turned the second page." Claude's example, he added, got him out of the office, out on the streets, into the grit of the city, and made him a better reporter—and a better writer—in the process.

In 1930 Claude got a telegram from France: He'd been drafted, and had to return home. My father and his colleagues gave him a going-away party, then poured him onto the Sunset Limited to San Francisco, whence he would sail back to France the long way around, through the Panama Canal. As the train pulled out, Claude promised to be back. "I never saw or heard of him again," my father wrote in *A Corner of Chicago*. He'd assumed that Claude had been killed during World War II. When the book was published, in 1963, however, an old *Chicago Daily News* reporter wrote to my father to say that Claude was very much alive, and had had a good career in journalism, eventually becoming the administrative director of Associated Press France. The two reconnected by mail and planned a reunion when my father could manage to route himself through Paris on one of his trips to the Far East. When I told Dad that I was going to Paris myself, in 1966, he arranged for me to meet Claude first.

If I resembled my father as Claude had known him in Chicago, I could have recognized Claude, likewise, from my father's description of him in those long-gone days: "The battered beak of a dissolute Napoleonic eagle hung crookedly in his pale, old-young face. His sparse blond hair stood up like the uneven bristles in a worn-out bathbrush." All still true. Pepita, on the other hand, was elegant and stylish, with a finely sculpted face and a short crop of silky white hair. She spoke no English, but Claude spoke it with great enthusiasm, sprinkling in slightly mangled slang terms he must have learned in the 1920s in Chicago. ("Hell bells!" he exclaimed halfway through our meal, to emphasize his displeasure at our waiter's slowness.)

We dined that night at Brasserie Julien, a busy bistro on the rue Faubourg Saint-Denis. I had steak frites again. After dinner, Claude and Pepita treated me to a tour of Paris by night. We drove up to Montmartre, where I saw the Sacré-Coeur washed in white light, as well as a few genuine Parisian prostitutes, mostly plump, with bleached or henna-dyed hair, wearing fishnet hose and garter belts, lounging with bored looks in doorways. We circled the Madeleine, then careered through the place de la Concorde, dodging taxis and motorbikes, Claude exclaiming "Salaud!" and "Espèce de crétin!" at various other drivers. Crossing the river, we worked our way to the boulevard Saint-Germain, found a place to park, and drank cognac at the Deux Magots. Then Claude and Pepita dropped me at the Esmeralda, and I collapsed on my bed.

At some point in the course of the evening, Claude and I realized that we got along pretty well together, connecting on some as yet undefined level that had surprisingly little to do, at least for me, with my father. Our meal at Julien turned out to be the first of what must have been close to two hundred lunches and dinners we were to share, sometimes with Pepita but mostly not, until his death in 1994. They had never had children of their own, and at some point I think I must have become a kind of part-time stand-in son for them. Before long, I had taken to calling Claude, only half in jest, mon père adoptif.

AFTER MY FIRST BRIEF VISIT to Paris and my summer on the Dalmatian coast, it took me about eighteen months to get back to Europe again. Once I did, I started making regular trips whenever I'd sold enough freelance articles or saved enough of my meager paychecks, flying across the Atlantic at least twice a year, usually going straight to Paris and installing myself at the Esmeralda and spending time with Claude. Later, as my travels extended into other parts of France, to Italy, and back to Eastern Europe, I'd still manage to route myself through Paris; sometimes just for a few hours, long enough for lunch, between planes.

When I was staying longer, I often dined at Claude and Pepita's apartment near Père Lachaise, where Pepita prepared her excellent boeuf à la mode or blanquette de veau or some other classic of French cuisine bourgeoise. (Claude's one specialty, which he made for me on several occasions, was homard au whisky, good Normandy lobster flambéed with scotch.) The three of us had glorious restaurant meals together, too, not just in Paris but in Provence, Burgundy, Alsace, and the Charente-Maritime, where they used to visit a friend on the Île de Ré, a monkey-wrench-shaped island off La Rochelle, famous for its shellfish. But Pepita drank little and ate lightly and preferred not to spend long hours at the table, and she recognized early that, however improbably, I had turned out to be one of the few people her cranky old French husband could actually talk to. Thus she was content, time and again, to send us off to dine without her.

Claude loved to eat and drink. He belonged to gastronomic societies with names like the Académie Rabelais, La Bedaine (The Belly), La Queue de Poële (The Pan Handle), the Académie des Poètes Chevelus (the Academy of Hairy Poets—the joke being that most of them were bald or balding), and Les Francs-Mâchons de Lyon (difficult to translate, but something like the Serious Eaters of Lyon). The last of these held its occasional meetings at various Lyonnais-style bistros in Paris at breakfast time, beginning around 8:00 A.M., and Claude took me to one of them. We ate platters full of pâté, ham, and saucisson, then boeuf bourgignon and assorted chèvres, washed down with plenty of Beaujolais. We were done by ten, and, no, we didn't meet again for lunch.

Over the years, Claude and I went out to meals both classic and contemporary, good and bad, mostly French but with an occasional Chinese, Indian, Lebanese, Portuguese, or even American excursion thrown in. What we liked most of all, though, was simple, hearty, honest French stuff, as served in restaurants of a kind that achieve their apotheosis in Paris: the massive, perfect côte de boeuf in the bustling downstairs dining room at Ma Bourgogne on the boulevard Haussmann (better than Taillevent's, as we once proved to our mutual satisfaction at lunch on two successive days at one place and then the other); the oysters and choucroute at Le Muniche or Le Petit Zinc; the fillets of mackerel poached in court bouillon and the roasted woodcock on toast at the now-defunct L'Artoise, a block from Aux Amis du Beaujolais.

It is hardly an exaggeration to say that most of what I know about eating in Paris—and about Paris in general—I learned from Claude. He knew food, not with the knowledge of the dilettante or the culinary professional but with the intimate, affectionate confidence of the genuine connoisseur. He took pleasure in the way the dishes he chose looked and smelled and tasted, and—the mark of a true food lover—he took pleasure in anticipating them before they appeared and then remembering them long after they had been digested. He was perfectly capable of enjoying the complicated contemporary fancies of the younger generation of French chefs, but he always approached such food with some measure of skepticism: It was guilty until proven edible. He preferred food—and restaurants—he could count on.

That didn't mean that he was uncritical of the older places, though. His standard comment when I'd ask about various restaurants that had been around for decades seemed to be "Well, it's not what it used to be." One of the first McDonald's in Paris—

maybe the first—opened in Les Champs, a shopping arcade on the Champs-Élysées, not far from Claude's office on the rue de Berri. One day I asked if he had eaten there. "Yes," he said. "It was all right at first. But it's not what it used to be."

The conversations Claude and I had over our long, wine-fueled lunches and dinners, meals often quite heroic in proportion, were never exclusively about food. One night, as we were polishing off one of Pepita's excellent home-cooked dinners, Claude casually mentioned that he had been part of the evacuation of Dunkirk as a cavalryman attached to the British army. He escaped across the channel on a boat belonging to the North Western railway line, a boat usually used to ferry passengers between Ireland and the north of England. "The soldiers weren't given berths," he said, "but were told to make up their sleeping bags in the dining rooms and salons. In the morning they were given breakfast—and then presented with bills! There was consternation all around, as few of us had any British currency, but eventually everybody paid, borrowing money if necessary. We left Dunkirk around midnight, and arrived in Dover late the next morning. There, in the bright sun, beneath the castle, there were officers in white playing tennis. The soldiers onboard taunted them, and the officers couldn't understand why."

Another time, we were dining at the Moulin du Village, next door to Steven Spurrier's wine shop in the now-vanished Cité Berryer off the rue Royale. The place was run by an Englishman I'd come to know, Mark Williamson, also proprietor of the famous Willi's Wine Bar, and one of the items on the menu, which Claude ordered, was côte de boeuf with "petit pudding de Yorkshire." This got him reminiscing about being sent with his younger brother to live in England for a few months when he was sixteen, to learn English. The boys had a pair of maiden aunts in Odiham, in

Hampshire, and they arranged for the two to lodge there with the family of a baker—whose name was Baker. The aunts kept a formal home, with maids who wore gray in the mornings, black in the afternoons, and would take Claude and his brother to church on Sundays—where the sermon, he recalled, was read by Neville Chamberlain, who lived nearby. The baker had two daughters, a blonde and a brunette, and Claude fell in love with both of them. His aunts found out about his infatuation and told him, "It is not correct to fall in love with a baker's daughter." Claude said "Okay," and that was that—an easy capitulation that seemed, all these many years later, to embarrass him. He suddenly stopped talking, looked confused for a moment, and said, "Why the hell am I telling you this?" Then he remembered. "Ah," he said, "once a week the baker would make roast beef with Yorkshire pudding, and to this day it was the best I have ever had."

We used to go sometimes to La Coupole, eating oysters with Alsatian Riesling and then steak au poivre or lamb curry with Beaujolais or Côtes-du-Rhône and enjoying the crowd. La Coupole was the quintessential Paris brasserie, legendary in the old days for its good food but also its illustrious clientele. Everybody came sooner or later: Joyce, Hemingway, Cocteau, Picasso, Matisse, Giacometti, Henry Miller, Man Ray. I once saw Jean-Paul Sartre and Simone de Beauvoir having lunch there, and, one afternoon, Anaïs Nin taking tea, surrounded by a gaggle of adoring young ladies in white blouses and plaid schoolgirl skirts. My favorite "sighting" at La Coupole, though, wasn't of a celebrity, at least not one I recognized. For several years, almost every time I went there in the late evening, I'd see the same tall, elderly gentleman, always dressed in white tie and tails. He would dine alone, looking up from the table occasionally to exchange a few words with a passerby, then pay his bill, stand up with some obvious effort, and move slowly across the room in the approximate direction of the front door, stopping whenever he saw a pretty woman, bowing to her, and wishing her a pleasant evening. Then he'd disappear into the darkness outside. I remember thinking that there must be worse ways to spend the twilight of one's life.

Claude could be prickly. Even in his Chicago days, my father wrote, "he had the feisty belligerence that was born in poodles until Park Avenue popularity bred it out of them." At Alain Dutournier's upscale Carré des Feuillants one warm summer evening, he was put out because two men at a nearby table had removed their jackets and were dining in their shirtsleeves. "In a restaurant of this quality, at these prices," he sniffed, "they should tell them 'I'm sorry, monsieur, but one must wear a jacket.'" On another occasion, at a place, long since vanished, called Alain Rayé, his word of the evening was "fulminate." He complained about the food, then added, "But I don't mind. The food gives me something to fulminate about, and I like that." He told me about an elderly Spaniard who covered sports for the AP, and who still came in and filed stories about Spanish sporting events every day even though he should have been retired. "It keeps him going," said Claude, "just as fulminating keeps me alive."

On my own one night, I "discovered" Guy Savoy in his first small restaurant on the rue Duret, and subsequently wrote about the place for *Metropolitan Home*. (Savoy still tells people that I was the first person to publicize him in America.) I also found another interesting chef, Jean-Paul Duquesnoy, who had had a two-star restaurant in Troyes and had just moved to Paris to try his luck. I coaxed Claude into coming to both places with me a number of times. (Savoy has enjoyed great success, and now has a well-deserved three Michelin stars at his main restaurant, a number of busy bistros, and an outpost in Las Vegas; Duquesnoy fared less well in Paris, and the last I heard of him was as chef at a French restaurant in a hotel in Tokyo.)

One Christmas Eve in the early seventies, Claude and Pepita took me to a wonderful old-style restaurant called À Sousceyrac, run by the grandchildren of a couple from the town of Sousceyrac, near Cahors in southwestern France. That part of France is known particularly for its wild game, its foie gras, and, in general, its hearty dishes full of concentrated flavors, and that's exactly the kind of food the restaurant served. I shocked Claude and Pepita a bit, I think, by arriving with Lyn, my girlfriend of the time, who was about a dozen years my senior. But Pepita was always très correcte, and Claude, as usual when addressing my foibles, displayed something closer to avuncular bemusement than parental disapproval, so the evening went well, full of chatter and champagne. Lyn might even have impressed Claude a bit by the way she held her own at a table fairly heaped with foie gras, grilled boneless pigs' feet, whole braised sweetbreads, and the restaurant's famous lièvre à la royale—an elaborately old-fashioned dish of wild hare stuffed with foie gras, truffles, and its own innards, then stewed in wine.

THE RESTAURANTS OF PARIS, high or low, were endlessly alluring to me, fascinating, compelling. They offered me experiences unlike anything I'd known in Los Angeles. The basic form may have been the same, the tables and chairs, the china and the glasses, even the accents on the waiters and the names of some of the dishes. But this was something else. It wasn't just the oysters with pigs' feet or the snails with cèpes; the radishes and the butter were different, the bread was different, the pâtés and terrines had a different consistency, more unctuous, more genuine somehow. And ultimately it wasn't even just the food. It occurred to me at some point that restaurants were in a way more essential to Paris than they were to other places; that they were an expression of all the things that make the city so seductive: not just food and conversation but art and fashion, politics and history, eroticism and romance. The restaurants of Paris, I thought, formed a kind of arterial system without which the city would hardly seem alive. They didn't just nourish Paris and its millions of visitors; they gave the city shape, and heart. This was true above all of places like Aux Amis du Beaujolais, the neighborhood staples that animated almost every quartier of the city.

The story of Aux Amis du Beaujolais is a tale of family continuity. Philibert Bléton, a young man from a wine-growing family in Fleurie, a grand cru Beaujolais village, opened the bistro in 1921. Some twenty-eight years later, Philibert's brother Georges bought the place from him. Georges married Marie-Clothilde Picolet, who came from a family with roots in Chénas, another grand cru Beaujolais village. Her brother Maurice, in turn, started helping out at Aux Amis, and then took it over in 1963, when Georges retired. Maurice was a character, mock-gruff, wisecracking, hardworking. Sometimes Claude would call ahead and ask Maurice to serve us something special, meaning not a dish but a wine. Maurice would then go down to the cellar and dust off an old bottle—a Moulin-à-Vent with twenty years of age on it, for instance, still surprisingly rich and lively. I noticed one day that Maurice had burn scars on one arm. These he'd gotten as a young man, Claude told me, in that very cellar. Wine used to be shipped up from Beaujolais in barrels, to be bottled at the restaurant. It was Maurice's job, after the corks were inserted, to dip the necks in molten wax to seal them, and one day he had dropped a bottle in . . .

One autumn lunchtime in 1980, Maurice brought a young man wearing a polyester necktie and a narrow-collared suit over to our table and introduced him as his son, Bernard. Bernard would be taking over the restaurant for him the following year, when he retired, he said. Bernard seemed very nice, but to me he didn't look anything like a bistro keeper. When they left, I said to Claude, "When I come here next year, there'll be rare tuna with pineapple beurre blanc on the menu instead of boeuf bourguignon."

I was wrong, as I quickly learned the next time I met Claude for lunch at the restaurant. Bernard had redecorated, with the off-white walls and red banquettes redone in shades of brown, but the menu was virtually the same, and Bernard wore a dark blue apron just like the one his father used to wear, and had the sleeves of his white shirt rolled up. He wasn't standing behind the bar: He was in the kitchen cooking, and doing it well. His hachis Parmentier, the French version of cottage pie, was noticeably better than it had been in the old days. Best of all, Bernard's own son, Christian, was apprenticing in the kitchen, and learning the old ways, too. Clearly, Aux Amis du Beaujolais was going to last for a good deal longer.

IN 1993, THE YEAR that Claude turned eighty-seven and I turned forty-eight, I decided to celebrate my birthday in Paris. On my first night in town, I had a good meal with my chef friend Jonathan Waxman at Alain Passard's superlative Arpège. We shared an oversize sole de l'Île d'Yeu belle meunière, accompanied by a slightly earthy, slightly sweet gratin of paper-thin celery root, then one of the house specialties, duck impeccably roasted in its own juices with a crisp little gâteau of its own abats and some pommes soufflés dusted very lightly with cumin—simple food, done absolutely right, full of flavor, elegant in a sensibly unornamented way.

The next night, Claude and I had a more complex but equally memorable dinner at Carré des Feuillants: an exquisite chestnut cream soup with a bit of pheasant as amuse-bouche; a strange but delicious "cake" of oil-moistened bread crumbs with slices of black truffle on top for me and a Jerusalem artichoke tart with foie gras and truffles for Claude; then a shared veal shank with cèpes; and finally cheeses and coffee-flavored crème brûlée.

On my birthday night itself, Claude joined me, along with Jonathan and a few friends, for dinner at La Régalade, a pioneer in the "bistronomie" movement. I ordered a puff-pastry "pissaladière" with seared rare tuna and black olives, then an hachis Parmentier de boudin noir (in effect, a blood sausage cottage pie, superb and wonderfully peppery), followed by a piece of brebis des Pyrénées. Elsewhere on the table were pumpkin soup, duck foie gras with puréed prunes, leg of lamb with white beans, côte de boeuf with potatoes cooked in goose fat, dove wrapped in ventrèche (pork belly)—all pure, hearty, and fine. We drank a Provençal rosé and a Mâcon-Clessé from the wine list, then three wines I'd brought from Los Angeles for the occasion. I loved the evening, and wished it could have gone on for hours more. Claude was tired, though, and I'd had enough to drink, so we said good night before midnight and repaired to our respective beds. This wasn't quite the last meal I was to have with Claude, but it was the last big, good, celebratory one.

In September of the following year, Claude and Pepita, both beset by a number of ills ("It's awful getting old," Claude would say repeatedly), were admitted together to a hospital outside Paris, sharing a room with side-by-side beds. I went to visit them there. They both looked weak and were all but immobile. After about an hour, I left, saying to Claude, "The next time I'm in Paris, you'll be up and around and we'll go to Aux Amis du Beaujolais and have a good lunch." "Yes, that's right," he said, though I'm pretty sure both of us knew it wasn't.

I flew back from Paris to New York, where I was working on one of the early issues of *Saveur*, and called Claude several times. He sounded reasonably good, and we had long talks. Twice he said, "You know, I just keep talking like this because it makes me feel better." One day when I called, he said, "Oh, I am having some trouble with my ass. Can you call back?" I said I would but got involved with the magazine close, and forgot until too late in the day. The next day I called, and he sounded very bad, drugged up; he told me that he had had trouble breathing, and now had "I don't know how many tubes in me." He wasn't comfortable talking, so I promised to call again the next day. When I did, I was told that both he and Pepita were in intensive care. On September 30, I called again. A man answered, and when I asked for Claude, he asked me who I was. When I told him that I was an old and good friend of Claude's, he said, "Well, you know, he came to us with a very grave problem. He was very sick. Il est fini." This had happened, he told me, about an hour previously. "Excusez-nous," he said in hanging up. Pepita died three days later, and on October 7 they were buried together at the cemetery in Saint-Cloud, which overlooks Paris from the distance.

The following year, I went to Paris to collect a few boxes of things that Claude had left for me—mostly books, photographs, and little oil paintings he'd done on boards over the years, many of the Île de Ré. He had always talked about making me his heir, but never seemed to get around to it, and that wasn't the kind of thing I felt comfortable reminding him about. A cousin of his from Geneva materialized shortly before his demise and ended up with almost everything. What I did inherit was roughly three decades of memories of Claude and of endless meals enjoyed together over endless hours at so many tables.

I WENT BACK to Aux Amis du Beaujolais one more time after Claude's death. Bernard had redone the place again, restructuring it from top to bottom, moving the bar and turning what had been the front room into a two-level space. The walls were now mustard yellow and the tablecloths a faint, sophisticated pink, and set with Beaujolais-themed place mats. There was more fish served than there had been in the old days (back then, marinated herring, salt cod gratinée, and the occasional sole meunière were about the only things piscatorial on the menu), but there was still plenty of good, unpretentious bistro fare, too: jambon fumé, assorted terrines, various cold vegetables in vinaigrette, thin slices of dry Lyonnais sausage, beef stewed with carrots, grilled entrecôte with pommes frites, cold smoked pork with lentils, crème caramel, mousse au chocolat. I ate well and drank too much and left with promises to return soon and often, even though Claude was now gone. I never had the heart.

Bernard Picolet closed Aux Amis du Beaujolais in early 2009. The magazines and newspapers whose journalists had been the restaurant's best customers for decades had all decamped to other parts of the city, and, Picolet told the *New York Times* shortly before the restaurant's demise, the global economic downturn had changed French eating habits. "The French are no longer eating and drinking like the French," he said. "They are eating and drinking like the Anglo-Saxons."

The site of the restaurant stood empty for several years. A

rumor went around that the lease had been taken by the son of a famous French actor, who planned to open a nightclub there, but that never occurred. Today, the place houses an eatery called Qualité & Co., whose website assures potential customers that "Our nutritionist works with all our salad recipes to maximize their nutritional qualities and balance."

Chapter Seven

SCANDIA,

West Hollywood (1946–1989)

B ACK IN THE MIDDLE OF THE TWENTIETH CENTURY, decades before a young Ethiopian-born, Swedish-bred chef named Marcus Samuelsson introduced elegant Scandinavian-inspired dining to New York City at Aquavit, and even longer before a Dane of Macedonian descent named René Redzepi galvanized international haute cuisine with his thoroughly original, locally derived creations at Noma in Copenhagen, sparking a craze for "New Nordic" food around the world, the culinary traditions of Scandinavia were represented in America primarily by smorgasbord. This was an ample buffet of cold and warm dishes, heavy on the herring, common (with slight variations in makeup and in the spelling of the name) to all Scandinavian countries.

In Los Angeles, Smorgasbord Central was a place called Bit of Sweden, which occupied a three-story, half-timbered building, surmounted by a large clock bearing the legend GRUEN TIME, on the corner of Sunset Boulevard and Doheny. Like other restaurants on the Sunset Strip, Bit of Sweden—which described itself as "the World's most unique [*sic*] restaurant featuring the largest Smorgasboard, fine foods and liqueurs"—drew a show business crowd. This was supplemented by a clientele of local businessmen, Beverly Hills matrons, and members of L.A.'s small Swedish and Danish communities, hungry for a taste of home. In 1942, while *Casablanca* was being shot at Warner Bros. studios in Burbank, the gossip queen Hedda Hopper reported that Ingrid Bergman was teaching Humphrey Bogart Swedish on set, and that Bogey was "so set up with himself he drives out to Bit of Sweden for lunch just so's he can impress the waiters—the big showoff."

The chef at Bit of Sweden was not a Swede but a taciturn Dane from Copenhagen named Kenneth Hansen. Hansen had shipped out as a kitchen apprentice on the Scandinavian America Line in 1919, when he was fourteen, and ended up in New York City two years later, where he found a berth cooking at the Waldorf-Astoria. By 1929 he had found his way to Los Angeles, where he made hors d'oeuvres at the Brown Derby before landing a job at "the World's most unique restaurant."

In 1946 Hansen found financing to open his own place. He called the new restaurant, which was just a block east of Bit of Sweden—"As close as possible, so my former partner could watch the lines," he once told Craig Claiborne—Hansen's Scandia, dropping his own name after a few years. It quickly turned into an early "power restaurant," long before that term came into general usage, where politicians, businessmen, and movie business figures gathered to drink and to eat such dishes as gravlaks with dill sauce, an assortment of planked steaks, and kalvfilé Oskar—a veal cutlet garnished with asparagus, crab legs, and béarnaise sauce, said to have been invented in honor of Oskar II, king of Sweden and Norway.

One contingent of local citizens used to meet at the old Finnish Baths in the basement of the Bing Crosby Building, across the street from Scandia, then troop over to the restaurant after their saunas and massages. Among their number was the L.A. County sheriff, Peter Pitchess. By the mid-fifties, Hansen felt the need to expand and constructed a new restaurant nearby with a flagstone façade, sleek Scandinavian lines, and a soaring chalet roof. In 1957, when the new location was ready to open, Pitchess obligingly closed down the stretch of Sunset between the old and new places, and a parade of regulars—among them Johnny "Tarzan" Weissmuller, the Danish pianist-comedian Victor Borge, the Air Force hero General Jimmy Doolittle, the comedian Nipsey Russell, and the Arizona senator and future presidential candidate Barry Goldwater (an assemblage of unlikely table fellows that hints at the breadth of Scandia's appeal)—trouped across the street, led by a horse-drawn Carlsberg beer wagon, bearing a pianist, an accordionist, and the famous Danish tenor Lauritz Melchior.

In its new home, with an expanded menu, two distinct large dining areas (one sunny and airy, the other dark and clubby), and a remarkable wine list, Scandia soon evolved into one of the best restaurants of any kind in Los Angeles, offering a level of cuisine and service that would have done any classic French place proud. The new Scandia no longer mounted a smorgasbord—the closest thing was the restaurant's lavish holiday buffets—though the menu did offer, under "Hors d'Oeuvres," "Our individual 'Cold Cabaret' served at your table and consisting of all the delicacies for which the smörgåsbord is famous." That menu was huge, both physically (it measured about twelve by sixteen inches) and in the sheer quantity and breadth of what it offered. All the "continental" standards of the era were there: shrimp cocktail, wilted spinach salad, vichyssoise, gazpacho, Lake Superior whitefish, chateaubriand, baked Alaska—and the planked steaks that Hansen had been serving since he first went out on his own continued to be a point of pride for the place. But there were also many dishes that made you feel as if you were someplace else, somewhere with a different sensibility—somewhere, well, Scandinavian.

IF CHASEN'S WAS MY FIRST RESTAURANT and remains my romantic ideal of what a restaurant should be, and Trader Vic's was for many years my fantasy eating place, Scandia was the first restaurant I came to think of, when I was more or less an adult, as my own. Sometimes at fancy places, I'd get pointedly seated in the establishment's version of Siberia, no matter how empty the dining room was or how long ago I'd made my reservation; this was obviously because, while I may have been decently dressed, I was still one of them long-haired hippie kids. I eventually figured out what to do if this happened, though: order good wine. This dawned on me one evening when I went with my friend Allen Daviau to dine in the pretty downstairs dining room at a place called Au Petit Café, on Vine Street in Hollywood. I was a regular at the restaurant, but because I was a habitué of the upstairs room and went there mostly for lunch, the host didn't recognize me, and—probably taking one look not only at my own hair but also at Allen's dense, curly mop and matching beard (picture a slightly rounder version of Levon Helm of the Band)—he seated us at a cramped corner table as much out of public view as possible. It took a while for a waiter to approach us, and when he did, I immediately commandeered the wine list and ordered us a bottle of good champagne, to be followed by a bottle of one of the great white Burgundies, Chassagne-Montrachet. Almost immediately, the host came over and conducted us ceremoniously to a splendid table in the middle of the room, where immaculate service was lavished upon us for the rest of the evening.

At Scandia, I never had a problem. At first, this was doubtless because I'd been introduced to the place, and its staff, by my parents, but before long I had gotten to know many of the key players on my own terms—John the bartender; Angel, who ran the front most evenings; Freddy, the maître d'hôtel. They'd greet me by name, joke with me a little, and always give me a good table in the dark, clubby dining room adjacent to the glamorous bar. This room was decorated with copper pans, blue-and-white ceramics, and Scandinavian coats of arms, and the best seats weren't the banquettes but the tall, broad, reddish brown leather swivel wingback chairs with embossed heart-shaped backs. Once I was ensconced in one of these, I'd order good wine not for defensive reasons but because the list was long, imaginative, and astonishingly reasonable in price, and then would settle in and eat some of the best food in town.

It was at Scandia that I discovered that I loved herring, which came marinated in vinegar, steeped in sherry, or cloaked in sour cream. I always ordered a combination of the three, along with the almost-frozen aquavit and icy Danish beer with which all the real connoisseurs seemed to wash herring down. Norwegian lobster tails—frozen, certainly, but flavorful nonetheless—came fried, with fried parsley (a great delight that I first encountered here), and also, even better, in the form of "The Great Hamlet Dagger," for which they were "deviled and broiled on the skewer, served with an ice-cold sauce made with caviar and aquavit." There were also, among many other things, oysters baked in their shells with herbs and aquavit, gravlaks with dill sauce, mushroom caps stuffed with snails in garlic and walnut butter, something called "The Crêpe" ("Thin pancake wrapped around tiny coral-pink Shrimps in Dill and Hollandaise, glazed under fire"), sweet-and-sour stuffed cabbage that remains the best I have ever tasted, a tasty tenderloin steak buried under heaps of butter-fried on-

ions called bøf med løg, the inevitable veal Oscar, and a changing selection of simply cooked fresh North Atlantic fish—turbot,
plaice, sole—flown in "via S.A.S. over the Pole." I also had the
first venison of my life at Scandia, overcooked by today's standards but luxuriating in a classic sauce veneur, and fell in love
with the meat's woodsy intensity.

The big production on the menu was a tourist-pleasing show-
piece called the "Viking Sword," which was described as "Large
brochette of broiled breast of turkey, small Chateau-Briand [sic],
center of a smoked pork chop, tomatoes and mushrooms, served
on a flaming sword with many kinds of vegetables and sauce bear-
naise." The sword was not ignited at the table, mind you: It was carried high through the dining room, boldly aflame, with more than
a little pomp, stopping conversation and eliciting oohs and aahs
and occasional shrieks of delight or fear (or both) from the children
in the room.

At lunchtime, the fare was simpler. There was a long menu of
smørrebrød, open-face Danish sandwiches inspired by those at the
world-famous Oskar Davidsen in Copenhagen. These included everything from smoked whitefish with sliced onion, homemade liver
pâté with mushrooms and bacon, and thick-cut Danish salami on
duck fat with meat jelly to Burgundy-baked ham with scrambled
eggs and chives. Even better, though, was the blackboard lunch
menu, which offered two courses for some unbelievably low price,
maybe five or six dollars in the seventies. I realized fairly quickly
that the secret of this menu was that it was constructed largely of
by-products of the previous night's dinner. The spinach salad was
made with the ribs, not the leaves, of the spinach; the irresistible
frikadeller (ground veal croquettes) and Danish meatballs were
made with scraps from the veal Oscar and the various steaks. Five
or six appetizers and main dishes each were offered, similarly de-

rived from recycled foodstuffs. Occasionally, when I explained this to a luncheon guest, he or she would take exception to the practice, as if the kitchen was trying to pass leftovers off as fresh food. I thought the contrary: that this practice showed intelligence, creativity, and even a kind of environmental responsibility. I loved the whole idea.

IN 1967, WITH GOOD GRADES from Cal State, I transferred to UCLA, still a philosophy major but taking history courses on the side. I got student loans to pay my tuition, theoretically with enough left over for living expenses, but I was already spending far too much money on food and wine, and so needed to supplement the loans somehow. I started digging through *Writer's Digest* and *The Writer* at the library, and sending unsolicited articles and reviews off to an assortment of obscure publications—the *Ford Times*, *Mankind* ("The Magazine of Popular History"), *The New-England Galaxy*—and occasionally selling one for fifty dollars here, a hundred dollars there.

The following year was a tough one for me: I was let go from my museum bookshop job and evicted from my castle apartment near El Coyote, because the owners of the building were converting the apartments there to offices. Then my car, a 1949 pink Cadillac Fleetwood with an impeccable interior, which I'd bought for a thousand dollars and into which I subsequently poured many thousands more, finally expired from a cracked engine block. The really awful thing, though, was that my best friend at UCLA, John Lydon, a black sheep from a Boston family prominent in the media, dropped dead while having lunch with his wife one afternoon—he sneezed, and a vein in his head burst. I walked around feeling hollow for months.

I needed a place to live and a new job. I found the former quickly, an inexpensive one-bedroom on Fountain Avenue in West Hollywood where a friend of a friend, the writer Robert Gover—whose first novel, *One Hundred Dollar Misunderstanding*, had been a cult best-seller a few years earlier—had been living. There was no air-conditioning and there was traffic noise day and night, but Fountain was equidistant from Sunset and Santa Monica Boulevards, both good hitchhiking streets, and my rent was $87 a month at first, and never rose above $125. I ended up staying there for ten years.

Around the time I got my new place, I also found a new job, through the student employment office at UCLA: I became a shipping clerk and film inspector at Medallion TV, a minor-league distributor of old movies and television series. The office was a few blocks east of Scandia on the Sunset Strip. I only made seventy-five dollars a week, but the hours were flexible, so I could keep going to classes in the mornings—and leave in the evenings early enough to hitchhike to downtown L.A., where I had a second job teaching English as a second language three nights a week.

My boss was crass, erratic, well-to-do, and sometimes unexpectedly generous (he let me drive his custom-painted electric blue Coupe de Ville convertible when he was out of town, and later bought me an old VW Bug with a whiny transmission). He also practically lived at Scandia, and every weekday at half past twelve, he'd drive a few blocks down the street to the restaurant to meet his buddies and, as far as I could determine, drink his lunch. This inspired an almost comical Jekyll and Hyde situation: He'd do business as usual in the mornings, occasionally calling me in to ask about the disposition of a print of some old British film like *Dick Barton at Bay* or *The Crimes of Stephen Hawke* that had been returned slightly damaged from a TV station in Fargo,

North Dakota, or Bellingham, Washington. He'd bid me good-bye as he left out the film vault door into the parking garage. He'd reenter, postlunch, scarlet-faced and swaying, and demand, in an aggressive tone, where this or that was, what I'd done about something or other, when was I going to clean up the back room or find those missing dupe negatives. Then he'd go into his office and, if I was lucky, I wouldn't hear a word from him for the rest of the day.

His other hangout, besides Scandia, was the Classic Cat, directly across the street from the office. This was—depending on the latest ruling by the L.A. County Board of Supervisors or the California Department of Alcoholic Beverage Control, and these seemed to change almost monthly—a bikini or topless or all-nude bar. He got to be friends with the owner, and ended up buying an interest in the Cat, at which point he put me to work moonlighting there, running errands, repairing the light-show paraphernalia, even writing scripts for the shows, which featured a revolving cast of "amateur" dancers and an energetic Mexican master of ceremonies named Raul, who was by nature immune to the charms of naked women. In return I received unlimited free drinks, and got to know everybody in the place, which sometimes turned out quite nicely.

IN 1978 KEN HANSEN was ready to retire and sold Scandia to one of his longtime regulars, the magazine publisher Bob Petersen (*Tiger Beat*, *Motor Trend*, and *Guns & Ammo* were among his titles), whose offices were a few blocks down the street. The restaurant continued on more or less as before at first, with few personnel changes, though regulars noted that the ship wasn't as tight as it had once been. During one of the Christmas lunches I had annually there with a group of fellow wine lovers, a waiter dropped a large tray full of dirty dishes and glasses, with a resounding crash and clatter. The dining room was silent for a moment as the last resonance died out. Then the wine writer Roy Brady said drily, "In Hansen's day, that fellow would have been dead before the dishes hit the floor."

But Hansen's day was gone. By the time Ken died, in 1980, the restaurant itself was ailing. In a restaurant guide I published in 1984, I noted that the food was at least decent and the wine list still excellent, but that the service was a mess. "The restaurant's founder and original owner, the late Ken Hansen," I wrote, "was a terror—with suppliers, in his kitchen (and it was always finally *his* kitchen, not the chef's), and most of all with his captains, waiters, and busboys. He demanded the best from them and almost always got it. Today, the service is a joke—an unorchestrated dissonance of bewildered novices, bored old hands, and bumbling captains in whose hands a can of tableside Sterno becomes a dangerous weapon. Somebody's still at the stove here, but nobody's at the stick."

Even if the old standards had been maintained, Scandia would have had a rough time. The Sunset Strip had once had an aura of glamour, but by the eighties it had grown increasingly tacky, and fancy cars turning in to the Scandia driveway sometimes had to thread their way through crowds of drug-addled teenagers. Tastes in food had changed, too, and the children of the generation that had built Scandia into an institution were now going to hipper, more casual places, like Spago, Trumps, and Morton's, or even heading to (or staying on) the Westside to eat at Michael's, Chinois on Main, or 72 Market Street. Prime-time reservations at Scandia had once been as hard to get as they are today at the latest hot restaurant in Manhattan; now the dining rooms were half empty at eight on a Saturday night. In 1989 Bob Petersen gave up and closed the place.

I mourned it. Sometimes I think that if I could summon back to life one vanished restaurant from my past, bringing it into the early twenty-first century intact, with all the same food and drink and people and vitality, it would be not Chasen's but Scandia—so luminous, so perfectly designed for conviviality and indulgence. Sometimes.

Chapter Eight

CAFÉ SWISS,

Beverly Hills (1950–1985)

A PART FROM THE ODD STOLEN TIPPLE OF PLONK AS a teenager or the occasional desultory plastic cup of jug wine at parties where the more common intoxicant was something you smoked, I didn't start drinking wine until I went to work at the L.A. County art museum. I had discovered by that time that I liked the way wine tasted, and besides, it seemed like the thing to have when I went out to gallery openings on Monday nights on La Cienega Boulevard or to nice restaurants with Martin and later other women—part of the worldly image I was anxious to project. Not just drinking but knowing about wine, I decided, was something a young gentleman should aspire to, so I tried to pay attention to what I drank, and read a wine book or two along the way. I was starting pretty much from scratch, though. I had a hard time remembering the difference between Bordeaux and Burgundy for at least a year. Once, trying to impress a sexy blonde at Chianti in Hollywood, I ordered Château d'Yquem, one of the sweetest and most unctuous of dessert wines, with the scampi (it was the most expensive white on the list, so I figured it had to be the best). Fortunately, our waiter politely steered me toward a crisp, dry verdic-chio instead.

I got better on my own, little by little, but I think it's fair to say that I didn't start to actually learn anything worthwhile about wine until I met Roy Brady, and began spending my Saturday afternoons at the Café Swiss. I first became aware of Roy at a tasting lunch devoted to the wines of the eccentric, legendary Santa Clara County vintner Martin Ray in Hollywood in 1971, the first such event I had attended. There were all kinds of Wine Experts bouncing around the place, among them my parents' old friend Robert Lawrence Balzer, the so-called dean of American wine writers, who at one point tasted Ray's 1963 pinot noir and announced, "This wine is an effrontery, just an effrontery!" A bit off to the side, not bouncing at all (or saying anything audible), was a distinguished but vaguely roguish-looking gentleman, sipping wines and making notes as if he and the contents of his glass were the only creatures in the room. "Who's that?" I asked somebody. "That's Roy Brady," somebody answered, in a tone of respect bordering on awe.

A year or so after the Martin Ray event, I chanced to sit next to Roy on a flight to San Francisco, and introduced myself. We'd both been invited to a luncheon in the Bay Area hosted by Browne Vintners to introduce a new line of "branded" imported wines. Roy and I started talking on the plane, and I ended up sitting next to him at the event as well, continuing our conversation. Along the way, I shared with him some of my budding-oenophile insights, and he listened politely enough—and before we parted company, he suggested that I drop by a modest Beverly Hills restaurant called Café Swiss the following Saturday with a bottle of wine in hand, to sit in on an informal wine lunch he enjoyed there weekly with some friends.

I don't remember what I brought that Saturday, but it must have passed muster, because I was invited back the next week and soon found myself a regular member of the group, spending most of my Saturday lunchtimes at the Café Swiss (and most of my Saturday afternoons sleeping off the results). I think I can safely say that no young man in the world, during that period, was more regularly exposed to so large and diverse an array of wines, good, bad, and indefinable.

CAFÉ SWISS WAS THE KIND OF RESTAURANT that has pretty much disappeared from major cities around the country, or at best languishes on the periphery of local dining scenes. It was, in other words, friendly, comfortable, and dependable, with a large menu of American and "continental" dishes, supplemented by specialties that were at least a little exotic, in this case from the exotic land of Switzerland. Swiss cooking was never as much a part of the menu there as, say, Scandinavian cooking was of Scandia's, but there were still ten or twelve offerings that were undeniably more Swiss than anything else—émincé de veau zurichoise, ravioli tessinoise, croûte au fromage valaisanne, and so on—and in some ways, Café Swiss was a bit like a less elegant, less expensive counterpart of Ken Hansen's place.

The restaurant belonged to a Swiss chef named Fred Hug and his wife, Laura. They opened Café Swiss in 1950, on the site of a former coffee shop on Rodeo Drive. Beverly Hills in those days was less than fifty years old, and was still basically a village. The house I grew up in was technically in West Los Angeles, but we did our shopping in Beverly Hills, and I remember well, from my childhood, the lazy streets with plenty of unmetered parking by the curb and the small shops owned by nice men and women who'd greet us by name when we walked in and let us buy things with house charge accounts. (I loved ElGee's, the butcher shop, with its museumlike display cases full of rosy beef tenderloins and long racks of lamb with pastel paper cuffs on the protruding bones; I hated Livingstone's, a dress shop that I thought smelled like old people, where Mom would spend what seemed like hours trying on clothes and gossiping with the salesgirls while I sat on the floor and drew.) A couple of decades before it became one of the most famous shopping streets in the world, Rodeo Drive had a gas station, a hardware store, a big independent bookshop (Marian Hunter's), and at least twenty beauty parlors that never would have thought to call themselves "salons." There may even have been a camera shop. What there weren't were marble edifices housing fancy boutiques selling Louis Vuitton and Yves Saint Laurent, tour buses full of gawkers hoping to see Richard Gere and Julia Roberts skipping out of a lingerie store giggling, or millionaires clogging the streets with their canary yellow Maseratis or metallic blue Maybachs on their way to buy ten-thousand-dollar suits at appointment-only menswear stores. The "real housewives" of Beverly Hills in those days were Mary Pickford, Lana Turner, and Dinah Shore.

Café Swiss fit right in. It was in the middle of things, casual, easy, the kind of place you could decide to stop by at the last minute on the way home from the office or the studio; you didn't have to dress up like you did for Chasen's, and the lighting was dim enough to facilitate discretion. The place didn't even have a liquor license until 1955, when the Hugs became American citizens. With alcohol on offer, its popularity grew. Clark Gable, Barbara Stanwyck, Gary Cooper, and Groucho Marx were among the regulars; studio executives from Twentieth Century–Fox, which was only a ten-minute drive to the south, liked to come for lunch, sitting on the umbrella-shaded (and later Astroturfed) back patio eating spaghetti bolognese and chicken-liver omelettes and downing vodka martinis or Michelob on draft. For some reason, Café Swiss also became the preferred hangout for a large number of songwriters, composers, and arrangers. One group of old-timers, including Harry Ruby, who wrote music for Marx Brothers movies, and Arthur Hamilton, who wrote "Cry Me a River," met every week for a patio lunch. In the evenings, a more famous crowd, including Johnny Mercer, Sammy Cahn, Bronislau Kaper, Harry Warren, and Jimmy McHugh, gathered around the piano, where Joe Marino, both a studio musician and a credible jazz performer, played most nights.

The group of decidedly nonmusical gentlemen that Roy Brady invited me to join had gotten its start one Saturday morning in 1964, when a wine distributor named Martin Weiner was visiting one of his customers, Bill Shapiro, manager of the old Vendome wine and liquor store on Beverly Drive. The two decided that day that instead of tasting wines in the back of the store, they'd pack up a bunch of bottles and go to lunch together at Frascati, an attractive Italian-French restaurant nearby, across the street from the Beverly Wilshire Hotel. It was a pleasant experience, so they decided to do it every week, sampling not just wines that Marty brought in but other samples that had been dropped off for Bill at the store. Roy, a customer of Bill's, joined them almost at once, and gradually the group expanded to include a core of other Vendome customers, including three local businessmen, an attorney, and an ophthalmologist.

By the time I started coming to lunch, Frascati had closed, and the group had migrated a few blocks away to Café Swiss, assembling promptly at 11:30 every Saturday morning, rain or shine, at a long table at the back of the patio. They abided by simple rules: Everybody brought at least one bottle of wine, which could be anything from a curiosity to a treasure; the bottles could be presented as they came or "blind" (concealed in paper bags), as their owner preferred; everybody ordered an appetizer and a main course; nobody ordered dessert, but one of the group always brought a wedge of Brie from the nearby Cheese Shop of Beverly Hills; and the check got evenly split, with our long-suffering regular waitress, Judy, getting a handsome tip.

Bill continued to use the lunch to open samples from suppliers: a complete line from some new California winery; the most recent vintages from some prominent Burgundy shipper; something we'd never heard of from Italy or Spain. Marty kept us up to date on his latest wares, which might mean new low-priced chardonnay from Fetzer or drop-dead wonderful Chianti or barbaresco shipped from Italy by the Enoteca Internazionale de Rham, and he sometimes threw in a good German wine from his own collection. The businessmen, the attorney, and the ophthalmologist liked to bring show-off wines from their cellars—pricey white Burgundies or older red Bordeaux, expensive offerings from Italy or California, vintage port. My own contributions were often oddball bottles I'd found wherever I'd just been (Majorca, the Canary Islands, Morocco, Luxembourg, the Valle d'Aosta). Roy was the wild card, showing up with anything from an old Madeira to a homemade wine a friend of his had fashioned. On one occasion, he brought a Château Mouton Rothschild decanted into a California cabernet bottle, to illustrate his contention that most people, even wine distributors, drank with their eyes more than their palates. One of the more vocal of our number, predictably, dismissed the wine as not very interesting at first and then, when its identity was revealed, said, "You know, it's starting to come around, yes, I'm really getting the breeding now." Roy just smiled.

Guests were sometimes invited to the table—one Saturday when I wasn't there, one of the businessmen brought Gloria Steinem, under circumstances whose particulars now elude me—and visiting winemakers sometimes attended, at their own peril: Wines were opened with no ceremony, passed around, tasted, and, if they were found lacking (as they often were), quickly poured out—even if their creator was sitting right there. More than one winemaker, beginning to explain the subtleties of his masterwork, realized to his horror that it had already been consigned to the dump bucket.

The wines at some of our lunches were just remarkable, random collections of celebrated bottlings both domestic and imported, hundreds and hundreds of dollars' worth. One Saturday in 1975, for instance, my notes remind me that we had a 1969 Heitz McCrea Vineyards pinot blanc, four top-of-the-line California cabernets (1963 Louis Martini, 1969 Chappellet, 1968 Beaulieu Vineyard Georges de Latour Private Reserve, and 1971 Ridge Eisele), three distinguished Bordeaux (Troplong Mondot, Ducru-Beaucaillou, and Pichon-Longueville) from the highly rated 1966 vintage, a Ficklin ribosa piave—an extraordinary and very rare red wine made from an obscure Italian grape for only a few vintages by an old-line California port producer—and a Mayacamas 1968 late-harvest zinfandel, an unusual and superb Napa Valley dessert wine. Another week, in contrast, we grumbled through a couple of barely drinkable white zinfandels, two wan California gamays, a tired 1961 generic Graves from a mediocre shipper, and a pair of thick, coarse Amarones.

If the wines varied widely from meeting to meeting, there was a certain predictable, almost ritualistic quality to the occasions nonetheless: same time, same table, same food, same people making the same jokes. One of the group was married for a time to a rather humorless European woman who once exclaimed, with undisguised disapproval, "I don't know how you can stand to just sit there and say the same things to each other week after week!" She didn't understand that the very predictability of the lunches was part of their appeal.

I came to lunch at Café Swiss, wine in hand, almost every week for probably ten or eleven years, and then managed to appear sporadically for another few years after that—though by that time I was married and living in Venice, a twenty- or thirty-minute drive to the west, and couldn't always manage the logistics. My sessions with the group exposed me to wines from probably every corner of the world that produced them, and to every style and quality imaginable. Because the selection was so arbitrary, so unpredictable (and often so mysterious, if the labels were concealed), I was pretty much forced to consider each wine on its own merits, without expectations or preconceived ideas. I can't imagine how I could have had a better training in how and what to taste.

But then, too, there was Roy. Roy was a mathematician who'd worked as an aerospace systems analyst at the Rand Corporation and elsewhere before retiring to devote his time to writing about wine and teaching wine classes. He had a good head start on almost everyone else in the field: He'd decided, back in the 1940s, to teach himself about wine—a decision, he once said, that "just came out of the blue, no more courted than web-footedness." In pursuit of wine knowledge, he studied most of the available texts on the subject, which at that time were primarily the work of British wine merchants or historians from the early years of the twentieth century, and started visiting the California wine country, where he got to know many of the pioneers of the state's modern wine industry. He also started buying wine—back when nineteenth-century Madeira, his greatest passion, went for five bucks a bottle and twenty-five would get you a case of Château Margaux—and installed it in an underground "cellar" he had dug himself, with the help of friends, next to the token grapevines in the backyard of his home in the San Fernando Valley. Before long, he was writing about wine, too, initially for the quarterly published by the urbane British-based Wine & Food Society, and later for a variety of other publications both scholarly and popular.

Roy was a laconic fellow, alternately avuncular and curmudgeonly, with white hair and white muttonchop whiskers and a limp from childhood polio, which worsened as he aged. Though he would probably consider this a libel, were he still around, Roy was the closest thing I had to a wine mentor. Over the years, by his example and not by the usual wine-expert pedagogy, he taught me many valuable lessons about wine. Chief among these was to judge it by the way it smells and tastes, not by its label or reputation or price—and then to keep my mouth shut about it unless I had something smart to say.

From the beginning, Roy's writing showed not just intelligence and humor but also unusual good sense and restraint. He was an enemy to jargon and cliché. If he read somewhere that a certain wine had "flavors" of raspberry, he'd ask, "How many flavors does a raspberry have?" If somebody quoted the wine merchant and writer Frank Schoonmaker's description of Almadén zinfandel as being "brambly," he'd say, "Have you ever tasted a bramble?" And this was one of his favorite jokes: "Did you hear the one about the famous wine writer who was so fat when he died that they couldn't find a coffin big enough to bury him in? Well, they gave him an enema and buried him in a shoe box."

It wasn't that Roy didn't appreciate the romance and lore of wine; it was more that he didn't like it when the romance and lore were mistaken for the reality. He had strong opinions about what he tasted but was stingy with them, and you drew them out of him at your own risk. When a fellow diner pressed him, once, about why he obviously disdained a wine that had been poured, Roy finally replied, in exasperation, "Because it's no damn good." He was similarly economical with praise: The definitive Roy Brady story, which he told on himself, was about the time he once sat through a long, boring wine and food dinner at which "it became all too apparent that absolutely every soul present was going to be called on to comment at length on a wine or a dish." When it was his turn, he stood up, drained his glass of whatever vintage it contained, and, after a suitable pause, said "Mighty tasty"—then sat down.

I GRADUATED FROM UCLA in 1969 with bachelor's degrees in philosophy and history, avoiding a ticket to Vietnam through a series of student deferments and then the good luck of a high draft lottery number. Professionally, I'd gradually been able to establish relationships with several publications that would take my writing. I did book reviews and a number of little music features for the Chicago *Sun-Times; The Christian Science Monitor* bought several brief travel pieces from me; and I somehow got linked up with an underground paper out of Miami called *The Daily Planet*, reviewing albums and covering music events in L.A. I never understood why such events would be of interest to the citizens of southern Florida, but, hey, I got paid (a pittance)—and better still, my pieces brought me to the attention of the record companies, and they started sending me advance copies of new albums and inviting me to opening nights at the Troubadour and the Whisky a Go Go. This, in turn, brought me to the attention of more outlets.

Before I knew it, *The Hollywood Reporter* was assigning me to cover concerts by Nana Mouskouri, John McLaughlin, and Gladys Knight and the Pips; Lester Bangs at *Creem* was basically letting me review any albums I wanted to; and I was getting lots of work from a publication called *Phonograph Record Magazine,* published by United Artists Records, and also writing liner notes and artists' bios for the company. (I'm pretty sure I'm the only food writer who has ever been nominated for a Grammy, an honor I was accorded in 1975 for the extensive notes I'd written for a two-disk Miles Davis reissue. I lost to Sam Samudio of Sam the Sham and the Pharaohs, of "Wooly Bully" fame, who had penned heartfelt autobiographical notes for his own album.)

I became part of the music business for real in 1972, when I was hired by Atlantic Records. I used to like to describe my position as (in reference to an early Rolling Stones song) "under-assistant West Coast publicity man." My job included following up on invitations to rock critics for concerts and club dates and writing press releases for forthcoming releases. I did this for, among other landmarks, the first Bette Midler album and Jackson Browne's debut LP. Atlantic also gave me my first expense account, a fairly generous one. Though I'd only just started writing about restaurants, I was apparently already known in some circles as something of a gourmand, because when I got the job, a columnist for the music business trade magazine *Cashbox* observed that "suddenly, everybody in town wants to interview Atlantic acts over lunch." (The truth is that I didn't care for the company of a good many of the music writers in town, and often just went to lunch alone, ordering expensive bottles of wine—I was in a white Burgundy phase—and three-course meals and charging it off to one act or another. I owe you guys one, Delbert and Glen.)

I got into magazine editing, indirectly, through a freelance job for United Artists Records. They'd hired me to write a press release about the new Traffic album, *The Low Spark of High Heeled Boys.* I was a fan of the group, but didn't care for the LP that much, and my feelings must have shown through, because the company turned down my release. Not out of any desire for revenge, but simply as a way to make a little more money out of my efforts, I rewrote the release into an overt critique of the album, which I dubbed "The Low Marks of Well-Heeled Boys," for a strange little local arts and entertainment monthly called *Coast*. (Today, I can't imagine what I was going on about. I quite like the album, and a few years ago, in the bar at the Mansion on Turtle Creek in Dallas, I got the chance to sing informal drunken backup, with my chef friend Tim Keating, on the LP's title song, behind Steve Winwood himself.) The editor of *Coast* liked my piece enough that when he decided to leave his post a few months later, he offered me the job. I'd never edited anything outside of school, but I thought it sounded like fun, and the magazine's publisher agreed to hire me away from Atlantic for the princely salary of twenty thousand dollars a year, which seemed like a fortune to me at the time. My first magazine job, then, was as an editor in chief.

I had great fun at *Coast*, even though the staff consisted of only a managing editor, a part-time art director, and a combination receptionist, fact checker, and copy editor. Our entire editorial budget was a thousand dollars per issue, to pay for every piece of text, every photograph, every illustration. Somehow we got pretty good stuff anyway. *Coast* was probably the first glossy magazine to publish Armistead Maupin, several years before he started writing "Tales of the City" for the *San Francisco Chronicle*. We ran stories by Lester Bangs, the *Los Angeles Times* media critic David Shaw, the English critic and novelist Sally Beauman, onetime *Interview* editor Glenn O'Brien, the author and journalist Sheila Weller. Our art director, a rangy North Carolinian named Don Owens, somehow seduced artists and illustrators like Ralph Steadman and Milton Glaser into working for us; Annie Leibovitz shot a cover for us.

One of Don's few failures was with Andrew Wyeth: I listened in on the phone one day, agog, as he tried in vain to talk the aging icon into painting a cover image for the exceptional price, to us, of $150; Wyeth, of course, said no, but in a manner that was not only polite but sounded genuinely regretful.

It was in the pages of the magazine, in October 1972, that I published my first piece on wine. It was called "Variety or Varietals? The Small Wines of Bordeaux," and it made the case that, while California cabernets—there were no California merlots to speak of at the time—were well worth drinking for their quality and consistency, similarly priced minor Bordeaux offered "a far wider range of wine-drinking experiences." Because I didn't have much confidence in my abilities as a taster of wine at the time—this was shortly before Roy first invited me to Café Swiss—and had never tested my oenological observations in public discourse, I decided to publish under a pseudonym, then see how people reacted. As my surrogate, I invented a mysterious Frenchman (for who knew more about wine than the French?) named Gaston Pinard—*pinard*, literally "red ink," is French slang for cheap red wine—whom I identified as the author of a made-up book I dubbed *Le Vin, la vanité, et la vantardise* (*Wine, Vanity, and Bluster*). This first wine article of mine appeared shortly before I met Roy, and when I had the chance, I asked him if he'd read it and, if so, what he thought of it. "Not bad," he replied, which I had already figured out was, from Roy, a veritable encomium.

Another man who taught me at least some good lessons about wine—and also about spirits and, most notably, cigars—was William Anthony Furness, better known as the Viscount Furness, or simply Tony. Tony was the son of the British shipping magnate Marmaduke Furness and Thelma Morgan Furness, an American diplomat's daughter and twin sister of the elder Gloria Vanderbilt (Tony was thus the uncle of Vanderbilt's grandson Anderson Cooper, the TV journalist). My parents knew Thelma socially, and dined with her frequently, but though Tony had visited Beverly Hills off and on for years, somehow I'd never met him. Learning from my parents that I would be passing through London on one of my first trips to Europe, however, he wrote to invite me to dinner, preceded by cocktails at his club.

When I arrived to meet him, wearing my only suit—a badly wrinkled concrete-gray double-breasted Carnaby Street mock-Edwardian number with exaggerated lapels, hand-rolled cloth-covered buttons, and twin vents in back—I found Tony standing at the bar with rosy cheeks and a look of perfect calm on his face. He greeted me warmly, and either didn't notice the sorry state of my attire or (more likely) was too polite to acknowledge it. "Now, what can we give you to drink?" he inquired. I ordered an Irish whiskey, probably not the thing to drink at a Tory watering hole. He didn't grimace, but simply asked, "Have you ever tried single-malt scotch?" I hadn't. My scotch-drinking experience at that point had been pretty much restricted to Cutty Sark on the rocks at the jazz clubs of central Los Angeles. He said something I didn't quite understand to the bartender, and a little glass of twelve-year-old Glenlivet arrived, with no ice but moistened with a few drops of bottled water. I picked up the glass and brought it to my lips and encountered something smoky, tart, a bit woody, and thoroughly extraordinary. It was, as the French say, a *coup de foudre*—a lightning bolt—at first sip. (A few years later, Tony introduced me to another great spirit: vintage rhum agricole from the French Caribbean—another lightning bolt.)

Tony was a sputtering, stuttering, corpulent man, beset (judging from the collection of pills he carried) by countless ills, but he was also a gentleman, generous and (when you could understand him, which sometimes took some doing) witty and knowledgeable on a wide range of subjects. He had, among other things, a particular interest in Mongolia (he founded the Anglo-Mongolian Society), and was a proud member of the modern-day Knights of Malta (he was devoutly Roman Catholic); he belonged to the politically influential Hansard Society; he enjoyed the theater, and had once produced plays; he imported wine for a time and had a serious cellar.

He also seemed to have an inexhaustible store of jokes, everything from arch anecdotes to rambling shaggy dog stories, which he'd tell at the slightest provocation. ("Do you know," he once asked me rhetorically as we studied the cheese cart at some establishment or other, "the three stages of ripeness in a Brie?" "Unripe, medium, and ripe?" I asked tentatively. "Not exactly," he replied. "Firm, runny, and 'Quick, Mildred, it's heading for the door!'")

After Thelma died, in 1970, Tony kept her house in Beverly Hills and spent some months a year there. Sometimes he'd invite me to small dinner parties, and we'd sit in huge leather chairs afterward and smoke the best available Dominican or Honduran cigars. (As a foreign citizen, he would have been allowed to bring Cubans into the country, but, he once explained to me, he felt enough like an American that he thought he should abide by the country's laws, whatever his citizenship.) It was Tony who showed me how to light a good cigar, taking my time, slowly rotating it, using several matches, never inhaling the smoke from the sulfurous match tips, but letting the flame reach out toward the tip of the tobacco, tentatively at first, then with greater ardor as the cigar grew warm; he also helped me perfect the art of letting a long ash grow, never flicking it off, until it dropped naturally into the ashtray. One thing I did not emulate, however, was Tony's disconcerting way of clipping his cigars: He kept the nail on one little finger long and sharpened for that purpose.

We'd eat meals out sometimes in Los Angeles, too. He liked the Café Swiss, which was only a few blocks from his mother's house, though he preferred the indoor dining room to the patio. He loved Scandia, for the food but possibly even more so for the wine list. It wasn't one of his regular haunts, but for some reason, one day we had lunch at Musso & Frank's in Hollywood, sitting in a booth near a window looking out onto Hollywood Boulevard and ordering squab with peas and Beaulieu Vineyard Private Reserve cabernet. When our waiter asked if he should let the bottle he had just opened stand on the table to "breathe," Tony replied, "It's my theory that the wine will 'breathe' considerably more freely if it's poured into the glass"—and then, when the waiter had departed, added, "And of course more freely still if we start pouring it down our throats" (which we did).

Tony was bemused by American waiters and waitresses. He liked to tell the story of the time he'd ordered a cognac at El Padrino, the casual dining room at the Beverly Wilshire Hotel, and been brought a Grand Marnier instead. When he called the error to the attention of the waitress, she replied, "Wow, Mr. Furness, you can really tell the difference between cognac and Grand Marnier?" "Yes," Tony replied. "And I can even tell the difference between garlic and ice cream."

In the eighties Tony sold the Beverly Hills house and moved back to London, and then to Rome and finally Montreux as a tax exile. He no longer came to Los Angeles, he wasn't a very diligent correspondent, and we lost touch. The last time I saw him was one evening in what must have been late 1995, when I encountered him, most unexpectedly, sitting at a table in the King Cole Bar at the St. Regis in Manhattan. He didn't seem very happy to see me, or perhaps he wasn't very well, and after a few attempted pleasantries, I said good night and departed. Tony died in 1996, of complications from the diabetes that had plagued him for decades. In its obituary of him, *The Times* in London noted that he "refused to conform to rules not of his own making."

I RESIGNED FROM *COAST* in 1975, after the publisher pulled the cover image my art director and I had decided on and substituted one he thought was more "newsy"—a classic betrayal of the editor-publisher relationship. In the next few years, I managed to surive, barely, with freelance assignments. At first, I wrote mostly about music, but gradually, as the rock-and-roll business became increasingly corporate and the L.A. jazz scene seemed to be waning, I turned my attentions more and more toward food and wine.

People ask me all the time how I "got into" food writing, and I never know quite what to say. Sometimes I think I should sit down for a couple of hours one afternoon and write myself an origin myth. The truth is that it just happened. It started, of course, with restaurants. Because they'd always been so much a part of my life, I naturally thought I knew something about them. I talked my way into my first restaurant review in 1970, when I was twenty-five. I wrote, on a whim, to Silas Spitzer, the food and restaurant editor of *Holiday,* a large-format, upscale travel magazine. He also oversaw the restaurant award section that appeared annually in the magazine, assembling the listings with the assistance of an informal crew of "anonymous eaters," as he called them. These were volunteers, scattered all over America, who filed reviews of restaurants that he had determined to be of interest. They were unpaid, but reimbursed for the price of a single representative meal for two at the establishments to which they'd been assigned. This sounded like a pretty good deal to me, and I thought I might be qualified to join Spitzer's squad. He apparently thought so, too, because he promptly replied to my letter, asked for some sample reviews, and then assigned me to write a report on Dan Tana's in West Hollywood, an old-style Italian place that was (and still is) a show business favorite.

I went off for dinner, then wrote and rewrote my assessment of it, and rewrote it again, until I thought I'd gotten it right. Then I mailed it to Spitzer, confident that I'd taken my first step toward a glamorous and well-fed life as a restaurant critic. Unfortunately, the day after I sent him the review, I got a letter from Spitzer that had crossed mine in the mail, announcing that *Holiday* had been sold and that the awards, at least in their old form, were being discontinued. My career reviewing restaurants was over before it began.

After this false start, I had to wait another year to officially become a published critic. In October 1971 an editor for the new *LA Flyer*—a short-lived regional supplement to *Rolling Stone*—hired me to review my old haunt Musso's, then as now "the oldest restaurant in Hollywood." I did so, and went on to write four more reviews for the *Flyer* before it folded. After the *Flyer*'s demise, having tasted blood (or at least fettuccine Alfredo and pâté maison on somebody else's dime), I created for myself what I hoped would be a more enduring critic's post: At the time, the reigning underground newspaper in the city was the *L.A. Free Press*, but several of its editors had walked out over a dispute with the publisher and started their own paper, *The Staff*. I knew the man in charge of *The Staff*, and convinced him to let me write a weekly restaurant review for him. I was paid thirty-five dollars per critique, with no expenses reimbursed, but you could still get a pretty good dinner for two for thirty-five bucks in L.A. in those days, so that seemed like a fair deal.

Instead of reviewing under my own name, I decided to invent a character called Mr. Food, a larger-than-life gourmand and world traveler with a penchant for Victorian elocutions and food-related puns and homonyms ("Mr. Food wanted to take it on the lamb"; "It made Mr. Food quail"). It was all very silly, and a lot of fun. (For the record, my Mr. Food made his debut in print three years before a onetime butcher named Art Ginsburg started doing local television shows under that name.)

I'm not sure how seriously the local restaurant community took Mr. Food's reviews, but they did catch the eye of Lois Dwan of the *Los Angeles Times*. Dwan was easily the most important and influential restaurant critic in town in those days, and in 1975, when she was going on vacation for a couple of weeks, she asked if I'd temporarily take over writing the featured review in the Sunday Calendar section of the paper. Would I! For a young, aspiring restaurant reviewer, this was the big show. I went on to have a long, peculiar, and ultimately unsatisfying relationship with the *Times*, but I consider having taken over Lois's column for a few weeks, more than thirty-five years ago, to have been the real beginning of my food-writing career.

I did other writing, too, having nothing to do with food—mostly profiles of celebrities. One of my best customers was the *Radio Times*, the weekly BBC program log cum entertainment magazine. The English writer Sally Beauman, who'd done a few pieces for me at *Coast*, had gone to work as an editor for the magazine, and she assigned me to write about a wonderful assortment of famous and accomplished people. I coaxed a reluctant François Truffaut to talk about his early films instead of the BBC special he was supposed to be promoting; I watched Jane Fonda switch on her talking-to-journalists persona in a hotel room in Colorado when she was shooting *Comes a Horseman* and then switch it off again like a light; I followed Marta Feuchtwanger, the ninety-two-year-old widow of the German anti-Nazi writer Lion Feuchtwanger,

around her big house in Pacific Palisades while she pointed out me-
mentos to me ("Maybe you've heard of the Dreyfus case?" she asked
as she pointed to a framed copy of the front page of the Parisian
newspaper *L'Aurore* from January 13, 1898, devoted to Émile Zola's
famous defense of Dreyfus, under a huge black headline reading
"J'Accuse.") One of my less pleasant interviews was with Leonard
Nimoy, who bristled when I mentioned his autobiography *I Am Not
Spock* ("I resent it when people who haven't read the book think
they know what the title means," he said, just a little bit ingenu-
ously, I thought) and then fairly stunned me by refusing to talk
about *Star Trek*—as if there were any other reason anyone would
care what he had to say.

That experience was more than made up for when I got an assignment to interview Jeanne Moreau, who had just finished her
first film as director, *Lumière*. At the time, Moreau was married to
the director William Friedkin and living in Bel Air, and she invited
me to do the interview at her home. Like any normal artsy fellow
of my generation, I was madly in love with Moreau and, of course,
nervous as hell to be in her presence. She turned out to be warm,
accessible, charming, and professional, and I got a good story. After
the interview, Moreau walked me to my car, asking along the way
if I wrote only for newspapers and magazines. I replied that I did,
but added that most of what I wrote about was food and wine.
Her face lit up, and she said, "You know, I am a very good cook.
Gault et Millau have written that the best table in Paris, it is Jeanne
Moreau's. If you would like, you can come again, for dinner, and
we will talk this time only about gastronomy. I am leaving town
Tuesday for two weeks, but call my husband's secretary after that
and we will arrange it." I promised that I would and added that I
would bring some good California wines to accompany her cuisine.
A few weeks later, I called Friedkin's office and explained Moreau's

invitation. I was told that someone would call me back, but they never did. This was quite possibly the most disappointing missed connection of my professional life.

I FIRST STARTED TO BELIEVE that I might actually know a little bit about wine—that I was really learning things at the Café Swiss and not just taxing my internal organs—in 1978, when I was invited to judge wines at the Los Angeles County Fair. This turned out to be a grueling exercise. Judging was conducted in the heat of summer at the county fairgrounds in Pomona. Several score of us—wine writers, winemakers, wine sellers of various kinds—sat four to a table in a cavernous room, with endless rows of glasses lined up in front of us. Pourers circulated, filling the glasses about a third of the way up, in succession, out of bottles swathed in brown paper bags. In two long sessions, morning and afternoon, we'd taste literally hundreds of wines a day over a two-day period.

Over the three or four years that I participated in the judging, I'd taste with Roy, a mainstay at the event, but also, in various combinations, with such knowledgeable folk as the Sacramento grocer Darrell Corti (known in wine and food circles as the Professor for the breadth and depth of his wine and food knowledge) and blue-chip winemakers like Dick Arrowood, Mike Richmond, and Dimitri Tchelistcheff (son of the legendary André). We were instructed to make our own notes and to score the wines, and then discuss the scores among ourselves so that each table could arrive at a consensus. Through this process, I discovered, to my great surprise and pleasure, that my perceptions of the wines were usually not that different from those of my vastly more experienced professional colleagues. Sampling so many wines and assessing them with some degree of intelligence and consistency demanded a lot of concentration; it was both mentally and physically tiring, and I remember later trying to make the case to someone that, jokes aside, this kind of tasting really was almost a sport, demanding not just sensory evaluation but a kind of physical coordination and a measure of real strength.

I was able to further verify my abilities as a taster a few years later when my friend Tim Johnston—today the proprietor of Juveniles, a sympa wine bar and mini–wine shop in Paris—got me invited to participate in the Saint-Bacchus in southeastern France. The Saint-Bacchus (who but the French would canonize the Roman god of wine?) is an annual competitive tasting of the wines of France's Roussillon region. The format was not unlike that of the L.A. County Fair, in that tasters gathered in small groups, made their own judgments, and then compared notes. But instead of being stuck for two days in a large hall in Pomona, at the Saint-Bacchus we sat for an hour and a half in an upstairs room at the Station Viti-Vinicole du Comité Interprofessionnel des Vins Doux Naturels, with windows open to the countryside, on a breezy, vine-covered hilltop in the village of Tresserre, a few miles from the Spanish border. And instead of making detailed notes and applying numerical scores to the wines, my fellow tasters and I were charged with simply deciding which wine in our judging category we liked best—not necessarily which one *was* best in some abstract, platonic sense, but which one pleased us the most; which one gave us, in the words of our hosts, *un coup du coeur*.

I loved the informality of the tasting and the collegial atmosphere at the Saint-Bacchus. ("If Bordeaux or Chablis tried to do a competitive judging this way," Tim Johnston remarked one day, "there'd be people out with knives and guns.") I also loved the lunch after the tasting, downstairs, outside, under the Station's porticoes—typically Collioure anchovies and grilled red peppers, assorted roasted vegetables, a platter of mixed fish and shellfish (rouget in vine leaves, mackerel, and squid, all grilled over vine cuttings), and Roquefort (always superlative in this part of France, for some reason). And I loved the fact that my *coeur* was nearly always *coupé* by the same wine the other fellows had liked.

THE CAFÉ SWISS CLOSED IN 1985. Rodeo Drive had by then become a shopping mall for the one percent (and the one-percent wannabes), and glittering palaces of upscale retail commerce had forced out most of the locally owned shops and more modest merchants. Café Swiss lasted as long as it did because the Hugs owned the building, so were able to resist encroaching developers. Finally, though, someone made an offer for the property so outlandish that it was impossible to refuse. Laura Hug invited some of the regulars to show up after she'd closed the doors for the last time and partially demolish the patio walls with sledgehammers. Then she announced that she planned to reopen in another Beverly Hills location, with the same menu and the same staff, in as little as four months' time. For whatever reasons, that never happened. The lot on which the restaurant stood for thirty-five years is now the site of a two-story building with thirty-five-thousand square feet of retail space.

After Café Swiss closed, the Saturday lunch group moved on to a succession of other places, none of them permanent. I'd show up occasionally, but by the end of the eighties, I was married for the second time, with a baby, and I pretty much stopped going altogether. Even Roy seemed to be enjoying it less. "The Saturday group seems more frenetic every time," he wrote in a note accompanying some wine articles he sent me. "It's just not possible to make reasonable notes on all the wines. I take more time to have lunch with two wines and one brandy." I still met Roy for lunch or dinner every once in a while, and he remained as smart about wine as ever, and as acerbic in his comments. A few days before I moved to the East Coast in the final week of 1994, I had dinner with him at a French restaurant in the San Fernando Valley. Though we exchanged letters after that, and he wrote a few short items for *Saveur*, that was the last time I saw him. He died in 1998 at the age of seventy-nine. It was rumored that, like André Simon, one of the old wine writers he'd read in his early days as a wine lover, he only had one bottle left in his cellar when he left the planet. "Must have miscounted," I can imagine him grumbling.

Chapter Nine

PICCOLO MONDO,
Rome (1954–)

F ROM AN ENTRY IN MY JOURNAL, DATED OCTOBER 25, 1978:

Leaving St. Peter's I took a cab to the Via Veneto, and walked a few blocks to Piccolo Mondo for lunch. I asked for a table with the waiter Guido, on the chance that he'd remember me, and he did, and very well. He embraced me, asked how long it had been, how Karen was, etc. I had a wonderful meal, attentively and affectionately served, with the usual Roman songs in the background (though not by the usual singer-guitarist: he'd died recently of cancer, Guido told me, adding, "La vita non è giusta"). I started with the little mozzarella "eggs" and crudités and pizza bread that are brought automatically; then funghi porcini, roasted and then sautéed with bits of garlic that were almost caramelized, then abbacchio al forno (the sweet charred flesh of Roman lamb!), then cheese, then banana ice cream with Strega, then coffee and sambuca, and all the while the very good house red wine (of which I drank nearly two bottles). I felt surprisingly fit after the meal, maybe because I felt so recklessly contented while eating and

drinking it. I felt as if I were really in Rome, and on my own
terms this time.

Throughout the sixties and early seventies, I was very much
what they used to call a "film nut," and one of my favorite directors
was Federico Fellini. It was he who gave me my first conscious look
at Rome, through his 1960 classic *La Dolce Vita*, which starred
Marcello Mastroianni as a promiscuous, disaffected tabloid journalist navigating his way through the city's caffè society and the
midcentury Italian celebrity whirl. It was through this film, more
than through any other source, that I was first seduced by Rome,
or rather by a romantic notion of the city. I loved the whole idea
of the Roman "sweet life"—of glittering, smoky caffès on the Via
Veneto, of fast cars and overnight affairs, of sophisticated, sleazy
parties thrown in medieval castles or sleek apartment suites by
aristocrats of questionable moral character. Of course, the Dolce
Vita era was over by the time I first got to Rome, but I always felt
as if I got a small taste of the spirit of those times through the restaurant called Piccolo Mondo.

My entrée to Piccolo Mondo, and to Rome itself, came through
an old friend from my Serrano Gay Bar days. One of the few
women who sometimes showed up at John Stachowiak's house
was a pretty, statuesque young woman of Irish and Italian origins
named Karen Kelly. She had known the Serrano regular Allen Daviau since grade school, and he sometimes invited her to join us for
one of our dinners out, or for one of my Sunday evening meals of
spaghetti with hamburger meat and canned corn.

Karen ended up marrying John, and they moved into a house
in the Hollywood Hills. The two traveled a lot in Europe and
the Middle East in the first years of their marriage, and then, in
the early seventies, Karen went off by herself to study Italian in

Rome for a few months—and more or less stayed there. She and John eventually divorced, and she found a good-natured Roman boyfriend named Gianfranco, who sold Ferraris for a living, and a dreamy old-fashioned fifth-floor walk-up apartment with white-washed walls and red-tile floors in the heart of the city, near the Piazza del Popolo. We stayed in touch, and when she learned that I was planning a trip to Paris, she insisted that I make a detour and come visit her in her adopted city.

I fell in love with the place my first day there. It felt both exotic and familiar, Mediterranean and Californian. I liked the radiant terra-cotta-colored buildings framed by vivid blue skies; I liked the way the streets smelled—that weird, alluring bouquet of diesel fumes, roasting meat, the moss in fountains, the piney cologne on small men wearing pastel shirts with pastel sweaters tied around their necks; I liked the Roman light, warm, thick, ancient. It excited me to be able to take a casual walk through the urban center and traverse not just centuries but millennia, from Caesar to Mussolini, St. Peter to Sophia Loren. I felt benevolent envy at the way people lived in Rome, or at least my perception of the way they lived—unhurried, sybaritic, sometimes bawdy, usually equanimous. And of course I loved the food.

Traditional Roman cuisine is rarely mentioned as one of Italy's best or most important culinary traditions, but when it's good—as it certainly was in Rome in those days (less so now, I think)—it is wonderfully accessible and immensely satisfying. To begin with, many of the pasta sauces that have become favorites all over Italy and in the United States and beyond claim Roman origins: carbonara (made with the cured pig's cheek called guanciale, along with pecorino romano, egg, and lots of black pepper, a reference to the charcoal sellers for whom it is supposedly named), arrabbiata ("angry," a tomato sauce with lots of garlic and red peppers), amatriciana (from the town of Amatrice northeast of Rome, made with tomato, guanciale, and pecorino), Alfredo (invented at the restaurant Alfredo alla Scrofa on Rome's Via della Scrofa, and correctly made with only butter and parmigiano—no cream, and certainly no ham or peas), cacio e pepe (Roman dialect for "cheese and pepper," a wonderfully minimalist seasoning, more than sauce, of nothing but pecorino romano and black pepper). I ate all of these and more in trattorias all over the city and its surroundings.

I also devoured saltimbocca, little veal scallops topped with prosciutto and sage, whose name means "jump in the mouth," and the stewed oxtail called coda alla vaccinara. I ate kilos of the roast baby lamb dish abbacchio (whose name derives from *abbacchiare*, meaning to beat down, which some say is a reference to slaughtering the tiny animals with blows to the head), the defining protein of the city and its region. In America, artichokes were big elongated globes that you ate by pulling off leaves and scraping off a thin film of meat with your teeth; I never saw the point. In Rome, the artichokes were either small and poached alla romana, in olive oil with garlic until they were as soft as butter, or were larger but prepared alla giudia, Jewish style, deep-fried and splayed out like delicious blossoms that crackled when you bit into them. I tried literal blossoms, too, fiori di zucca, squash flowers filled with mozzarella and anchovies, battered, and deep-fried—unbelievable. I steeled myself and tried trippa alla romana, tripe in tomato sauce flavored with nepitella, a relative of mint; I even sampled rigatoni con la pajata, in which the little ridged tubes of pasta were tossed with other little tubes—sections of milk-fed veal intestines that still contain cheese-like coagulated milk (to my surprise I actually liked this better than the tripe, though I didn't go out of my way to order it subsequently).

To call these food experiences revelatory would be a gross un-

derstatement. For a young American, even a comparatively experienced restaurant goer like myself, eating like this in the 1970s
was sheer exotica; I might as well have been sampling the cuisines
of Ethiopia or Nepal. You have to remember—or imagine—what
our perception of Italian food was in America back then: A sophisticated Italian meal meant "shrimp scampi" and veal parmigiana.
Unless you came from an Italian family that had maintained strong
culinary ties with the old country, you very likely would simply
have never heard of, much less tasted, porcini, pancetta, mozzarella di bufala, sun-dried tomatoes, or even arugula (called rucola
in Italy). Radicchio, which now gets tossed into salads at McDonald's, was a pricey import. My old friend Piero Selvaggio of Valentino remembers buying radicchio from Italy for seventy-five dollars
a crate, including air freight, and having to throw half of it, wilted
and moldy, away when it arrived; when he'd put the good leaves
into salads and charge a bit more than usual for them, he says, customers would ask, "What's so special about a little red cabbage?"
You couldn't even buy baby greens; when I gave a dinner party and
wanted to serve an Italian-style salad, I'd go to a nursery and come
home with little pots of seedling lettuce meant to be planted in the
garden, then uproot and clean the leaves and toss them with some
shredded beet leaves (standing in for radicchio) in good olive oil;
that was as close as I could come.

At home when I was growing up, mushrooms were rubbery
little nubs that came in tiny cans and squeaked when you chewed
them, and I couldn't stand them. I'll never forget the first time I
saw big porcini mushroom caps, the size of steaks, grilling on hot
coals at Piccolo Mondo; I found it hard to believe what they were at
first, and it took me a few visits to be brave enough to order them,
but the moment I finally did, I became an instant mushroom lover.
Spaghetti, even in the better Italian places in the States, tended to

be slippery noodles unevenly coated in a thick, sweetish tomato sauce (American recipes in those days invariably called for the spaghetti to be rinsed off after cooking, an idiocy that flushed away the starch that helps the sauce to cling), usually garnished with big, bready meatballs. In Rome, spaghetti was more likely to be sturdy, rough-textured, maybe even square-cut strands, cooked just north of al dente—a texture Romans call *filo di ferro,* or "iron string," meaning that there's a firm, wheaty core to each piece of pasta—tossed with a few flavorful ingredients.

When we ate "garlic bread" in America, it came in the form of spongy loaves, halved and sprinkled with garlic powder and maybe powdered industrial-strength "parmesan"; Karen and Gianfranco introduced me to real garlic bread, a Roman specialty called "bruschetta"—slabs cut thick from a big rustic loaf, toasted on the grill, rubbed with raw garlic cloves, then seasoned with olive oil and salt. One place we went to sometimes got fancy in the summertime and served it with some chopped fresh tomatoes on top. (How this simple, definitive rustic specialty became the "broo-shedda" served in America today, which typically involves multi-ingredient toppings on insignificant pieces of toasted bread, sometimes lacking even the garlic and the oil, is a mystery to me. It is now common to see containers of chopped tomato salad labeled "bruschetta" in the supermarket, as if this extraneous accoutrement were the thing itself.)

I ALWAYS STAYED with Karen when I went to Rome, sleeping on the couch in her apartment near the Piazza del Popolo. Our days were built around food. In the mornings, as soon as we woke up, she'd call the latteria downstairs and say a few words in her by then fluent, Roman-accented Italian, then put on the espresso pot. By the time the pot had finished sputtering, the delivery boy would have shuffled up the stairs, bringing us a tub of warm, just-made ricotta. We'd spread it on slices of crusty, lightly toasted country bread, either salting it generously or topping it with little spoonfuls of apricot preserves. We'd sit there and drink our strong, muddy espresso between bites and talk about where we were going to have lunch.

We'd end up at places like La Buca di Ripetta, a neighborhood trattoria a few blocks from Karen's place, where we'd have penne all'amatriciana or fettuccine with clams (or porcini, if they were in season), then saltimbocca or roast chicken. Or we'd go to Ambasciata d'Abruzzo and attack the huge basket of assorted mountain-style sausages presented the moment we sat down, before moving on to linguine with artichokes or spaghetti alla carbonara and some thick, juicy veal chops or roast suckling pig. Sometimes, around one in the afternoon, Gianfranco would come by and spirit us off in a borrowed Ferrari (or a battered-up, traded-in Land Rover) to a place out on the Via Appia, one of those famous old Roman roads that lead you-know-where, to an eighteenth-century country inn turned restaurant called Casale. There, we'd pile our plates high from a long, two-tiered antipasto table—meat-and-rice-stuffed vegetables, borlotti beans in olive oil, fresh ricotta and bufala mozzarella glistening with olive oil and sprinkled with spicy red pepper flakes, marinated anchovies, grilled squid, grilled zucchini, grilled radicchio, marinated beets, thin slices of hard sausage in several varieties, three or four kinds of olives, and on and on—then move on to something like tagliatelle with baby shrimp or spaghetti sauced with squash blossoms cooked down nearly to a marmalade, and always slices of rotisserie-roasted baby lamb accompanied by rough-cut potato chunks cooked in the dripping fat beneath the rotisserie.

One lunchtime we went to another of our favorites, Sabatini, on the Piazza Santa Maria in Trastevere, sitting on the terrace and eating grilled scampi, pan-fried slices of porcini with crisp bits of garlic, spaghetti with clams, and coda alla vaccinara. There seemed to be some to-do around the old octagonal fountain in front of the church of Santa Maria: twenty or thirty people milling around, frames of pipe being erected with big lights attached, a little Fiat van pulling up. Suddenly a clutch of motorcycles roared out of the background and started circling the fountain, their engines revving, their tires squealing. Then we noticed a big movie camera emerging on a dolly from the far side of the fountain, and as the crowd parted, we saw a robust-looking man with a leonine profile standing on a step like an orchestral conductor. It was, I realized, Federico Fellini, directing a scene from what we later learned was his paean to the city, *Roma*—a film which was ultimately to feed my fantasies of the place even more than *La Dolce Vita* had done.

Of all my Roman restaurant experiences, though, nothing more vividly defined the cooking of the city—and the city itself—to me than my many meals at Piccolo Mondo. Piccolo Mondo was opened in 1954 by one Tommaso Camponeschi, who came from a mountain village not far from Amatrice. His timing was perfect. He set up shop just as the Italian economy was beginning to recover after World War II, and the massive Cinecittà film studio, founded by Mussolini, was beginning to thrive as a major European production center, luring even American filmmakers. (*Ben-Hur, Cleopatra,* and Franco Zeffirelli's *Romeo and Juliet* were to come out of Cinecittà, as were most of Fellini's films, including *La Dolce Vita*.) As the alluring, self-indulgent Roman "sweet life" flourished, with the Via Veneto as its main artery, Piccolo Mondo—unpretentious but still glamorous, near the Via Veneto but refreshingly not quite in the thick of things—became a kind of celebrity nerve center, an institutional expression of the giddy spirit of the era. It was the Chasen's of its place and time.

The restaurant's walls, when I first ate there, told the story: Two decades' worth of photographs, faded, cracked, and curling, were taped or thumb-tacked haphazardly around the dining room—glossy shots of Cary Grant, Burt Lancaster, Marcello Mastroianni, Gina Lollobrigida, Audrey Hepburn, Brigitte Bardot, and other stars, but also studio portraits and large-format snapshots, mostly taken at the restaurant's tables, of scores of heartbreakingly beautiful and optimistic-looking young men and women who are now long since forgotten.

By the seventies, production at Cinecittà was slowing down, and Rome no longer drew the big-name stars, and I never saw anybody I recognized at the restaurant. But the dining room always bustled furiously, at lunch and dinner both, full of models (real or aspiring) in high-heel shoes and gauzy dresses, fat-cat businessmen or politicians with open shirts and potbellies, artsy-looking earth mothers in shifts and copious costume jewelry, sun-darkened septuagenarian roués with long gray manes. I used to imagine—and I'm sure I was right—that more than a few of them had been habitués of the place in the good old days, and still came back regularly to forget, if only for a few hours, how much their world had changed. I used to imagine that I was one of them.

We had a regular waiter at Piccolo Mondo, a round-faced, bald-pated little fellow named Guido, who clearly loved Karen. We'd typically arrive around one-thirty for lunch, or close to ten o'clock for dinner. Someone would show us to our table, always one of Guido's, and he would appear in an instant with a bottle of the red house wine and a basket of bread, which included the first focaccia I'd ever had, a Roman interpretation of this basic bread, seasoned with olive oil and salt, which they called "pizza bianco," white pizza. Next would come a dish of mozzarella bocconcini—little bites—about the size of plump cherries, and some pinzimonio, which was more or less what restaurants in America used to call a "relish tray," an assortment of cut-up raw vegetables, but here served with a metal bowl of olive oil seasoned with lots of salt and pepper, into which the pieces of carrot, fennel, red pepper, and the like were to be dipped.

After we'd nibbled for fifteen minutes or so, and probably worked our way through most of our first bottle of wine, Guido would reappear and ask, "Now, what would you like to eat?" Whatever we decided on, we'd get more. We might order the penne all'arrabbiata or the homemade meat-filled ravioli tossed with butter, garlic, and a confetti of tomato bits. Then, before it arrived, Guido would come by with the remains of a platter that he'd just served to another table and say, "Have a little lasagne," or "I bring you some cacio e pepe." If our main course was, say, abbacchio al forno, we were likely to be treated to a few scampi quickly cooked in olive oil or some strips of porcini fried with garlic first. I loved this way of eating: simple, savory, relaxed, appreciative, joyful. I loved just being in this ancient city, and part of me, as I sat there, would sometimes get a little sad, knowing that in a day or two, or even a week or two, I'd have to pack up and leave and go back home to real life, whatever it might have been at the moment. But then another part of me would remember that, hey, at least for the foreseeable future, I could always come back.

BY THE MID-SEVENTIES, I had become something of a traveling fool. When I had a steady job, I would work business trips into the routine as often as I could. When I was freelancing, I sometimes spent more days of the year on the road than at home, carpentering together complicated transcontinental or overseas itineraries based on whatever assignments I could cadge. What I liked so much about traveling was the wonderful sense of dislocation it brings. I'd let myself get sealed into a gigantic metal tube, then hurtle through the ozone for a few hours or overnight and step out into another place entirely, with different smells and sounds, different people, and, of course, different food.

On so many occasions over the years, finding myself someplace else, someplace *other*, I'd get suddenly flooded with a kind of euphoria, a rush of figurative and quite possibly literal adrenaline. I remember standing on the quai above the Adige in Verona at sunset in the warm springtime air, watching the old stone buildings on the other side of the river luminesce for a minute or two in the falling light and then turn cool blue-gray, and feeling unreasonably, simplistically happy. I remember stepping out of a water taxi, driven by a beautiful dishwater blonde with an amber tan and stevedore hands, onto a stony beach framed in tamarisk and myrtle trees and sprawls of rock roses on the Île de Porquerolles, and turning almost breathless with wonder at the idea that not even twenty-four hours earlier I'd been sitting at my desk on Sixth Avenue in New York City editing an article about common crackers from the Vermont Country Store.

One time, lunching alone at Harry's Bar in Venice, I was so overcome with sheer joy at the music of the multilingual chatter and the clink of silverware on china all around me, and at the aromas of the food, and at the sight out the window of gulls perched on the blue-and-white-striped mooring poles rising up from the Grand Canal and the sparks of sunlight leaping across the water, that I started clawing my fingernails across the pale yellow tablecloth, like a dog pawing for a bone, until I realized how silly I looked and made myself take a sip of Soave instead.

Some of my more exotic eating was in Finland, where I went at the suggestion of my girlfriend Lyn, who had a boutique in Beverly Hills devoted to a Finnish designer. When I got to Helsinki for the first time, I quickly figured out a few key food terms in the Finns' impenetrable language, and I ate pretty well. I learned to savor, and pronounce, pöronpaïsti (thin-sliced, smoked reindeer tongue) and tried stewed bear at a Russian restaurant (once was enough). I ate herring with mica-thin onion slices in curried oil and pike-perch in red wine sauce at Havis Amanda, then the city's leading seafood restaurant; reindeer steaks in Madeira sauce at the Hotel Marski; roasted riekko, or willow ptarmigan, at the Hotel Hesperia. At a lively bistro near the opera house called Bulevardia, I had what I described in my notebook as "the best steak tartare I have ever encountered," which had shredded beets added to the mix.

On one occasion, I flew to Bulgaria, as a guest of the government tourist office. My flight connected through Brussels, with a layover of almost twenty-four hours, so I had the chance to enjoy two consecutive meals there, dinner and then lunch the next day. I took both at a place called Au Filet de Boeuf on the rue des Harengs (Herring Street), which I'd read about in one of the British wine merchant Harry Waugh's entertaining books about his travels. He had singled it out not only for its more than decent cuisine but for the fact that the wine list was packed with excellent Burgundies at surprisingly low prices. My dinner was escargots, filet de boeuf Clément (in a sauce of cream, tomatoes, and tarragon) with potato croquettes, chèvre, and vanilla ice cream, accompanied by a half bottle of Chapitre de Beaune 1970 and a full one of Drouhin Grands-Echezeaux 1961, topped off with two framboises (lord, but I could drink in those days) and a Don Pedro cigar. My more modest lunch, before I headed to the airport, was smoked salmon, quail with Armagnac sauce, and meringue Saint-Hubert, along with a bottle of Corton-Charlemagne 1966 and a cognac.

That night, I found myself sitting, with my Bulgarian hosts, at a place called Boiansko Hanche, a touristic tavern in the village of Boiana, just outside Sofia, and eating shopska salata (cucumbers, cherry tomatoes, and fresh white cheese) with pitka (moist round bread, to be dipped into a mixture of salt, pepper, and coriander), sirene gyuveche (cheese baked with tomatoes and peppers and topped with a fried egg, which I of course avoided), and kavarma—which, I jotted down in my notebook, was "an intricate folksong of hot peppers, pork, onions, mushrooms, garlic, and cheese." Quail with Armagnac and shopska salata in the same day? I felt *very* cosmopolitan.

I later returned to Brussels on assignment for the *Los Angeles Times*, and spent what I think was the most grueling eating week of my life there. The Belgian tourism people had assigned me a guide whose brief was apparently to wine and dine me with abandon and make sure I got a taste of the range of restaurants Brussels and the surrounding countryside had to offer. That meant two big meals a day. Two big *Belgian* meals a day. (There is a story that Victor Hugo was once dining in a Brussels café when a man at the next table looked over and remarked, "You must be French to be eating so much bread"—to which Hugo replied, "You must be Belgian to be eating so much of *everything*.") At the Villa Lorraine, which several years earlier had become the first-ever Michelin three-star restaurant outside France, we drank champagne en carafe and assorted Burgundies while we tucked into two kinds of foie gras—duck, faintly perfumed with ginger, and goose with truffles and a gelée of malvoisie wine—followed by oysters in champagne sauce, sole with miniature mussels, and noisettes of venison with a muscat grape feuillcté and a purée of celery and chestnuts. At Comme Chez Soi, another three-star place, we had lightly smoked, thinly sliced cow's udder with asparagus, mousses of wood pigeon and ham, crayfish in a veal demi-glace, and pheasant with braised endive, mushrooms, and celery root. Everything was just wonderful—hearty, obviously, but intensely flavorful and finished with real finesse. Even dinner at En Plein Ciel, the rooftop restaurant at the Brussels Hilton, was impressive—thin-sliced sweetbreads glazed in orange juice with onion confit and mâche and wild roast duck with shredded brussels sprout and potato cakes.

On expeditions outside the city, we lunched at Edgard & Madeleine, a little roadside place overlooking the rolling farmlands of the Hainaut, on trout en escabeche, simply roasted woodcock, and Chimay cheese. At Le Sanglier des Ardennes in the tiny village of Durbuy, we feasted on Ardennes ham with whole-wheat sourdough bread cut from huge round loaves, subtle woodcock mousse, grilled river perch in cress sauce, and saddle of hare in cream sauce. I wish I could report that when I got back to Los Angeles I gave up food entirely for a couple of weeks, but of course, as grueling as my Belgian experience had been, it seemed to have stimulated my appetite, and I started planning almost at once for my next gastronomic foray.

IN 1982 KAREN WENT HOME to California to be near her parents, her Roman adventure—and thus, to a large extent, mine— over. We saw each other from time to time (she'd moved to San Diego), and kept up with the other's progress. I went back to Rome a couple of times for brief visits, on one occasion returning to Piccolo Mondo, where I ate pretty much as I had in the seventies. A decade passed, and then most of another one. Karen got remarried. My first wife and I split up, and I got remarried, too. In late 1994

I moved to New York to edit a new food magazine that I'd help to found, *Saveur*.

One day in 1999, as I was in the process of developing some Italian story ideas for the magazine, it occurred to me that I could probably write a pretty good article about Roman cooking by returning to the city and revisiting all the old places—or as many of them as still existed—contrasting my experiences then and now. I had started mapping out my trip when I got a crazy, impractical, Roman sort of idea: What if I not only revisited my old haunts but could somehow revisit them with Karen and Gianfranco? Of course, this was absurd on the face of it: Karen's husband was an easygoing and generous sort, but he was hardly likely to approve of his wife traipsing off to Rome with a couple of men from her past; Gianfranco, though he was still selling Ferraris in Rome, had gotten married, too, to a quiet Ukrainian woman he'd met on a business trip to Moscow. But Karen and Gianfranco had kept in occasional touch over the years, and . . . Well, I thought it might be worth a couple of phone calls.

Remarkably, Karen and Gianfranco both loved the idea, and Karen could make the time for it; even more remarkably, both spouses gave their dispensation (as did mine). The next thing I knew, the three of us were sitting down to lunch at Sabatini again, for the first time in twenty-five years, addressing a tableful of food: roasted peppers, prosciutto di Parma, mushrooms preserved in oil, carciofi alla giudia, clams in marinara sauce, red mullet baked in parchment. . . . We may have been older, but we were still hungry.

Over the next week's time, we went back to La Buca di Ripetta, delighted to find that though it had new owners, some of the old waiters and cooks were still there and the menu was little changed; to Ambasciata d'Abruzzo, where the same big basket of sausages came out the moment we sat down; to Casale, where the antipasto table was as big as ever and the lamb tasted just like it used to. And of course, we went to Piccolo Mondo. This turned out to be a sad mistake. Tommaso Camponeschi's son Benito had been running the restaurant, but he died in 1997 and his four children took over. They added a pizza oven and dumbed down the menu. Guido had retired fifteen years earlier, and the new waiters had none of his warmth and generosity. We were seated in a dingy back room and ate food that was merely okay. Some of the photographs from the Dolce Vita era had survived, but they were now neatly aligned on the walls behind Plexiglas shields. The place was almost empty.

Karen, Gianfranco, and I left in a gloomy mood that lasted until dinner that night, which turned out to be a delightful meal at another relic of Rome's glamour days, Taverna Flavia. This was reportedly Liz Taylor's favorite Roman restaurant, and has always held a special place in my ravenous heart because it's the first place I ever tasted white truffles. These were shaved into a tangle of lattughella (mâche), celery, ovoli (*Amanita caesarea*, one of the most delicate and delicious of wild mushrooms), and scales of Gruyère, a dish called Insalata Veruschka, in honor of that stunning, lanky German-born model-turned-artist. Of course I had to have it again on this visit, and though the frisson of discovery was lacking, it was still pretty good. So were the big platter of delicious fried things (whole little long-stem purple artichokes, stuffed zucchini flowers, polenta croquettes, olives crusted in ground veal) and the small lamb chops called scottadito, finger burners, because you're supposed to eat them with your hands. Unlike Piccolo Mondo, the place was buzzing. We even saw some local celebrities: members of the Roman soccer team, A.S. Roma.

Over dinner we agreed, with melancholy, that Piccolo Mondo

was finished, at least for us. Now, though, we're not so sure. In 2005, three of Benito Camponeschi's children decamped, leaving his son Roberto in charge. The following year, Roberto completely refurbished the place. The kitchen was remodeled, the dining room brightened up, and a false ceiling that had been installed along the way was removed, revealing the original brick ceiling from 1954. The menu has been modernized—in the seventies, we never could have imagined finding artichoke flan with pecorino cream, ricotta gnocchi with lamb ragout, or sliced beef salad with arugula in balsamic dressing here—but there is a section of Roman specialties, including spaghetti alla carbonara, bucatini all'amatriciana, and saltimbocca. Many of the raw materials come from around the Camponeschis' rural hometown. Roberto, people say, is charming. Karen plans a trip to Rome with her husband, and wants to try the place again. So, I guess, do I.

Chapter Ten

PORTS,

West Hollywood (1972–1992)

F OR SLIGHTLY MORE THAN SEVEN YEARS, FROM THE
day it opened in early 1972 until I got married for the first
time, in April 1979, and moved out of the neighborhood, my social,
romantic, gastronomic, and, well, alcoholic life revolved around an
unassuming if eventually legendary restaurant and bar called Ports,
a few blocks from my apartment on Fountain Avenue. Ports was
my hangout, my second home, my great good place. I went there
almost every night, either to spend the evening or before or after
going someplace else. I ate there, anything from casual snacks to
huge dinners, and drank mind-numbing quantities of wine and liquor perched on one of the barstools or installed in one of the plain,
marginally comfortable booths. I ran up huge tabs, and ended up
prowling the floor as an evening manager off and on for a year or
so to work off part of the debt. I cooked banquets there a few times
when the proprietors were gone. I acquired scores of friends and
girlfriends there.

Ports, which was owned by an eccentric couple named Jock
and Micaela Livingston, looked a little like one of the so-called
brown bars of Amsterdam (where the proprietors had briefly

lived), maybe crossed with one of those multicultural bistro-dives you used to happen upon in the East Village. The floors were bare concrete, the tables were covered with green oilcloth, and the walls were faced with cheap wood veneer. Some of the regulars had their names on small brass plaques nailed up over their regular perches. (I had two at my favorite corner table in the small front room: one with my name and one, at my request, reading "Pseud's Corner," after a column of pretentious press clippings in the British satirical magazine *Private Eye*, of which I was a devotee.) The menu at Ports was all over the culinary map: Moroccan eggplant salad, Chinese chicken salad, "Greek pie" made with watercress and feta cheese, cold curried chicken consommé, chicken livers in marsala sauce, stuffed game hen with plum sauce, choucroute garnie, couscous every Thursday. My favorite Ports dish was albóndigas en chipotle—parsley-flecked meatballs of finely ground beef in a thick, spicy, smoky, luminescent brown chile sauce, topped with a thick blanket of well-browned melted cheese. I would usually eat the cheese off the top first, seasoned with bits of sauce and meat clinging to it, and then send the dish back to the kitchen for another layer.

The night my father died, I'd gone to visit him at his apartment—my mother had died a year earlier—and found him in a bad way. I drove him to St. John's Hospital in Santa Monica, where he expired after an hour or so, with that chilling "death rattle" you hear about. I signed some papers, then headed straight for Ports, where I had the albóndigas, which I sent back twice that time for extra cheese, and drank two bottles of Rioja. I couldn't think of what else to do.

The clientele at Ports was even more diverse than the menu. The restaurant drew artists, writers, actors, directors and producers, photographers, and musicians, but also bankers, tailors, architects, shopkeepers, and every sort of hanger-on and ne'er-do-well. There was a core group of men and women sprawled around the bar almost every evening who didn't quite do anything but were always talking about what they were about to do; I called them "les perdus de Ports." There were also often unexpected visitors. When you walked into Ports, a habitué once noted, you were always running into somebody you had last seen in Marrakech.

Celebrities great and small came to the place. Sometimes we'd peer through the smoky light and notice Warren Beatty having a quiet supper in the front room with Julie Christie, or Robert Redford in a booth at the back, talking deals with a couple of fellows in jeans jackets. In the late seventies and early eighties, Francis Ford Coppola's Zoetrope Studios was located across the street, and he would preside over big wine-laden tables at lunchtime with an ever-changing cast of associates. Dave Garroway, the affable, jazz-loving host of the original *Today* show, used to come in sometimes, and I bought him dinner one night—in return, I told him, for all the pleasure I used to get out of the jazz performers he had booked on the show. A snarky sometime Yalie and NYU film school graduate with Hollywood aspirations named Oliver Stone would be there in the evening on occasion, holding court and insulting the waiters (the journalist Maureen Orth once told me that he had pursued her one evening at Ports, and that she might have been interested if he hadn't been wearing a red patent leather belt). Tom Waits liked the place, and the Eagles often came in, separately. Tom Wolfe stopped by whenever he was in town. One night I walked into Ports and saw sitting, separately, at four adjacent tables, by coincidence, Claes Oldenburg, Michelangelo Antonioni, Milton Glaser, and Rip Torn. It was that kind of place.

There was music at Ports, both recorded and live. A wonderfully bizarre jukebox blared out everything from bebop and Italian pop to Argentinian tangos and Finnish polkas; one particularly strange disk, which Jock had probably found at a garage sale somewhere, was of a men's chorus singing a lusty shanty about "rowing to Madagascar"—in German. When he was in a particularly surly mood, Jock loved to play it over and over, no doubt alienating at least some of the clientele. The independent filmmaker Henry Jaglom, who came to Ports almost nightly, seemed particularly offended by it. I didn't like him, so I used to put it on whenever he walked in. I believe he threatened me with violence one evening in response.

There was also a battered old upright piano just inside the door. For some time the underrated jazz pianist Freddie Redd—who had written and performed the music for the famous Jack Gelber play *The Connection*—played it every evening for tips and dinner, sometimes letting me stand behind him and sing "Lush Life" or "Blame It on My Youth." One night the left-wing songwriter Earl Robinson, author of "Joe Hill" and the Paul Robeson classic "Ballad for Americans" (which had the curious distinction of having been used as a theme song by both the Republican and the Communist party national conventions in 1940), somehow found his way into Ports and sat down at the piano and started playing—at least until Jock, who had no idea who he was and probably wouldn't have cared if he did, told him to shut up and leave.

Jock was an imposing presence, big and bearded, with a deep voice and a manner that could go from avuncular to menacing in an instant. He could be impressively theatrical when he wanted to be, which wasn't surprising: He'd cowritten and starred in an experimental film called *Zero in the Universe* (with a score by the avant-garde jazz trumpeter Don Cherry), and won a distinguished performer Obie in the 1959–1960 season for his portrayal of the

General in the American debut of Genet's play *The Balcony*, off Broadway. He later had a memorable cameo as Alexander Woollcott in the Julie Andrews vehicle *Star!*, and continued to turn up in small but usually meaty roles in all kinds of movies made by friends and habitués of Ports.

Jock was widely traveled and well read; he spoke fluent, often impolite Spanish and used to bid me good night in Serbo-Croatian. At his best, he was great company, charming, erudite, obscure. But he had demons, which he tried constantly and unsuccessfully to drink away. Over the years that I knew him, his charm became more and more ephemeral, his erudition ever vaguer. He would end many evenings at Ports sitting almost comatose at a back booth, rising occasionally to lurch across the floor in search of another drink—sometimes, with no warning, erupting into an outraged roar. He was always acutely aware, through his haze, of any hint of condescension or disrespect to him, or of any stylistically inappropriate (in Ports terms) behavior, and he was quite capable of tossing even regular customers out with a contemptuous bellow. (If you mattered to him, you'd get a sheepish call the next day, not exactly apologizing but asking, "Was I all right last night?") A number of us, at various times, made sure that he got home safely and that the restaurant got locked up after Micaela had departed with a look of resigned despair.

I once asked the Hollywood photographer David Strick—a well-liked Ports regular whose father, the director Joseph Strick, had neglected to cast Livingston in his film version of *The Balcony*—whether he had any photographs of the restaurant in the old days. "I remember taking almost no pictures at Ports," Strick told me, "maybe because the first time I did, Jock went berserk and tried to choke me. . . . Maybe he sensed my genetic link to the plateauing of his acting career. Anyway, after that encounter, I tended to confine myself to repartee."

PORTS HAD ITS ORIGINS in another restaurant, the Studio Grill, three blocks west along Santa Monica Boulevard. The Grill was opened in 1970 by Jock and his friend Ardison Phillips, an artist. Neither had any previous restaurant experience, but they'd been neighbors in Hollywood and used to cook for large groups extemporaneously, and they thought they could make a go of a modest bistro serving the kind of food they liked to prepare and eat themselves. They made a sort of Odd Couple. Ardison was punctilious and chipper, and liked to wear ascots. Jock was more nonchalant and sometimes sulky, and used to greet guests at the restaurant garbed in a long white lab coat, which made him seem at once authoritative and vaguely sinister.

The Grill had an appealingly casual, bohemian feeling to it, and it quickly gained a local following. Lois Dwan summed the place up pretty well in the *Los Angeles Times* when she called it "Greenwich Village in Hollywood" and hailed its "fearless menu that ranges from caviar aspic to zarzuela." The Grill was only a few blocks from my apartment on Fountain Avenue, and I thought the place looked interesting from the outside, so stopped in one night shortly after it opened. I was intrigued by the large lab-coated man who seemed to be in charge, and I liked the eclectic menu—I think I probably had the roasted red peppers with anchovies followed by that zarzuela, a seafood stew that Jock had learned to make in Spain. I soon became a regular, and started getting to know Jock, often over two or three shared bottles of good Rioja after dinner.

It turned out that running a business together emphasized the considerable differences in temperament between Jock and Ardison, and they began disagreeing about everything from the menu to the air-conditioning. Eventually they cut a deal to manage the restaurant on alternate days, and regulars would often make it a point to show up only on Jock's night, or Ardison's, depending on where their loyalties resided. The arrangement didn't last for long. Micaela once told me, "On 'his' days, Ardison would not let me in while I waited for the butcher [next door] to prepare my meat for the empanadas I used to make at home for the restaurant. One fine evening, I put on an evening dress, walked into the Studio Grill, and threw a brandy cream pie at him, managing to hit his shoulder. After that I always walked on the other side of the street and never spoke to him again. Shortly after, we moved down the street to open Ports."

Ports got its name for purely practical reasons. The space had housed a bar called Sports Inn. When the Livingstons took over the lease, in late 1971, Jock climbed up on a ladder (which must have been a sight) and pulled down the "S" and the "Inn"—and Ports was christened. It opened for business in February of the following year.

Micaela was an artist—her painted furniture contained whole cosmos full of characters and signs—and a kind of offbeat beauty, simultaneously earthy and ethereal. She was quick with a devastating mot, and infinitely long-suffering with her difficult husband. She was also a wonderful cook, preparing savory make-ahead specialties (like those empanadas) and desserts that always seemed to take classic preparations just one step beyond the merely good. One of the best of these was a perfect flan improbably flavored with Pernod. The one that made diners swoon, though, was her brandy cream pie. This was Micaela's exaltation of cheesecake, an appropriately creamy, opulent confection so addictive that some of its fans would probably have licked it straight from Ardison's shoulder if they'd had the chance.

The day-to-day cooking at Ports fell to Jock, overseeing whichever quiet Mexican he had hired to work the line. Jock was a natural, instinctive cook, the kind of guy you'd want around to whip up something delicious on a beach in Morocco or in a borrowed finca on Ibiza, and he had a bagful of tricks. His borscht, enhanced with an island of sour cream, was just the liquid from big supermarket jars of shredded beets (the beets themselves didn't interest him, and he'd toss them in the garbage can); the pesto that stuffed the giant mushroom caps was based not on basil but on carrot tops, and he put enough garlic and parmigiano in the mix that I don't think anyone ever noticed. For years, every main course was accompanied by the same vegetable: crescents of thin-sliced banana squash seasoned with salt, pepper, and paprika and broiled on sheet pans until they cooked through and started to brown. Jock also made a pretty good "char-broiled" steak—seared directly on the high gas flame from his old cast-iron range.

Lois Dwan's take on Ports was that it was "just a place, battered as it was found, its age softened by books, pictures, and purpose." Micaela once added another dimension to that description: "It was a forum. We welcomed participation." The week after I got back from my trip to Bulgaria, Jock let me take over the place to prepare a Bulgarian meal, basically the one I'd had on my first evening outside Sofia: a salad of cucumbers, cherry tomatoes, and fresh white cheese; some slightly spongy bread I'd found at an Italian market with a Bulgarian spice mixture I'd brought back; and a pork stew with onions, mushrooms, garlic, and hot peppers.

I wasn't the only Rome-loving regular at the place, and on another occasion, three of us—one was a writer named Richard Adams (not the *Watership Down* one); I can't remember who the other one was—got into a heated discussion about how to best make pasta, and ended up deciding to have a pasta cook-off. Jock and Micaela loved the idea, so an evening was set aside and we each prepared one pasta for the customers. I made spaghetti with an intensely flavorful American-Italian red sauce, but Adams trumped me with pappardelle con la lepre, a Tuscan specialty of broad noodles in hare sauce—though he cheated and used domestic rabbit. Ports even got turned into a sort of theater-in-the-round one night, with a production of Julie Bovasso's restaurant-set play *Schubert's Last Serenade,* produced by my friend Bill Stern and featuring the artist Paul Ruscha (in the role created by a young Robert De Niro in New York) and the actor-stockbroker Michael Schwartz.

The queen of Ports—the woman who defined it most of all, after Micaela—was Ruscha's longtime girlfriend, Eve Babitz, a prolific, stylishly undisciplined writer and woman-about-town who penned such classics of the era as *Eve's Hollywood, Sex and Rage,* and *Slow Days, Fast Company,* and who knew simply everybody, except, of course, the people she didn't want to know. Eve had had an affair with Jim Morrison, been photographed nude playing chess with Marcel Duchamp at the Pasadena Museum of Art, and appeared in *Five 1965 Girlfriends,* a book by the artist Ed Ruscha (Paul's brother). Besides writing, she designed record album covers for Buffalo Springfield, the Byrds, and Linda Ronstadt. Igor Stravinksy, a friend of her violinist father, Sol Babitz, was her godfather. Earl McGrath, onetime president of Rolling Stones Records (and now an art gallery owner in New York City), once remarked that "in every young man's life there is an Eve Babitz; it is usually Eve Babitz."

For a time in 1973, Eve turned out a makeshift publication called *Port's* [sic] *Echo & Semi-Bimonthly Dispatch.* She and I both wrote nonsense for it, as did Jock (under the anagrammatic byline Lion V. Sting), and Eve's friend Steve Martin published some of his first short humor pieces in the *Echo,* including "Cruel Shoes" (which became the title story for his first officially published collection) and "Poodles—Great Eating!" which began, "These days it's hard to look at a poodle without thinking what a great meal he would make." Martin was already well known, of course, but not yet as much of a star as he is today. We knew where he was going, though. One night, Martin, who had just arrived at Ports with Bernadette Peters, told Eve, "You look like a million dollars"—to which she replied, "Your favorite amount."

SOME SNAPSHOTS OF EVENINGS at Ports in 1977 and '78, from my journal:

> *Party at Ports for* Slow Days, Fast Company [Babitz's second book]. *Eve was effusively polite and had made superb burritos, which her mother passed around with her customary unobtrusive grace. Her father, off wherever it is he goes when he's out in public, was there. Also her sister, Mirandi, in a very sexy, rather outdated Cacherel dress—a gamine working for the UFW. The screenwriter Kit Carson (whose canyon wedding to Karen Black I'd been to a few years earlier), leered rather cheaply and hailed me as a character in the book—which I am, but I won't tell you which one. Others I can recall: Ronee Blakley (still luminous), Paul Ruscha (of course), the screenwriter and television producer Michael Elias (a sharp dresser these days), Joan Tucker (likewise), Nick Meyer (of* The Seven-Per-Cent Solution *fame), Ed Begley, Kinky Friedman, Warren Hinckle . . . and quite a few more whose names I don't quite know. Jock stayed behind the bar most*

of the time, not looking well. Micaela came in late, nervously, and left on a long errand. . . .

Geraldine and I went to Ports for supper. . . . Jock and Micaela came in late and, after a time, sat with us. There was a new, tall, sun-tanned waiter. What did we think of him? Jock asked. "He's an 8 x 10 glossy," said Geraldine. "Yes, but only on one side," Micaela added. Geraldine later told Micaela, meant as a compliment and taken as one, that she looked like "This year at Marienbad." . . .

Tuesday dinner with [Anthony] *Haden-Guest at Ports. His date was a bizarre woman called D., one of those walking talking characters no writer would dare to invent—a blowsy floozy who looks 40 and claims to be 30, who apparently used to fool around with Tom Jones and Elvis, and who has every possible area of conversational authority firmly held (early poverty, famous friends, acting career, violence done to one, Scotland Yard, diamonds, cities of the world, etc., etc.). A moll, says H-G. Eve put in a brief appearance (when the name of* [the photographer] *Norman Seeff somehow came up, she commented, "Norman Seeff is where people go when they first leave home"), and then left abruptly. . . .*

M. and I went to hear Michael Ford read at a small bookshop-gallery in Westwood called George Sand. Waiting for the reading to begin, as M. and I browsed, I picked a copy of Italo Svevo's Further Confessions of Zeno *off the shelf. M. said, rather derisively, "Do you really know who that is, or were you just reaching for the most obscure-sounding volume you could find?"—the kind of ignorant remark she comes up with once in a while and which strikes out large portions of her great beauty and charm in my mind. The next night I stopped at Ports for a quick light supper, which grew considerably longer, though no heavier, when Nick Meyer came in alone and asked me to join him. He remarked the coincidence that we had spoken on the phone for the first time in some months that very afternoon and now had run into each other at Ports. . . . I replied that I had been reading recently about a theory of coincidence—of some sort of cosmic concentricity or maybe intersection of patterns which did in fact cause certain occurrences to coincide. I gave as an example a person mentioning an uncommon proper name to someone on, say, a Thursday, and having that same name turn up the next day under (seemingly) totally unrelated circumstances. "You mean like somebody mentioning Italo Svevo one day and then you see a book by him the next?" said Meyer.*

I SPENT NEW YEAR'S EVE, 1977, at Ports, having champagne and caviar with Jock and Micaela, then helping them work their way through a number of bottles of 1972 Grivot Clos de Vougeot before going home with a woman named Adele—Micaela insisted on calling her "Adèle H.," after the Truffaut film—who was a newcomer to Ports and seemed as much at loose ends as I was. Waking up at seven in the morning in a strange bed on the first morning of the new year, I got up, slipped out, and headed home, where I went promptly and very deeply to sleep. I was awakened, in the early afternoon, by my ringing phone. It was a man named Jay Levin, who'd gotten my number from an editor we both knew at *Esquire*. He'd just taken over as editor at the *Los Angeles Free Press*, he said, and he wondered if I'd consider coming in once a week as an "editorial consultant" for $100 a day. The previous day, I'd computed that I'd written approximately 125,000 words for pay during 1977, for which I had been paid exactly $17,016.79—just over thirteen cents a word on average. At that point, a steady income of an additional $400 a month sounded pretty good to me, so I said yes.

The *Free Press* had just been bought by Larry Flynt. This was what I think of as Flynt's surrealist period: He had recently undergone what turned out to be a brief conversion to evangelical Christianity, in the course of which—it had been widely and incredulously reported—he had gotten down on his knees and prayed with Ruth Carter Stapleton, Jimmy Carter's evangelist sister. Suddenly, the onetime Dayton sleaze-bar owner and *Hustler* publisher was hanging out with Dick Gregory and claiming to be on good terms with Tom Hayden and Coretta Scott King. His best friends in Los Angeles, he said, were the novelist Harold Robbins (*The Carpetbaggers*), the comedian Marty Allen, and the pop poet Rod McKuen. He announced plans to publish "a spiritual magazine" about "lifestyles for the Christian female" with Mrs. Stapleton. And he hired not only Levin, a scrappy New York–born journalist, but also, as publisher of *Hustler,* Paul Krassner, the counterculture hero and editor of *The Realist.*

Almost as soon as I reported for duty at the *Free Press*, Jay asked me if, for extra money, I'd like to interview Flynt and write a profile of him for the paper (this was Flynt's idea, he said, as a way to introduce himself to L.A.). I didn't see why not. He intrigued me. I figured that he had his income of $20 million or so a year, his private jet, and his skanky publishing empire, and was looking for something else: credibility, legitimacy, influence? He was, in any case, a great interview, saying things both intentionally and unintentionally funny in his reedy, Ozark-inflected voice. About Magoffin County, Kentucky, where he was born and raised, he cracked that "the major source of income was jury duty"; revealing his plans

to publish a pictorial version of the Bible, he told me, "We're looking for a Jesus in Los Angeles right now."

When my piece appeared, Flynt flipped out. The problem?
Apart from the fact that I had stupidly given him the wrong middle initial, he objected to a sentence reading "Part of the Flynt
legend—which he denies—is that . . . with Ruth Stapleton, he went
into a trance and spoke in tongues." He had *never* denied having
spoken in tongues! he raged. In fact, I realized when I looked back
at my notes, he hadn't denied it in so many words; but he *had* denied going into a trance, and every definition I could find of glos-
solalia said that it occurred in a state of ecstasy or trance. Flynt
dictated to Levin a "retraction" that was to appear on the front page
of the next issue of the *Free Press,* in which he called me "a liar"
but added "overall Andrews' article was magnificent and without a
doubt an accurate description of [my] personality and background."
(Flynt was later diagnosed with bipolar disorder.) He also invited
me to submit a "rebuttal" to his retraction for the following issue.
I penned an eloquent rejoinder, which began "Fuck you, Flynt."
Levin chose, perhaps wisely, not to print it. In early February, Flynt
sent me an informal apology, through Jay, for having called me a
liar. In late February, a few weeks before he was to be shot outside
a Georgia courthouse and partially paralyzed for life, he fired Jay,
and my short-lived gig at the *Free Press* was over.

IN THE EIGHTIES, living in Venice, a thirty- or forty-minute
drive west of Ports, I got there only once every month or so. Eve
and I did cohost a Halloween party at the restaurant, though, a few
nights before the holiday in 1982. It was supposed to be a costume
party, but the only people who played along were a suave Columbia
Records publicity guy, Charlie Coplen, who arrived in white tie

and tails, complete with top hat—he wore the getup as if it had been designed with him in mind—and Ed Begley Jr., who came in a rabbit suit. I remember the party most, though, because one of our guests was John Sweeney, a promising young chef at Ma Maison (I still have his recipe, from a class he taught at Ma Cuisine, for canon d'agneau à la crème d'ail), who came with his girlfriend, Dominique Dunne, the actress and daughter of the writer Dominick Dunne. They seemed as happily together as any other young couple. But two nights after the party, they got into a violent argument and Sweeney choked her hard on her front porch; she died on November 4.

JOCK SUCCUMBED IN 1980, while living apart from Micaela, finally run to ground by his demons (or the cure he sought for them). An actor named Philip Compton joined the restaurant as manager after Jock's demise, and helped Micaela manage it. The decor and clientele evolved, but the food remained more or less the same. "The menu's still going to be that same old melting pot," Compton announced when he came aboard. "Something will probably change somewhere along the line, but I don't know what or when." Micaela sold Ports to Compton in 1990, and it closed two years later. In its place there is now a restaurant called Jones Hollywood, which has red-and-white-checked tablecloths and a menu whitewashed onto big mirrors offering pizza, farro salad, and branzino on a cedar plank.

Chapter Eleven

MA MAISON,

West Hollywood (1973–1985)

&

SPAGO,

West Hollywood (1982–2000)

IN THE FALL OF 1973, A YOUNG MAN OF FRENCH and Russian origins named Patrick Terrail opened a casual-chic bistro on Melrose Avenue in West Hollywood. He called his restaurant Ma Maison, "my house," and indeed one of the buildings on the property had been a small house, painted pink, before he took it over (the other building was a warehouse for Angeles Carpets). He obviously didn't have the budget to transform the place too substantially. The interior was nondescript, in a sort of half-hearted rustic French style, with bentwood café chairs and French newspapers threaded through dowels. The patio, in front of the restaurant, was furnished with Ricard café umbrellas and the kind of sturdy white plastic chairs you'd find around the pool at a medium-range motel. The floor was a field of Astroturf. The patio was separated from the walkway leading to the front door by what looked like one long, transparent shower curtain, and there were plastic ducks in the corner that lit up at night. He had always planned to transform the patio into something more comfortable and attractive, Patrick used to say, but it became such a signature of the place that he ended up leaving it alone.

Patrick had emigrated to the United States in 1959, attended the Cornell School of Hotel Administration, and then worked at several prominent New York City restaurants, including the Four Seasons. A job with Adolph's Meat Tenderizer brought him to Los Angeles, but when the owner of the company began negotiations to sell Adolph's to Unilever in 1973, Patrick realized that he'd soon be out of a job and began trying to raise money—the goal was thirty-five thousand dollars—to open a restaurant of his own.

Patrick was descended from an illustrious French restaurant family: His great-grandfather Claudius Burdel ran the famous Café Anglais in Paris from 1856 to 1913. His grandfather André Terrail was chef to Kaiser Wilhelm II and took over another legendary Parisian restaurant, La Tour d'Argent, in 1910. Patrick's uncle Claude Terrail was running that institution when Patrick opened Ma Maison. Lineage notwithstanding, Ma Maison had no pretensions to haute cuisine. The specialty was brochettes of marinated chicken and beef—trendy Left Bank fare in those days—and there were things like salade niçoise, quiche lorraine, and the Greek egg-and-lemon soup called avgolemono (Patrick had lived in Greece with his mother and stepfather for some years, and spoke Greek). Claude Terrail sent some of his celebrity clientele Patrick's way, but Ma Maison didn't exactly set the L.A. restaurant scene on fire. The food frankly wasn't very good, and there were other French restaurants in town that offered far more agreeable surroundings, among them the nearby Le St. Germain and my old record business haunt, Au Petit Café.

Patrick's fortunes changed in 1975, when he had the perspicacity—or the blind good luck—to hire a young French-trained Austrian chef with the unlikely name of Wolfgang Puck. Puck was born in a small town in southern Austria, near the Slovenian border. His mother cooked at a local hotel, and his father—who left the family before he was born—was the town butcher. (Wolf takes his name from his stepfather, Josef Puck, a professional prizefighter.) There wasn't a lot to do where he grew up, Wolf once told me, so he hung around the hotel kitchen and watched his mother and the other cooks at work. By the time he was fourteen, he'd decided that he wanted to be a chef. He went to school to study restaurant and hotel management and then, at seventeen, headed for France. He eventually landed at the celebrated L'Oustau de Baumanière in the Provençal hamlet of Les Baux, which then had three Michelin stars. After three years at Les Baux, wanting to broaden his experience, Wolf moved on to Maxim's in Paris—in those days also still a Michelin three-star restaurant, and a golden name on any young chef's résumé. It was at this venerable institution, Wolf has said, that he first recognized the importance of attracting famous people to a restaurant: "It brings excitement into the place, both the dining room and the kitchen, and that's good for everybody."

While he was at Maxim's, Wolf decided that he'd like to try his luck in America. He couldn't find a job he liked in New York City, his first choice, but the respected Lyonnais chef Pierre Orsi had opened a fancy restaurant called La Tour in Indianapolis, and the young Austrian was offered a post there. Indianapolis surprised Wolf: Because it was the home of the Indianapolis 500, he had expected a certain level of sophistication; he thought it might be an American Monte Carlo. He ended up cooking almost nothing but well-done steaks, and couldn't wait to get out of the place. His biggest accomplishment in his year in Indiana, he once told me, was learning English.

The company that ran La Tour also had properties in California, and eventually Wolf moved to Los Angeles as night chef at one of them, Restaurant François, a French-Continental place of no particular distinction in a rather somber shopping mall at ARCO Plaza in downtown L.A. According to Patrick, he hired Wolf and a coworker and friend of his, Guy LeRoy, away from the place at the recommendation of a friend who worked for Maxim's back in Paris. According to Wolf, he ran into a young American cook whom he'd fired in Indianapolis—a kid, he has said, "who had like two left hands and two left feet and no taste"—and learned that he was cooking at a new little place called Ma Maison. The restaurant, said the young man, was looking for a lunch chef. However it happened, Wolf took the job several days a week, continuing on at François in the evenings, until Patrick's head chef quit and he offered Wolf the job full-time. When he went to deposit his first paycheck, Wolf remembers, it bounced, but Patrick offered him a ten percent stake in the business, so he stayed on.

Settling into Ma Maison, Wolf reproduced the old menu briefly, but his style quickly evolved, and before long he was serving things like cream of sorrel soup, lobster terrine, steamed oysters with baby vegetables, grilled chicken with sherry vinegar, and grilled squab with thyme and honey—deft interpretations of what was then the hottest thing in France, nouvelle cuisine, which may sound staid and archaic today but was pretty much cutting-edge at the time. He prepared this fare under difficult conditions: The kitchen was tiny, with only one oven, and instead of a walk-in cooler for fish, meat, and produce, Wolf had to rely on half a dozen home refrigerators lined up outside the kitchen door.

I met Wolf the year he started at Ma Maison, not at the restaurant but in Manhattan, at a big walk-around tasting event promoting the heroes of nouvelle cuisine—Paul Bocuse, Roger Vergé, the Troisgros brothers, and other such luminaries of the movement, all of whom were present, serving their specialties. Wolf was there as a guest, like me, not as a participant. Nobody knew who he was—except possibly Yanou Collart, the know-everybody Parisian restaurant PR woman who had wrangled all those big-name chefs, and who introduced me to Wolf. I liked him immediately. He seemed simultaneously self-confident and modest, and communicated a genuine enthusiasm for the possibilities for good cooking in America in an era when this was by no means a given.

I hadn't been to Ma Maison yet. It hadn't been very well reviewed. The prissy society columnist and restaurant reviewer George Christy, for instance, wrote after a meal there that "the pâté maison was a joke" and that the brochettes were "tough, stringy, not especially flavorful." Then there'd been a story in the *Los Angeles Times*, reporting that when Patrick took the coats of arriving female guests, he always looked at the labels before deciding where to seat the diners. Another version of the story was that he'd said that because even the well-to-do wore jeans these days, the only way he could tell if they were wealthy was by stealing a look at their watches or handbags. (Patrick always denied both versions, and maintained that if he had in fact said anything of the kind, he'd been kidding.) I thought that sounded really stupid, in any case, and I'd decided that Ma Maison wasn't my kind of place. Wolf said, "No, really, you should come. I'll cook for you."

By 1976 Ma Maison, which had survived early criticisms, had begun to thrive. Patrick—who wore sturdy Swedish clogs with a dark double-breasted suit, even on hot summer afternoons, ornamented with a Charvet tie, a silk pocket handkerchief, and a red carnation boutonnière—greeted the rich and powerful of Los

Angeles with a rapidly evolving sense of calculated snobbery that seemed to work like catnip on these fat cats. Wolf, meanwhile, continued to turn out some of the best food in town. Now the celebrities started arriving for real. One of Wolf's—and Patrick's—favorite famous customers was Orson Welles, who came almost every day and sat alone, or with his pretty Croatian girlfriend, Oja Kodar, at a table just inside the dining room, where you couldn't see him unless you were returning from the restrooms. Wolf charmed Welles and the rest of the illustrious crowd with his sense of humor, his guileless nature, and, of course, his excellent cuisine. Other regulars at the place included Cary Grant, Frank Sinatra, Jack Lemmon, Elizabeth Taylor, Rod Stewart, Ursula Andress, Goldie Hawn, Michael Caine, Fred Astaire, Gene Kelly, Lauren Hutton, Dustin Hoffman, Jacqueline Bisset, Sylvester Stallone, David Hockney (who designed a menu cover for the place); directors including Billy Wilder (Puck's fellow Austrian), Tony Richardson, and Steven Spielberg; other Hollywood heavyweights like the attorney Greg Bautzer, the agent Irving "Swifty" Lazar, and the financier Kirk Kerkorian; and even, on occasion, a couple of ex-presidents named Ford and Nixon. The not typically starstruck Michiko Kakutani, in *The New York Times,* called it "probably the most celebrated celebrity hangout since Romanoff's in the days of the Rat Pack."

Friday lunch became the essential see-and-be-seen occasion at Ma Maison. Alicia Buttons, wife of the comedian Red Buttons, once claimed that her Fridays at the restaurant were so sacred that she gave her young son a handwritten card reading, "Mommy . . . Fridays . . . 655-1991." There were people around L.A. who probably would have mugged the kid if they'd known about that note. When *People* published a short piece about Ma Maison and its talented young chef in 1975, the phone started ringing nonstop.

To avoid being completely swamped, Patrick decided to unlist the number—which, of course, only added to the cachet of the place. Another cachet booster was the "parking lot" facing onto Melrose Avenue: It had room for only five or six cars, and these were always the most extravagant trophy vehicles—Rolls-Royces and Bentleys, Ferraris, vintage Jaguars, and the like. Patrick always claimed that these expensive cars were parked there strictly for security reasons, so his valets could keep an eye on them. The fact that everyone who drove past on Melrose also noticed them was presumably just a happy accident.

I WAS ABLE TO BECOME A REGULAR at Ma Maison myself after I got a full-time job again, which meant both an expense account and a steady if modest income. One morning in the spring of 1978, I got a call from a woman named Leslie Ward, who had recently been named Southern California editor of *New West* magazine, asking if I'd consider writing restaurant reviews for the publication. *New West* had been launched the previous year by Clay Felker as a Californian analogue to his groundbreaking city magazine *New York,* though by this time, Rupert Murdoch had taken over both publications. I told Leslie that I wasn't interested—I already had a good relationship with the magazine's considerably older, more established rival, *Los Angeles*—but I was feeling the pressures of the freelance life, so I added that I might consider some sort of editorial position, especially one involving oversight of the magazine's food and wine coverage. She promised to discuss the idea with the editor, a recently transplanted San Franciscan named Jon Carroll.

Jon apparently liked the notion, and there followed a courtship of several months, a succession of phone calls, lunches, drinks. One afternoon, finally, I got a call from Jon, offering me a job as *New West*'s food and wine editor. I ran into trouble right away. There were two editions of the magazine, one in each half of the state. The San Francisco edition had two restaurant critics, trading slots in alternate issues of the biweekly publication: Sandye Rosenzweig, a health writer who had once been married to Jon, and Ruth Reichl, a transplanted New Yorker who lived in a communal house in Berkeley with her artist-husband and several friends. One of the first things I did when I arrived at *New West* was to ask the Northern California editor, a brisk professional named Rosalie, if the Bay Area reviews could come straight to me for editing in the future without going through the San Francisco office first, which didn't seem like an unreasonable request for the newly hired food and wine editor to make. "No," she said. End of discussion. Well then, I continued, I thought I might make a trip up to San Francisco in the next week or so to meet the two Northern California critics. "I think that would be premature," she sniffed.

Well, okay. I had business to attend to in L.A. In addition to a regular restaurant review, *New York* had had great success with a column called "The Underground Gourmet," covering budget-priced, usually "ethnic," restaurants. The idea was borrowed by *New West,* and taken on in L.A. by Jivan Tabibian, a dapper, diminutive political scientist and urban planner who loved good cigars and good wine and always seemed to be surrounded by a gaggle of pretty young women. He was also a friend of Milton Glaser, the designer who had helped Clay Felker create *New York,* and Jivan— who had coined the name *New West*—apparently considered the column to be a kind of sinecure. Jon didn't. He thought Jivan's columns were too fussy and old-style, and one of my first jobs, he told me, was to fire him. I did this over a civilized lunch at Club Elysée on Doheny, where a precocious young chef named Ken Frank was in the kitchen, and we remained friends. (Jivan subsequently became a restaurateur himself, as the designer Adam Tihany's partner in the Santa Monica branch of Remi. Later, after the collapse of the Soviet Union, he served as a high-level diplomat for the Republic of Armenia for more than a decade, before dying in his native country in 2009.)

In place of "The Underground Gourmet," I decided to mirror the Northern California edition and hire two critics to alternate reviews. One was my old wine mentor, Roy Brady, who also knew the local restaurant scene well; the other was a longtime *Rolling Stone* writer and editor named Charles Perry, who had roomed with the legendary black-market LSD manufacturer Owsley Stanley in Berkeley but was also a student of Middle Eastern languages and culture, an expert on the food of the Arab world, and a witty writer with a particular affection for obscure cuisines. At the same time, I hired Phil Reich, an eccentric wine merchant recently relocated to L.A. from Colorado, as wine columnist. When Reich begged off the task after a few months because he had become too busy creating and managing the wine list for a new restaurant called Michael's, I brought in the wine-loving screenwriter Jeffrey Alan Fiskin (*Cutter's Way, The Pursuit of D. B. Cooper*), whose columns compared certain aspects of various wines to the porn star John Holmes or the alternative singer-songwriter Tonio K. (Fiskin later endeared himself to me permanently by giving a New Year's Eve dinner party, based largely on recipes from a Troisgros brothers cookbook, for which he designed a menu patterned after the cover of a popular Devo album. It was headlined "Are we not men? We are Troisgros.")

I was finally given permission to visit the San Francisco office and introduce myself to our restaurant critics there. I met Ruth first, and we went out to lunch, walking a few blocks to a French restaurant of the kind by then pretty well vanished from L.A., called Lafayette. "The meal was straightforward and good," I recorded in my notebook a few days later, "and Ruth was a delight—tall and rangy, extremely pleasant, and extremely knowledgeable, apparently, about *les choses de vie*." That night, I had a dinner date with my wine business friend Rich Leland and his wife at Fournou's Ovens, the dining room at the Stanford Court hotel. Since Ruth had mentioned that she was going to be reviewing the place for the magazine, I invited her to join us. The food was up and down (I recall that I particularly liked a cream of artichoke soup), but the wines were excellent and abundant: '66 Bollinger R.D., '74 Albert Pic Valmur Chablis, '69 Coron Les Cent Vignes Beaune, '71 Henri de Villamont Chambolle-Musigny, and '71 Château Lynch-Bages. Ruth seemed a little stunned by the number of bottles we consumed, and certainly—since she had gamely offered to pick up the tab, on her expense account—by their prices. "Get used to it," I said.

The next day, I drove across the Bay Bridge to Berkeley to meet our other critic, Sandye, for lunch at the Café at Chez Panisse. She turned out to be very nice—she'd brought me a single red rose as an offering—and we had a fine meal of fresh tuna salad, cheese, blueberry ice cream, a bottle and a half of Domaine Tempier Bandol rouge, which I had never before seen in America, plus two half-bottles of Bourgueil. I left thinking that between Ruth and Sandye, both with very different sensibilities but both obviously pretty smart and possessed of real food sense, our Northern California restaurant coverage was probably in very good hands.

That night, I took Ruth and my short-lived wine critic Phil Reich, who was in San Francisco on other business, to Trader Vic's, the high-society Bay Area counterpart to my old favorite hangout in Beverly Hills. Ruth had been supervising a photo shoot all day for a story of hers and was tired and quiet. She liked Phil, though, and they became fast friends. In the course of the evening, I asked Ruth if she'd spent much time in Los Angeles, and she said no—with, I thought, the usual San Francisco (or, worse, Berkeley) tone that seemed to ask, "Why on earth would I go *there*?" Well, I replied, you should come down and see what's going on in our restaurants, just to give you some sense of comparison. She was skeptical but agreed to fly down the following week.

I thought of the San Francisco office as something of a rebel satrapy. It lived by its own rules, protected from unwanted incursions from the south (or the East Coast) by its tough, supremely self-assured ruler, Rosalie. To put it somewhat less dramatically, while the office wasn't willfully malevolent, and while its population included several very talented writers and editors, I thought it was rather provincial—not in an oblivious way but in that smug, self-referential manner that certain denizens of the Bay Area so skillfully affect.

I got into fights with the San Franciscans over the silliest things. Once I happened to notice, in galleys, that one of the photographs in a piece on wild mushrooms was misidentified—one of the toxic *Amanitas* was labeled as being edible—and pointed that out. The caption was corrected, but I was told that I wasn't supposed to be looking at galleys of stories I hadn't edited. Another time, in a short piece about jazz, somebody San Franciscan made a reference to "the late Roland Kirk." I pointed out that in the latter years of his life, in response to a dream he'd had, this quirky, talented saxophonist had renamed himself Rahsaan Roland Kirk, and suggested that it would be both respectful and accurate to call him that in print. I was told that this was a minor error and didn't warrant correction. I said, "It's my opinion that a magazine that lets its contributors use bylines like Susan Subtle [née Dittenfass] and

Futzie Nutzle [a.k.a. Bruce Kleinsmith] ought to damn well have the courtesy to call Rahsaan Roland Kirk by his proper name."

I think Jon was simply scared of Rosalie. One day there was a flap about the title Ruth had given to one of her restaurant reviews: She'd called it "Diary of a Fat Housewife"—prompting one editor to crack, "Ruth, you're not a fat housewife, you're a slender communard." Rosalie refused to let the title be used, on the grounds that it was "sexist." Everyone else liked the headline, but when Jon attempted to champion it to Rosalie on the phone, she told him that she was prepared "to go to the mattresses" to keep it out of the magazine. Jon, by his own admission, "crumbled like a little sugar cookie."

A few weeks after my first visit to the Northern California office, Ruth came to L.A., and we went to dinner at L'Orangerie, which was almost certainly the most beautiful restaurant in town, and one of the best. After a couple of bites of her first course—a wondrous fresh vegetable assortment, in which each vegetable was different and differently perfect—she looked around the elegant, flower-bedecked, candlelit room and exclaimed in delight, "There's *nothing* like this in San Francisco!" We went on to share a dish of sea bass with green peppercorns, then had calf's liver with sherry vinegar (me) and veal medallions with "three mustards" (Ruth), followed by the restaurant's signature apple tart à la minute. With this we managed a bottle and a half of Sancerre, a bottle of '70 Grand Barrail Lamarzelle Figeac, and a bottle of '76 Benôit-Trichard Moulin-à-Vent. The owner of the restaurant, Gérard Ferry, insisted on picking up the check, on the grounds that I was now editing food pieces and not writing about restaurants— and, somewhat to Ruth's surprise, I let him.

Ruth agreed to go to Ports with me afterward, and we drank more wine (when I snuck a bottle of mineral water in between sips of Châteauneuf-du-Pape, she accused me of "cheating"). After an hour or so, I walked Ruth to her car, and as we kissed good night, I told her that I would feel recalcitrant if I didn't at least *ask* if she would like to come back to my apartment. She was hesitant, she said, because if she did, she'd want to sleep with me, and she *didn't* want to sleep with me, though she *did* want to. . . . I talked her into at least stopping by briefly, and she finally consented. We walked to my place, where I made coffee and offered her some eglantine—eau-de-vie made from wild rose hips ("I have an eau-de-vie you've never tasted," I said; "I'll just *bet* you have," she replied).

Being a red-blooded boy, I kept trying to get her into bed. She wasn't the unfaithful type, she said, though she quickly added that that wasn't what was stopping her. What was? The friends she was staying with would be worried, and it was too late to call them. Anyway, I was her boss, and it would be a bad idea to start something. Her life was complicated enough already, et cetera, et cetera. Finally, I gave up and walked her back to her car at Ports.

For some months, since before I'd been hired at *New West,* I'd been planning a long autumn trip to New York and Europe to see friends, revisit old haunts, and research a freelance piece or two. "When will you be in Paris?" Ruth asked when she was safely back in Berkeley. When I gave her my dates, she announced that, coincidentally, she might be there at the same time.

In the last days of September, before my trip, Ruth contrived some flimsy pretext to come to Los Angeles for a few days. We met for a late lunch at Scandia, and then I went home to shower and change and went off to Ma Cuisine, the newly opened cooking school attached to Ma Maison, to give a wine class. Ruth met me at the restaurant for dinner afterward. In her book *Comfort Me with Apples,* she remembers the evening dramatically and romantically. When Patrick led her into the restaurant, she writes, she found me sitting with Orson Welles (in fact, though I saw Welles often at the restaurant, we never met). She remembers the menu as starting with caviar and champagne, and then letting "a man in a tall white toque . . . [with] a round face and a snub nose he kept rubbing with his finger, like a little boy"—Wolf—prepare us a meal of baked oysters wrapped in lettuce and bathed in beurre blanc, terrine de foie gras, duck "just like Tour d'Argent!," and, after that, some Roquefort and Brie, and finally a textbook dacquoise.

I don't remember the food myself, but I remember that we talked intensely about all kinds of things—food and restaurants, writing, the nature of perception, the challenge of reconciling sensual pleasure with political belief. . . . At one point she said that she was surprised at how easily she lied (to her husband about her reasons for this trip to L.A., for instance), but thought that her proficiency at it must have to do with the fact that she greatly valued her privacy. She was swept away, she suggests in her book, by the food, the special treatment, and, well, me. "It all felt unreal, as if our dialogue had been lifted from one of those 1930s movies where mink coats go flying out of windows and there are only happy endings."

After dinner, we went to Ports, had a few glasses of wine, talked a bit—weakly—about moral compunction, and then went back to my place. She'd known she was going to sleep with me, she told me, the first time we had lunch in San Francisco. "I don't know which would be worse," she said before we went to bed. "For us to end up hating each other or for us to end up liking each other too much."

A few weeks later, I went to Paris. Ruth arrived a few days later—she'd been offered the use of a friend's empty apartment on the rue Berthollet—and we met around six in the evening for apéritifs at Le Départ on the place Saint-Michel. From there, we went for a long walk, across the pont du Carrousel, up past the Louvre, back across the pont Neuf to the Île de la Cité, quickly into Notre-Dame, across to the Île Saint-Louis for a glass of Sancerre or two at the Brasserie de l'Île, then to a restaurant behind the church of Saint-Julien-le-Pauvre called the Auberge des Deux Signes, which had medieval beamed ceilings, an abundance of candles in wrought-iron holders, Lully and Couperin on the stereo, pretty good food (including "gothique" specialties like pounti, a savory but slightly sweet Swiss chard tart, and talmouses, which were pillow-shaped cheese beignets), and an endless supply of Cahors.

Ruth moved into my room at the Hôtel Esmeralda, and we spent the next ten days together, wandering around Paris, eating lunches and dinners both serious and casual. If we didn't have specific plans, I'd just ask, at some point, "Are you hungry?," to which she'd inevitably reply "I could eat," and we'd stop into whatever likely looking place we saw. Every morning, we'd have tartines and café crème at the Village Ronsard on the place Maubert—on days when the market was there—or the Le Départ or Le Saint-Séverin on the place Saint-Michel.

I introduced Ruth to Claude over lunch at Aux Amis du Beaujolais; he was impressed with her, he told me, when she got up from the table to negotiate the narrow, winding staircase down to the basement restrooms. A few nights after that, we went to dinner at his house—coquilles St.-Jacques and boeuf à la mode, cooked superbly by Pepita. Another evening, we ate choucroute at the Brasserie de l'Île with my friends Yves and Ursula. We had oysters and roast partridge at Artoise and côte de boeuf at Ma Bourgogne on the boulevard Haussmann. We drank at Le Petit Bar and the Closerie des Lilas. One night we ate sardines and lamb chops both grilled in a little fireplace in the dining room at a tiny spot called Robert. Another night, courtesy of Patrick Terrail, we dined at the

Tour d'Argent, at the perfect window table, eating impeccable foie gras (me) and scrambled eggs with truffles (Ruth), and then duck—"just like Tour d'Argent!" To finish, there were raspberries and assorted sorbets. We drank a good 1974 Meursault-Charmes and a 1945 Château Petit-Villages, then some superb reserve cognac.

We spent most of one day at SIAL, the major French food show. At one stand, belonging to a big commercial charcuterie company, a comedian on a closed-circuit TV monitor was importuning passersby, and he fastened on Ruth, engaged her in conversation, and talked her into playing a quick game of Pong with him. She brought this all off with aplomb, and in French so good that I doubt anyone realized that she was American. Another day we took the train to Reims, in the middle of champagne country, to have lunch at Boyer, then still a two-star in its original farmhouse location, ordering "la fameuse truffe en croûte"—a whole black truffle as big as a golf ball, coated in foie gras, then baked in a flaky pastry covering and moistened with an intense brown sauce in which there were additional truffle pieces, just to make sure you got enough—followed by a perfect pièce de boeuf with marrow, cheeses, and tastes of three desserts, among them a pear sorbet, pure concentrated fruit, that Ruth proclaimed the best sorbet of her life.

On our last night in Paris, we watched the sunset from a café near the Jardin du Luxembourg, stopped into Notre-Dame to hear a few minutes of an organ concert, met Claude and Pepita at a Left Bank bistro for dinner, had digestifs at Flore, and then—I'd already checked out of my hotel—spent the night at Ruth's friend's apartment. The next morning, we had our last tartines and cafés crèmes, at a café near the apartment, then I took her by Métro to the Gare du Nord and put her on the train back to London, whence she was flying home. I walked off down the platform, and when

I turned back to wave good-bye as Ruth's carriage pulled past, I found to my surprise that there were tears lightly clouding my eyes.

Back in California, for the next few months, we'd take turns visiting each other, Ruth sometimes flying down to L.A. for the day, I contriving trips to the wine country, where she'd meet me. One day she gave me a signed copy of a little booklet called *History of the World in Epitome* by Bertrand Russell, which consists, in its entirety, of these words: "Since Adam and Eve ate the apple, man has never refrained from any folly of which he was capable."

Ruth blossomed as a writer. From the beginning, her reviews had been literate and highly readable, framed more as semifictional vignettes than rote critiques, but having to write a regular column for *New West*, with occasional longer pieces on the side, seemed to liberate her and give her new confidence. Her structural devices evolved into a real style, accessible, even a little chatty, but full of authority. In 1979 we started hearing rumors about a young American chef with French training who was going to open a new kind of restaurant in Santa Monica—French in inspiration but Californian in decor and spirit, with a menu glorifying the state's best ingredients. His name was Michael McCarty, and he agreed to let Ruth hang out with him and his initial crop of chefs—Jonathan Waxman, Mark Peel, and Ken Frank, all of whom were to become culinary stars—as they worked to launch what was to become the celebrated Michael's, not just planning menus and developing sources for raw materials but literally painting walls and laying tiles themselves. I'm not sure if the lengthy, impressively detailed article that she produced for the magazine was the first-ever "birth of a restaurant" piece, but it remains one of the best.

Besides just writing about food, Ruth wanted to keep learning about it. On one of my trips north, we visited the remarkable wine and food expert Darrell Corti at his store in Sacramento, then went back to his house for a memorable dinner. He served us Russian sevruga along with some caviar he'd made himself from California sturgeon, alongside a vodka produced by Gilbey's for the English market in honor of Smirnoff's hundredth anniversary; excellent smoked salmon from Washington; beef consommé with little cubes of foie gras floating in it, matched nicely with a 1950 Sercial Madeira; a Tuscan dish of duck roasted with bitter oranges ("the original duck à l'orange," he explained) with three excellent Chiantis; and then plump asparagus spears drizzled with thick, dark umber drops from a little vial of aceto balsamico artisanale, artisanal balsamic vinegar. As difficult as this may be to believe in the twenty-first century, neither Ruth nor I had ever heard of balsamic vinegar, and I feel fairly safe in saying that if we hadn't, not very many other people in America had either. It was a revelation, something truly special, dense and complex and perfectly balanced between sweet and acidic. I don't know what we would have thought if somebody had told us that, twenty years later, there'd be cruets of "balsamic" on almost every restaurant table in America.

The next time I flew up north, Ruth picked me up at the airport in her old white, humpbacked Volvo and we went to lunch at an Italian restaurant we liked, Modesto Lanzone in Ghirardelli Square. As we ate, Ruth proposed that we consider renting a small apartment in San Francisco, sharing the cost, so that we'd have a place to go when I came to visit. ("I don't want to spend the rest of my life across a restaurant table from you," she said.) I suggested that we could take a place in the Napa Valley, where I could retire occasionally to write, and where I could even *tell* people I had taken a place. Over coffee, we reminisced about Paris, and she told me how alone she'd felt as her train pulled out of the Gare du Nord. As we walked back toward the car, we stopped behind a wall by the bay and necked, then later sat in the car in the parking lot and necked more. She kept asking where our relationship would lead. "We'll end up just friends," she said. "You'll find a girl and not sleep with me anymore. . . ." That, of course, is exactly what happened.

THE NEW WEST OFFICE was full of interesting and attractive women, among them the tall, lively, exquisitely sarcastic Maureen Orth, who became my drinking buddy; the serious, somewhat ethereal Meredith White, who seemed soft and sincere; and Leslie Ward, my original contact at the magazine, of whom I noted in my journal, after my first day at the magazine: "She has beautiful golden-green eyes and . . . will be a useful ally." Leslie and I did indeed become allies, and after-work confidants; we'd have lunch at El Padrino in the Beverly Wilshire Hotel or Carroll O'Connor's place the Ginger Man, drinks at the Mandarin or Mr. Chow, sometimes followed by dinner, sometimes not. We bitched to each other, made catty remarks about various personalities at the office, talked office politics. We gossiped. We had fun.

One day, the magazine's Southern California senior staff flew to the Bay Area for an all-day editorial meeting at Rosalie's house. I'd planned to stay overnight in San Francisco and drive up to the Napa Valley to see some friends the next day, and at some point asked Leslie and a couple of the other editors if they'd like to come with me. Leslie said yes, but the others demurred. Checking out of our hotels the morning after the meeting, we headed for St. Helena, along the way rehashing the meeting at Rosalie's house, excoriating the San Franciscans, making fun of Jon. When we got to our destination, we visited Joseph Phelps Vineyards and tasted some wines there, then went for burgers and shakes at the Yountville Diner. We ended the afternoon at Stags' Leap Winery, run by my friend Carl Doumani, sitting on the veranda of the property's big old stone house drinking old champagne and '61 Cos d'Estournel in the clean air and perfect light. Then we drove back down to San Francisco and caught a 9:30 P.M. flight for L.A. A few days later, having drinks with Leslie, I allowed as how the fact that the two of us had gone off to the Napa Valley together must have made a few people wonder. "I wondered myself," she said, which I liked. I was finding myself increasingly attracted to her, though she seemed scarcely any more available than Ruth (whom I was still seeing): She wasn't married, but she was living with a man.

One evening, Leslie and I both worked fairly late, then repaired to El Padrino for a drink, which turned out to be two bottles of red wine. At some point, it came out that I'd never been to Las Vegas. "Let's go right now!" she said, and that sounded like a good idea to me. I went to a pay phone (this was before cell phones) and reserved two seats on a flight that night and a rental car on the other end; we'd figure out accommodations when we got there, we agreed, or maybe just stay up and gamble till it was time to fly back. Leslie called her boyfriend and simply told him that she was going to Las Vegas with a coworker.

We drove to Ports to cash a check (this was also before ATMs) and stayed a little too long, and when we finally got to the airport we had missed our flight. There were no more seats on any of the remaining flights to Las Vegas, so after briefly considering a red-eye to New Orleans, we bought tickets to San Francisco. At the last minute, sitting at the gate, we decided that we didn't really want to go there after all, so I drove Leslie back to her car near the office. Sitting in my old Mercedes, we kissed and kissed, and she made no protest when I started the car again and took her back to my place, where she stayed.

About six months later, Leslie and I got married at Stags' Leap—secretly, to avoid complications at the office (the politics there were complex; I once bought a copy of *The Prince* and shelved it with the reference books, just to make a point)—with a local Episcopalian priest officiating and just a handful of friends in attendance. Back in L.A., we lived separately for a couple of months, sneaking out together whenever we could, and then found a rental house in Venice—in a part of the community, I used to tell people, where one saw more lawn mowers than Rollerblades. One afternoon, after we had set up housekeeping, we announced what we had done to the entire *New West* staff, which had assembled for an all-hands-on-deck editorial meeting. Some office wag cracked that the building shook from all the jaws hitting the floor.

We renewed our vows publicly in Paris in September, in a Malachite Orthodox ceremony at the church of Saint-Julien-le-Pauvre, across the street from the Hôtel Esmeralda. Claude, of course, was my best man. We'd brought a bottle of Stags' Leap petite sirah as a gift for the Lebanese-born monsignor who officiated—it seemed like a nice way to connect the two ceremonies—and when he gave me the ritual sip of altar wine during the ceremony, he asked, sotto voce, "Vaut-il mieux que le vin de Californie?"—"Is it better than the wine from California?" After the ceremony, we walked around the corner to the Auberge des Deux Signes for a banquet of foie gras, pike soufflé, roasted lamb, Cantal, and marzipan-frosted wedding cake. About fifty of our friends, from both Europe and the States, came to the wedding and the dinner afterward. At least three sets of the single guests, meeting for the first time, ended up spending the night together, which I took to be a sign of a successful wedding.

We honeymooned in Avignon, Saint-Paul-de-Vence, Nice, and Venice. On my first day back in the office, Jon took me out to a Swedish café a few blocks from the office and fired me. "You're good at the details," he said, "but not at the big picture" (or was it vice versa?). He told Leslie that I had been let go because he just didn't think I was any good at my job. "Around the office," Leslie told me years later, "people knew that wasn't true, and many subscribed to the 'too many roosters in the henhouse' theory." I just figured San Francisco had finally won.

I'D GOTTEN INTO THE HABIT of having a weekly lunch at Ma Maison with two writer friends of mine, the theater critic and mystery novelist Dick Lochte and the writer-director Nick Meyer. Because Friday was celebrity madness day at the restaurant, we agreed to meet on Thursdays—though there were plenty of famous faces on the patio on that day, too. Wolf always came out to see us, and sometimes recommended new dishes he was trying out. Patrick had decided that he liked me, and always greeted me effusively when I arrived and made sure that we had a good table. I remember remarking to Dick and Nick that it was too bad I wasn't in the film business myself, because the importance Patrick seemed to accord me at the entrance to the patio could probably double my asking price one day.

The food at Ma Maison remained superb. When my friend Margaret Stern, who was doing wine business public relations, brought the Austrian winemaker Lenz Moser to town to promote a new bottling of his, we had dinner at Ma Maison, and I asked Wolf to make us whatever he wanted. He dazzled his fellow Austrian (and us) with perfect big cold asparagus in lemon sauce, striped bass stuffed with fish mousse en croûte, and thin slices of duck breast over buttery apples, covered with green peppercorn sauce, followed by frisée salad made with crispy duck skin instead of the usual lardons. Another night, while I was still at *New West*, I came in late with Jon and discovered that it was Patrick's birthday, and that he was celebrating with a dozen or so friends at a table inside. Wolf served Jon and me endive salad, salmis de pigeon, and tarte au citron, a perfect supper, and when we had finished, ushered us into the party, saying, "Come see the cake we made for Patrick." It was decorated with a large white, sugar-frosted phallus, standing upright in the middle. Patrick invited us to sit down. Everyone at the table was asked to say a few words about him, and most speeches were a combination of insult and praise. When it was my turn, I said, "This is the best night I've ever had at Ma Maison: I had a good dinner with my friend and didn't have to look at Patrick once—and now that I do have to see him, he's pouring free champagne."

I always thought that part of the key to Ma Maison's success, beyond Wolf's cooking, was the fact that it never took itself too seriously. Patrick once overheard a couple of regulars joking that they'd rather have cheeseburgers than this fancy French stuff, so he promptly sent a busboy down the street to a place called Great American Burger to bring back a sack of those all-American sandwiches. Borrowing an idea from Paris, he launched an annual Waiters' Race, in which servers from restaurants all over town fast-walked a little over half a mile carrying a tray with a wine bottle and two full glasses of wine. (In case of a tie, the waiter who had the most wine left in the glasses won.) He once served lunch to Monty Python's hot-air balloon of a character, Mr. Creosote, in the parking lot, because he couldn't fit through the door. Another time, Chippendales dancers took over the place.

I was never sure exactly how Patrick and Wolf felt about each other. Patrick surely realized that much of the success of the restaurant was due to Wolf—not just his food but his easygoing personality, a counterbalance to Patrick's own more deliberate way of dealing with people. And Wolf surely realized that he had been given an extraordinary forum, a chance not only to develop his own culinary talents further but also to show them off to a moneyed and at least putatively refined clientele. But while Patrick let Wolf do pretty much what he wanted to do in the kitchen, he never fully involved him in the management, even though Wolf owned ten percent of the place, and didn't seem receptive to Wolf's suggestion that the restaurant's decor should be upgraded to suit the quality of the food. It was inevitable that Wolf would eventually want to open something on his own, and in 1981 he started making plans to do just that. Initially, he envisioned a fifty-fifty partnership with Patrick, but Patrick held out for a fifty-one percent interest, and Wolf refused. When he quit Ma Maison, Wolf has said, it was like a bad divorce. Patrick repossessed the car he had given Wolf and cut his company credit card in half in front of him.

Back when he'd been working at L'Oustau de Baumanière, Wolf and the rest of the kitchen crew used to spend their nights off at an eccentric little place called Chez Gu in Salon-de-Provence. A haphazardly appointed bistro with red-and-white-checked tablecloths, Chez Gu was a popular stop for French showbiz types driving between Paris and Cannes or Monte Carlo, and the walls were covered with white plates signed in Magic Marker by the likes of Charles Aznavour, Jacques Brel, Brigitte Bardot, and Jean-Pierre Rampal. The menu offered its illustrious clientele caviar, smoked salmon, and foie gras, but the specialties were steak (in eleven varieties) and pizza cooked in a wood-burning oven built by Gu—short for Auguste—himself.

This was precisely the kind of high-low place Wolf had decided that he wanted to open in L.A., but all the experts told him that wood-burning ovens were illegal in California, and good Provençal-style pizza was key to his vision, so he put the idea on hold. On a jaunt to the Bay Area one day, though, he happened by the newly opened Café at Chez Panisse in Berkeley and—voilà!—there was a wood-burning oven happily and efficiently turning out pizzas and more. The ovens weren't illegal after all. Wolf got the name of the oven's maker from Alice Waters and drew up a business plan. He found an available location: the rambling old bungalow, on a hill just above a car rental office on the Sunset Strip, that had most recently housed my old friend Misha Markarian's Armenian restaurant, Kavkaz. Wolf envisioned checkered tablecloths like Chez Gu's, and thought he might call the place Mt. Vesuvius.

By this time, Wolf and his first wife, a pretty French waitress, had split up, and he was living with a flamboyant Bronx-born interior designer named Barbara Lazaroff (they married in 1984 in an elaborate ceremony—the bride made her entrance riding sidesaddle on a white horse—at L'Oustau de la Baumanière). With her encouragement, he solicited investments from a couple of food-loving dentists he knew and from a small group of other Ma Maison regulars, and set about creating his restaurant.

Lazaroff quickly put a stop to the checkered tablecloths, and the name Mt. Vesuvius reminded her unfavorably of Arthur Avenue, the bustling Italian-American neighborhood in the Bronx, so she vetoed that, too. The Ma Maison regular Giorgio Moroder, who was to write the scores for films like *Top Gun* and *Flashdance*, suggested that Wolf call the place Spago—the Italian word for "string," the diminutive form of which is "spaghetti." Wolf liked it, both because it was simple and pronounceable and because nobody would know what it meant, and thus nobody would come to the place with preconceived ideas.

Lazaroff began designing the interior. Any hint of Chez Gu was banished, and instead Lazaroff came up with something that would seem ho-hum today but that was revolutionary thirty years ago: a dining room that was beach-bar casual, with bare floors, wire-mesh chairs, bright contemporary art on the bleached wood walls, and an open kitchen. It was informal, raucous, *fun*; it was unambiguously Californian.

When Wolf first opened Spago, though, local gastronomes and restaurant critics didn't celebrate; they groaned. Ma Maison may have been casual in decor, but it maintained the usual French-restaurant conventions in other ways, and Puck's cooking there would have seemed at home in the most formal of dining rooms. Why did this talented young man, then, leave haute cuisine to run an oversize bistro—something, remember, that simply wasn't done back in those days? And how could he be wasting his considerable abilities on pizza?

But Wolf, as it turned out, knew exactly what he was doing. He once told me that he thought there'd be a lot better food in the world if chefs cooked the kinds of things they liked to eat themselves, and that's basically what he did, celebrating California vegetables in his chopped salad of produce from the estimable Chino Farm near San Diego, roasting whole fish of impeccable freshness in his wood-burning oven, smoking duck over tea leaves instead of drenching it in sticky orange sauce. And those pizzas? Forget mozzarella and pepperoni; Wolf topped his with fresh Santa Barbara spot prawns, California goat cheese, and homemade duck sausage. Spago confounded the critics, delighted its customers, and ultimately changed the nature of dining in America.

Reviewing a new collection of Kurt Vonnegut's early work in *New York* magazine a few years ago, the critic Jacob Rubin noted that Vonnegut's "influence is so ubiquitous as to be invisible." The same could be said, in a very different context, of Wolf. The innovations, both culinary and stylistic, that were introduced and/or propagated by Spago are so many and have become so common-

place that it may be all but impossible to remember—or believe—
that they weren't always with us. Before Spago, pizza was almost
never seen outside pizzerias and was certainly never cooked by
people who called themselves "chefs"—and nobody topped pizza
with goat cheese or Santa Barbara shrimp. Wood-burning ovens
were virtually unknown (even the old-line East Coast pizzerias
burned coal, not wood). Pasta was rare outside Italian restaurants,
and restaurant guides had no "Mediterranean" category. Kitchens
fully open to the dining room were unheard of, unless you counted
sushi bars or coffee shops. And there were certainly no other restaurants where you could eat food of Spago's quality in your T-shirt
and jeans—especially not with Sean Connery at the next table and
Dolly Parton over by the window and Jodie Foster coming through
the front door.

Spago took the mystery and the ceremony out of great eating, and democratized the experience of dining out, which even
(especially?) the rich and famous loved. It also galvanized the local
dining scene, to the point that L.A. became, for more than a decade, the most exciting and trend-setting restaurant city in the
country. And it introduced America to what had been an utterly
unknown concept here: that of not just the celebrity restaurant but
the celebrity chef. "The original Spago on Sunset," the Pulitzer
Prize–winning restaurant critic Jonathan Gold later wrote, "was
to New American Cooking what the Armory Show was to modern painting or *Meet the Beatles* was to rock & roll: the one that
changed the rules."

On opening night in 1982, Wolf once told me, he and Lazaroff
stood by the counter that separated the kitchen from the dining
room and wondered if anyone was going to come. Some did, but
it took a few days for the restaurant to fill completely. And then it
never stopped. Wolf has always said that he never set out to have

a "Hollywood" restaurant, and that he got more pleasure out of providing a unique food experience to a tourist couple from To-ronto than he did from pampering the rich and famous—but he was smart enough to realize that the tourist couple from Toronto came to Spago at least partially because he was pampering the rich and famous there, and he cultivated his more luminary customers with great enthusiasm and skill.

All the movie business people and local power brokers who had frequented Ma Maison now came to Spago. (Actually, many of them remained loyal to both restaurants; Spago wasn't open for lunch, so it was possible to enjoy a midday meal on the Ma Maison patio and then come to Spago after dark.) Wolf was a matchmaker more than once; he engineered a flirtation at the res-taurant between the ur–Bond Girl Ursula Andress and the much younger actor Harry Hamlin, for instance (the two stayed together for four years and had a son). He juggled "don't-invite-'ems" like a diplomat—rival Hollywood columnists George Christy and Army Archerd, for instance, or two movie producers whose partnership had dissolved acrimoniously and were always trying to one-up each other for the best table—staggering their reservations or simply charming them so thoroughly that they forgot their feuds. And he indulged the whims of his regulars in the best of humor: Carol Channing brought all her own food, in silver containers, until somebody told her that Spago's vegetables were organic and she deigned to start ordering off the menu; Suzanne Pleshette would arrive carrying a Tupperware container of her own pasta sauce. At one stage, scores of Spago customers were on the then-trendy Pri-tikin diet, and Wolf would gamely prepare them dishes according to the Pritikin cookbook. They always claimed it was the best diet food they'd ever had. (He never told them why: that he was add-ing butter—a Pritikin no-no—to everything.) The only person he banned from Spago was Patrick—though years later, he relented and the two are now on cordial terms again.

Spago became absurdly successful; its phone number, unlike Ma Maison's, was listed, but it was very seldom answered (regulars called Wolf or one of the maîtres d'hôtel directly for reservations), and for years it was by far the toughest reservation in town.

The year after he opened Spago, some of his original investors wanted Wolf to duplicate his success with a similar place on the Westside. He wasn't interested in copying Spago, he said, so instead he rethought Chinese food and opened Chinois on Main in Santa Monica. This gave his wife (who liked to say, "I'm not his wife—he's my husband") the chance to develop what became her extravagantly colorful, artisanal-tchotchke style of interior design (a Venice artist friend of mine cracked, "Doesn't Chinois look like she just went to the Pacific Design Center and took one soap dish from every showroom?"). It also unleashed on the American dining scene what came to be known as "Asian fusion" food. For better or for worse, there'd be no P.F. Chang's or Roy's today if it hadn't been for Chinois on Main.

More restaurants and a host of brand extensions followed—most notably a line of frozen pizzas. (Wolf got the idea from Johnny Carson, he said, who'd take a dozen of his pizzas home after dinner at Spago on Sunday nights and freeze them himself to eat later in the week.) Wolf was on his way to becoming the most famous chef in America.

WHEN WOLF LEFT TO OPEN SPAGO, Patrick replaced him almost at once with a chef from the acclaimed La Ciboulette in Paris, Claude Segal, and at first the daily lunch scene on the patio hardly seemed to miss a beat. When Segal left to start his own place, Bistango, he was in turn succeeded by Jean-Pierre Lemanissier, who had apprenticed under Paul Bocuse and then cooked at L'Ermitage, an elegant French restaurant not far from Ma Maison. Both Segal and Lemanissier were excellent chefs, but neither won the hearts of the restaurant's blue-chip clientele the way that Wolf had (Segal came closer), and after a while, Ma Maison seemed to be losing steam. Patrick's reputation suffered a blow when John Sweeney, who was Segal's sous-chef, killed Dominique Dunne, and a rumor went around that Patrick had paid for Sweeney's attorney (he vehemently denied it). Dunne's father, Dominick, and her uncle, John Gregory Dunne, married to Joan Didion, called on their many influential friends to boycott the restaurant, which at least some of them did. When *People* magazine did a long, breezy profile of Patrick in the fall of 1983, linking him romantically to a pretty ex-model named Kathy Gallagher, ten years his junior, who ran a buzzy bar and grill down the street from Ma Maison, he shrugged off the seriousness of the relationship to me by saying, "C'est une bonne pub'"—it's good publicity—in a tone that made me think that he felt he really needed some.

In 1985 Patrick sold Ma Maison and its adjacent cooking school, as well as the half-acre lot they stood on, for something over $2 million. The following year, professing himself tired of French food, he opened a place he called the Hollywood Diner. Ruth, who had become the restaurant critic for the *Los Angeles Times*—the continuation of a career that was to later include the posts of food editor for the paper, restaurant critic for *The New York Times*, and editor in chief of *Gourmet*—reviewed the place shortly after it opened. "This is not, obviously, your ordinary diner," she wrote. "It has valet parking. It takes credit cards and reservations. It has caviar (with miniature pancakes and sour cream), fresh oysters and sauteed shrimp sprinkled among the hamburgers, hot dogs and pork chops. Unfortunately, what it does not seem to have at the moment is very good food." Her review was typical of the critical reception the place got, and Patrick closed it after about a year.

Patrick took one more stab at L.A. restaurant success: He sold the Ma Maison name to the French-based Accor Corporation, which applied it to the $55 million Sofitel Hotel property it built from scratch on the corner of Beverly and La Cienega Boulevards. When the hotel opened, late in 1988, the *Los Angeles Times* reported that "Jack Lemmon, Ed McMahon and Suzanne Pleshette arrived by horse-drawn carriages last Monday at the ribbon cutting." Patrick had the title of food and beverage director for the hotel, and his showplace was a large, airy, comfortable restaurant also called, of course, Ma Maison. This time, Ruth was a fan, writing that, "with its widely spaced tables, its carpet and its thoughtful service, the restaurant has the air of the old Ma Maison—but one that has grown up and gotten dignity." I went a few times, and always ate well enough, but, dignity or not, the place just never seemed very interesting to me. It was a good hotel restaurant, even a very good one, but not much more. Celebrities continued to come for a while, out of loyalty to Patrick, but the new Ma Maison never became the new Ma Maison.

Patrick left the hotel in 1991, and both the hotel and its dining room were subsequently renamed. He dropped out of sight for a few years, and it turned out he had been diagnosed with throat cancer. He beat the disease, got a consulting job with the Hiram Walker spirits company, and took an assignment from them in Atlanta. He stayed in Georgia, getting married to a woman he'd met there and buying an abandoned gas station in the town of Newnan, southwest of Atlanta, which he converted into Gaby's Café & Bistro Etc. (named in honor of his mother, Gabrielle Sirigo). He and his wife now live in Hogansville, down the road a piece, where he publishes a magazine called *85 South,* as in the I-85, which runs from Petersburg, Virginia, to Montgomery, Alabama.

Spago continued to thrive well into the nineties, but in a sense it became a victim of its own impact on the American food scene. A celebrity-filled restaurant serving pasta and pizza and organic vegetables was no longer a novelty, and Wolf began to retrench, revisiting the idea of cooking more serious food for a clientele that was becoming more serious *about* food. The original Spago had, in a sense, been cobbled together—the too-small parking lot out back sloped downhill, to the dismay of more than one high-heel-wearing beauty after a few glasses of wine; the "back room" had originally been an unheated, uninsulated storeroom and still always felt a little bit like one—and the open kitchen began to seem inadequate for the larger menu and more demanding dishes Wolf was introducing.

In 1997 Wolf convened a meeting of his original investors, telling them that his landlord wouldn't renew his lease at a reasonable price and that he was going to move the restaurant to Beverly Hills. He offered to buy them out. A few of them balked, and tied up the transition in arbitration for a couple of years. Wolf went ahead and opened the new place anyway, and for three years there were two Spagos in town, no doubt confusing out-of-towners—but giving them the chance to finally eat at the legendary original, since most of the famous people now patronized the Beverly Hills establishment, where Wolf was most likely to be found.

In 2000 Wolf and Lazaroff—who were by then personally estranged, though they remained (and remain) professionally entwined—finally closed the old place down. I was there on the restaurant's last night, sitting at a big table across from Warren Beatty and Annette Bening, listening to Don Rickles insult Aaron

Spelling on the mike, eating Chino Farm chopped vegetable salad, and toasting the demise of a great L.A. institution.

The new Spago was a larger, fancier iteration of the old place, with the kitchen concealed like kitchens used to be and a more serious menu. Under Wolf and his longtime executive chef, Lee Hefter, it is easily one of the best restaurants in Los Angeles, but a very different one from the original. There are other, more casual Spagos in Las Vegas, Maui, and Beaver Creek, Colorado. Wolf also runs (at this writing) twenty other fine dining restaurants around the country (and one each in London and Singapore) and his company has more than forty Wolfgang Puck Express and other casual dining units in airports, shopping malls, and museums nationwide. His lines of canned soups and frozen pizzas and entrées are sold in every supermarket. He has a huge catering business (for years, he's provided elaborate dinners for the Academy Awards' Governors Ball), has written five best-selling cookbooks, and grosses an estimated $20 million a year selling his signature line of cookware on the Home Shopping Network alone. His companies bring in almost $400 million annually. A recent survey reported that his name is recognized in seventy-seven percent of urban households in this country, and another calculated that his name is better known than Martha Stewart's.

Dad at his typewriter,
early 1930s
(Courtesy of the author)

Mom with Groucho
Marx in a scene cut
from *At the Circus*, 1939
(Courtesy of the author)

The house on Beverly Glen Boulevard, 1944 *(Courtesy of the author)*

Getting an early start at writing, circa 1946 *(Irene Andrews)*

Prematurely blasé at one of my parents' parties,
with Dad *(fourth from the left)*, circa 1951 *(Irene Andrews)*

At the table with Dad, Mom, and Merry, circa 1951 *(Courtesy of the author)*

At Buccone wineshop in Rome,
circa 1972 *(Karen Miller)*

tlantic Records: singing backup with
usic business colleagues Bill Yaryan
d Todd Everett, with Screaming Lird
tch and Noel Redding (ex-bassist
th Jimi Hendrix), 1972
urtesy of the author)

With wine business colleagues in a private room at Scandia, 1973 (Joe "Trader Joe's" Coulombe to my right) *(Antonin Kratochvil)*

From the left: me, writer Jan Short, actor-writer Tom Nolan, and photographer David Strick at Ports, 1978 *(Courtesy of the author)*

Dinner at home with Claude and Pepita, 1978 *(Leslie Ward)*

With writer-director Nicholas Meyer at Ma Maison, 1978 *(Courtesy of the author)*

Conducting a wine tasting for staff at *New York* magazine, 1979
(Courtesy of the author)

At Le Vieux Moulin, 1983
(Claude Caspar-Jordan)

With Pepita at Le Vieux Moulin, 1983 *(Claude Caspar-Jordan)*

Claude in Provence, 1983
(Colman Andrews)

With the Saturday wine lunch boys at Café Swiss on the restaurant's
last Saturday in business, 1985 *(Julian Wasser)*

At Sol-Ric in Tarragona. *From the left:* Charles Perry, me, Bradley Ogden, Lydia Shire, Sol-Ric chef, Alice Waters, Jonathan Waxman, Mark Miller, Ruth Reichl, Sol-Ric manager, 1986 *(Courtesy of the author)*

With Alice Waters, Jonathan Waxman, and
Ruth Reichl in Barcelona, 1986 *(Mark Williamson)*

Opening night, Coyote Cafe, Santa Fe, 1987. *From the left:* Larry Forgione,
Mark Miller, Stephen Singer, me, and Alice Waters *(Courtesy of the author)*

Roy Brady, my wine
mentor, 1991
(Colman Andrews)

After tasting wine with Steven Spurrier, St. Bacchus wine competition,
near Perpignan, 1991 *(Courtesy of the author)*

With Julia Child in her kitchen in Cambridge, 1992 *(David Graham)*

With Karen at the "new" Piccolo Mondo in Rome, 1999 *(Christopher Hirsheimer)*

Cooking at the Beard House with Gabrielle Hamilton, 2002 *(Courtesy of the author)*

With Erin and Ferran Adrià in the elBulli kitchen, 2006 *(Courtesy of the author)*

Teatre-Museu Dalí   6 de Juny 2011

Celebrating the 50th anniversary of El Motel, Dalí Museum, with prominent Spanish chefs and restaurateurs, including *(starting from the top row, second right)* Joan Roca, Carme Ruscalleda (partially obscuring me), Jaume Subirós, Ferran Adrià, and José Andrés, 2011 *(Jordi Meli)*

Chapter Twelve

HOSTELLERIE DU VIEUX MOULIN,

Bouilland, France (194?–)

W HEN I QUIT *COAST* IN 1975, ONE OF THE MAGA-
zines I started freelancing for was *Apartment Life,* a sort
of precursor to *Real Simple.* (I remember describing it to somebody
at the time as a magazine that told you how to make a coffee table
out of thread spools, which, of course, was a little unfair.) My first
assignment for it was a short piece on peppercorns—black, white,
green, and pink, the latter two just starting to appear on our tables
through the influence of nouvelle cuisine. My article was published
in December 1978, and for the next few years, I wrote fairly regularly on food and, increasingly, wine for the magazine.

In 1981 *Apartment Life* disappeared, or rather evolved into
a more grown-up publication, christened *Metropolitan Home.*
Met Home, as everybody was soon calling it, was to become my
lifeline—my best market as a freelancer, my training ground as a
late-twentieth-century magazine editor (it was at the magazine's
Manhattan office that I first tentatively tried using a computer),
and my entrée into the New York food and magazine worlds. It
was also where I learned a very important lesson about writing.

At first, I kept sending *Met Home* basically the same kinds of meet-the-contract pieces I'd done for *Apartment Life*. Then one day the editor in chief, a calm, confident Connecticut-bred professional named Dorothy Kalins, kicked something back to me. I had been assigned an article on vintage port, a genre of wine I'd been fortunate enough to be able to enjoy in some profusion, thanks to my Saturday lunch friends at Café Swiss. I thought I knew the subject pretty well, then, and I approached my article the way I'd approached similar pieces for years: I assembled some research materials and synthesized them into a dozen paragraphs of Port 101, then sat down with a tableful of bottles, bought at *Met Home*'s expense, tasted through them, and made notes on each one, to be crafted into prose that I hoped would evoke their flavors and aromas.

Sorry, said Dorothy when she read the piece, but this isn't what we want. You can get Port 101 anywhere. A little bit of background and some tasting notes are fine, but what we really want to know is how *you* feel about Port, how and when you first tasted it, what you thought when you did, what feelings it evokes in you now. Most of the editors I'd worked for up to that point had discouraged the use of the first person, on the grounds that what people were interested in was the subject matter, not the writer. Fair enough. But now that Dorothy mentioned it, I realized that what could make my stories interesting (I hoped) to other people wasn't that they were about *me* but that they were about the experience of discovery; I could be an educated, well-prepared novice taking readers with me as I learned about Port (or anything else). Years later, when Dorothy and Christopher Hirsheimer and I were developing the editorial voice for *Saveur*, we agreed that the proper tone for us to adopt wasn't one of impeccable authority but one of informed curiosity: Hey, we've never really stopped and taken a good look at Burgundy or Venice or the Anderson Valley, either, but we've done our homework and we have the right connections and we're going to go find out what these places are all about, and you're invited to come along.

My freelance relationship with *Met Home* turned out to be something of a dream job. In the magazine's first decade, I wrote dozens of articles for its pages. The majority of these were about food or wine, but Dorothy also let me cover art and design on occasion, which I loved. I interviewed and wrote about David Hockney, Terry Allen, and the architect Charles Moore. I even wrote the entire feature section for a special issue, in February 1989, on a DIFFA—Design Industries Foundation Fighting AIDS—showhouse, interviewing Michael Graves, Andrée Putman, Mario Buatta, Santo Loquasto, Hockney again, and all the other contributors to the project.

But food and drink remained my main beat, and I could pretty much pick and choose what I wanted to write about. My piece on "new American bistros" brought me for the first time to Houston, to visit Cafe Annie, whose owner-chef, Robert Del Grande, later became a good friend. I introduced American readers to the great Paris chef Guy Savoy, and trekked up into the eastern Alps to Merano to write about the ill-starred Villa Mozart. I covered the opening of the original Rattlesnake Club in Denver, first of a proposed chain created by Michael McCarty and the Detroit chef Jimmy Schmidt, and the launch of Mark Miller's Red Sage in Washington, D.C. I wrote about three-star restaurants and cafés alike, and offered detailed dining suggestions for Boston, Chicago, Washington, Barcelona, Paris, Berlin. I wrote about the wines of Long Island, the Napa Valley, the Languedoc; about Alsatian eau-de-vie and bourbon. Somehow, imperceptibly, along the way, I went from being just another freelance contributor to being part of the magazine, a sort of honorary editor. I was never officially employed by *Met Home,* but I was on the masthead, and on the circulation list for memos; my opinions of writers and proposed stories were solicited; I helped brainstorm and plan and plot direction.

In 1989, in partnership with a big British publishing house, *Met Home* launched a U.K. edition, edited by a delightful Australian named Dee Nolan, and this became another of my major markets. The U.K. *Met Home* used longer pieces than the American magazine, and paid more for them. I did a certain amount of recycling, in both directions, but also did a lot of original work for *Met Home* U.K. I had great fun writing about restaurants in Scotland that were developing a modern cuisine based on traditional recipes. (As an old philosophy student, I was fascinated to learn along the way that David Hume had retired from philosophical studies in later life to devote himself to cookery; sheep's head soup was his specialty.)

Another article I enjoyed doing was "Conran's Paris," for which I followed the estimable British designer and restaurateur Terence Conran around that city for a day, with Dee and a photographer in tow, while he introduced me to his favorite restaurants and shops. As a young man, Terence had worked briefly as a *plongeur,* or dishwasher, at a restaurant called La Méditerranée, and when we happened to walk past it, Dee suggested that we take a picture of him outside. I had a better idea, and went in, introduced myself to the proprietor, explained who I was with, and asked if we could possibly shoot the former plongeur down in the basement kitchen, at the sink. He was game, and so was Terence, and the photo (and the story of its origins) helped make the article.

In the first few years of our marriage, Leslie and I traveled together frequently, going to Europe at least once a year, usually for three weeks or so in the summer. Our trips, of course, were built around food, sometimes on assignment for *Met Home,* sometimes not. In Nice, we always dined at Barale, a kind of museum of old farm implements and Niçois bric-a-brac, where the energetic, wizened Madame Barale served a fixed-price meal of local specialties, from pissaladière and "le vrai" salade niçoise to ravioli with meat sauce and the emblematic Niçois dish of stewed air-dried cod called estocaficada—and then passed out song cards, cranked up an old Victrola, put on a scratchy 78 record, and made everybody sing along with the city's unofficial anthem, "Nissa la Bella." Or we'd go to the matchbox-size La Merenda, which had no telephone, took no credit cards, and seated only about twenty diners at a time, on tiny wooden stools—but served absolutely delicious versions of soupe au pistou, merda de can (literally "dogshit," but actually Swiss chard gnocchi), and tripe à la niçoise.

One day we drove up the coast to eat bouillabaisse in a form we had never imagined it at the vertiginous La Roquebrune, on a sliver of cliff above the Mediterranean, beginning with a rich stock dappled with rouille made at the table and continuing on with a veritable fleet of fish and shellfish—gurnard, wrasse, langoustines, the indispensable rascasse—presented on a huge tray of free-form cork and laboriously boned and shelled before our eyes by the slightly rakish looking white-haired patron; the process took almost half an hour, but the results were worth the wait.

Across the Italian border from Nice, we discovered Ligurian cuisine—things like lasagna with pesto and meat-stuffed ravioli with dried porcini at La Cambusiere in Albissola Marina; the addictive focaccia col formaggio at Manuelina in Recco; and, most memorably, an entire repertoire of definitive local specialties at an extraordinary establishment, now long gone, called A Çigheûgna, "The Stork" in the local dialect. A Çigheûgna was a one-of-a-kind place, way up, farther than you thought it could possibly be, in the hills above Rapallo. It was open only Saturday nights and Sunday afternoons, strictly by reservation. As far as we could tell, the signora of the house did all the cooking, alone, while her husband and a uniformed serving girl ran the dining room, which had big windows looking out on the far-distant coastline, and wooden furniture that was obviously homemade. There was no menu or wine list. We drank unlabeled Piedmontese dolcetto and barbera, made by relatives of the proprietors, and ate what they brought us, which was plenty, wheeled out to the tables on big three-tiered wooden carts. First came focaccia, glistening with olive oil. Then cima alla genovese (cold veal breast wrapped around a forcemeat of puréed organ meats studded with vegetables and thinly sliced, sort of a Genoese ballotine), rice croquettes, homemade salami served with fried beignet-like breadsticks, two kinds of ravioli (one filled with finely ground veal, sweetbreads, and liver and sauced with herb butter, the other with a stuffing of cheese and herbs and a light meat sauce), tagliatelle al pesto, meat-stuffed vegetables (onions, sweet yellow peppers, hot round green ones), roasted rabbit covered in fresh herbs, potatoes in a sauce of porcini mushrooms and parsley . . . and finally dessert: homemade peach ice cream, little meringues, and a square of golden tart dough topped with apricot preserves. This remains one of the most memorable meals of my life, and was one of the main inspirations for *Flavors of the Riviera*, the book I later did about the cooking of Liguria and Nice. I'm not sure why I never wrote about it for *Met Home*.

AT ONE POINT I set myself the challenge of finding an undiscovered gem of a restaurant somewhere in the French countryside, a kind of rural counterpart to Guy Savoy in Paris, a place I could "discover" for *Met Home* readers. My friend Michael Roberts, the chef at Trumps in West Hollywood and one of the underrated, unjustly forgotten pioneers of California cuisine, recommended just the place to me: a modest inn called Hostellerie du Vieux Moulin, hidden away in the tiny hamlet of Bouilland, near Beaune in Burgundy. (Michael, in turn, had heard about it from the American-born, Burgundy-based wine exporter Becky Wasserman, who lived in Bouilland and ran her business from the village.)

On my next trip to France, then, I found my way to the place, staying and eating there for a couple of days, and enjoying it very much. It was just what I'd been looking for. The morning of my departure, I paid my bill and then told the proprietors, a young couple named Isabelle and Jean-Pierre Silva, that I was a writer and would like to ask them a few questions about the place. They were astonished. This was not how French food critics worked at all, they said. I should have told them that I was a writer, so they could have taken care of me properly. I assured them that I had been very well taken care of, and that going anonymously and paying one's own way was how we did things in America. I added, jokingly, that Americans were better critics anyway. They laughed, and joked right back at me about how honored they had been to host a great gastronomic expert like me. (Ever after, when I'd call to make a reservation, I'd announce myself as "Le plus grand critique gastronomique du monde," which could mean either the greatest or the largest food critic in the world.) I decided right then that I liked the Silvas as well as their food, and for more than a decade after my first visit, Le Vieux Moulin was an inevitable stop on my frequent French itineraries—my home in Burgundy—connecting me to rural France as surely as I felt Claude had connected me to Paris.

Bouilland is an anomaly in the Burgundy region: a village with no grapevines. It's too cold, say locals. Set in a narrow channel of grazing land between high hills, more glen than valley, it doesn't get a lot of sunlight, and has a chilly microclimate that has earned it the nickname "the little Burgundian Switzerland." Bouilland has a population of fewer than two hundred souls, and there isn't much there other than a few farms, a small church, a café, and, on the banks of a slender stream called the Rhoin, the Hostellerie du Vieux Moulin.

There was once a working water mill on the site, hence the name (a *vieux moulin* is an old mill), but it has long since stopped functioning. The original millhouse, vintage 1860, and another old building were all that remained when, sometime after World War II, one Madame Lebreuil repurposed the place as a bar tabac with a large terrace giving onto the Rhoin. Trout ran in the river, and Mme. Lebreuil served them to her customers, *à la crème*—just trout, nothing else, according to the American wine writer Eunice Fried in her charming book *Burgundy*. Later, at the request of regulars who had probably had enough trout, she added pâté, sausage, and a few other dishes. In the mid-1960s, she sold the place to an amateur cook and former sportswriter for the Burgundian regional newspaper *Le Bien Public*, Raymond Hériot. It turned out that he had a natural talent in the kitchen, and he earned a good reputation and eventually a Michelin star for his straightforward interpretations of such traditional French dishes as veal kidneys in white wine sauce, poularde en vessie (chicken stuffed with foie gras and truffles and cooked sealed in a pig's bladder, a specialty of the legendary Fernard Point at his seminal La Pyramid in Vienne), and trout served not à la crème but au bleu—cooked live in vinegar-spiked court bouillon.

Hériot was reportedly an unpredictable character. The Gault-Millau guide, awarding him a more than respectable fifteen points out of a possible twenty, wrote that he was "a man with two faces: sometimes a thundering Jupiter denouncing those who dare to criticize, sometimes a delightful being in whom, when he talks about cuisine—especially his own—one finds a true poet." Elsewhere, it described him as *papillonnant*, flighty. When Michelin took away his star in 1978, presumably for reasons having more to do with his cooking than with his temperament, Hériot reportedly went into a funk and began to think about selling the place. In 1981, he did just that.

The new proprietors were the Silvas. Jean-Pierre, who was born in Lyon in 1957, had decided by the age of eleven or twelve that he wanted to cook for a living. After his family moved to the south of France when he was a teenager, he found a job apprenticing in a restaurant kitchen in Antibes. There he met Isabelle. The two got married in 1976, and the following year, he landed a good job cooking at a highly regarded restaurant called La Mourachonne, in Mouans-Sartoux, in the hills about halfway between Antibes and Grasse. The Silvas saved their money as Jean-Pierre honed his skills, and they started looking around the Côte d'Azur for a small restaurant they could buy. Such enterprises were expensive in that part of France, though, and one day, on a trout-fishing trip in Burgundy, Jean-Pierre discovered Le Vieux Moulin. A short time later, after a brief stint cooking at a ski resort in the mountains above Nice, he and Isabelle bought the place.

I CAN QUOTE from memory the first few lines of my piece on Le Vieux Moulin for *Met Home:* "One afternoon not long ago in Burgundy, I bit into a carrot. It was tiny and neatly beveled, lightly steamed and glazed in butter. . . . I thought for a moment that it was perhaps the most perfect thing I had ever tasted." If I had been offered a truffle instead at that very moment, I continued, I wasn't at all sure that I would have preferred it. The carrot was really *that good*, but it was also in part a metaphor for the quality of the raw materials the restaurant used in general. Long before "local" and "farm to table" became marketing clichés, Jean-Pierre used vegetables grown in a little market garden just across the road; his baby pigeon came from one nearby farm, his superlative goat cheese from another. It wasn't just the ingredients, though; Jean-Pierre's food was unfailingly fresh in conception and always full of flavor. He had a gift for matching flavors and textures (he used little wisps of grapefruit and a scattering of pink peppercorns, for instance, to turn paper-thin slices of raw sea bass and wild salmon into a kind of French ceviche, unlike anything I'd ever imagined), and his technique was flawless; never did he serve an overcooked piece of fish or fowl, an unbalanced sauce, a soggy bit of pastry. He didn't yet have the polish of a Guy Savoy, but he clearly had the makings of a first-rate chef.

Isabelle ran the dining room and schooled herself in wine, especially Burgundy, as Jean-Pierre kept getting better and better in the kitchen. In 1986, the Guide Michelin awarded Le Vieux Moulin a well-deserved star, and the Silvas responded by beefing up the staff—a maître d'hôtel was hired—and converting the dining room from its rustic original form (for a time there was actually a gently plashing little fountain in the middle of the place) into something sleek and hard-edged, with a shiny interior canopy and black-and-white color scheme. Before long, the place had earned a second Michelin star.

Jean-Pierre's cooking became increasingly sophisticated, but it continued to surprise and delight me. On one trip, I'd dine on exquisite, tiny Burgundian crayfish sautéed in pumpkin seed oil and an improbably sweet and tender suprême of capon that had been poached in a rich calf's muzzle broth, which seemed to me an almost medieval indulgence. On another, I'd sample sea trout with cabbage and goat cheese and ragout of sweetbreads and kidneys in foie gras sauce with vegetable-filled ravioli. The next time, it would be frogs' legs in a sauce of wine lees with young leeks, followed by caramelized pork cheek with a bouillon of Asian spices and capers in red wine—or, after I'd organized a trip for him to Los Angeles, to cook a banquet at a private club, his version of a cheeseburger, made with ground carp topped with goat cheese and homemade "ketchup."

The guest rooms at the inn were tiny and drab, but it was always a pleasure, after one of Jean-Pierre's superb meals, accompanied by great Burgundies chosen by Isabelle and concluded in the parlor with the chef, over good cigars and too many snifters of marc de Bourgogne or vieille prune, to be able to stumble up a flight of stairs and collapse for the night. In 1987, though, the Silvas improved the property by building a freestanding structure across the road, with four large bedrooms and a suite. The following year, they installed an indoor swimming pool on the ground floor of the building. I asked them when the tennis courts and golf course were going in, and started calling the place "the Bouilland Hilton." I was kidding, of course, but I honestly did imagine that one day the Silvas would be presiding over a luxurious property—a Relais & Châteaux, perhaps—with a three-star restaurant attached. I felt as if I had known a future culinary phenomenon almost since birth.

But then . . . "I woke up one day," Jean-Pierre later told me, "and realized that I wasn't a cook anymore. I was a manager and an accountant, which is not what I wanted to be." The Silvas were also worried that they weren't spending enough time with their daughters, Dorothée and Laure—especially after Laure had suffered neurological damage in an automobile accident on the narrow byway between Savigny-lès-Beaune and Bouilland. A year after Michelin had given the restaurant its second star—and a number of years before more celebrated chefs like Alain Senderens, Olivier Roellinger, and Marc Veyrat were to voluntarily give up stars and simplify their cuisine—the Silvas decided to take a step backward. Isabelle assumed control of the dining room again and stripped the service down to the basics, and Jean-Pierre re-cast his food, serving such fare as cannelloni stuffed with shredded coq au vin, pike perch in a vinegar sauce with lentils, and roast lamb from a nearby farm with a whole bouquet of exquisite, simply cooked local vegetables—perfect carrots among them. Michelin, as expected, promptly took away a star—but, Jean-Pierre told me, his business actually increased.

He felt better for a while, but he realized that he wanted some-thing even simpler. He and Isabelle also dreamed about living someplace warmer than this little Burgundian Switzerland. He flirted with the idea of moving his family to St. Barths and open-ing something there, but also looked back to the south of France. His dream, he said—I've heard dozens of chefs, even Wolfgang Puck, say something like this—was to have a tiny place where he could cook food he liked for a handful of customers. Unlike most chefs, he actually made it happen: In 2000, the Silvas bought a beautiful old stone millhouse in the hills above Cannes, in a village called Le Rouret, and began to renovate it into a family home with a small restaurant attached. In January 2003, they sold Le Vieux Moulin—to a Swiss buyer, appropriately enough—and moved south. (The place seems to be doing well under its new owner, the former director of a psychiatric hospital in Fribourg, who hired a Burgundian-trained chef.)

A few months after they'd left Bouilland, the Silvas opened a fourteen-seat dining room in their new millhouse, called La Table de Mon Moulin. This was a two-person operation: Isabelle was the entire dining room staff and Jean-Pierre, by himself, cooked one fixed-price menu daily, five days a week, based on foodstuffs he bought each morning at the market in nearby Cagnes-sur-Mer.

When I asked him if Isabelle ever helped with the prep work, he looked at me like I was crazy, as if to say that surely, after all the years we'd known each other, I realized *he* was the chef. She didn't even clean up afterward: The plongeur was an automatic dishwasher.

Jean-Pierre's food was no longer Burgundian, of course; instead, it was full of Provençal flavors. His cold tomato soup with a poached egg and a whole bouquet of herbs from the garden outside was like a field guide to the Côte d'Azur; his sea bass with scallion marmalade sang with freshness; his dorade coryphène, a kind of Mediterranean mahimahi, served on rounds of eggplant with a white bean cream and summer truffles, was an anthology of the Cagnes market; his pork loin with Perugia sausage in red wine sauce with new potatoes and wild chard was earthy and intense; his fig tart with pineapple sage leaves and apricot sorbet evoked a Provençal orchard. Like the food Jean-Pierre had served at Le Vieux Moulin, it was unfailingly good and redolent of its place of origin.

La Table de Mon Moulin was Silva's fantasy restaurant—but it wasn't the end of his story. His daughter Dorothée had studied architecture but had a hard time finding work on the Côte d'Azur, which she was disinclined to leave. She had literally grown up in the restaurant business, and one day she came to her father and said, "Can't we do a restaurant together?" As he puts it, "She got her mother on her side, and then I didn't stand a chance. There wasn't room for another person at Mon Moulin, so we looked around, and we found L'Ondine."

L'Ondine is a beachfront restaurant on La Croisette in Cannes, complete with a private enclosure full of chaises longues and umbrellas, a breezy terrace, and a large interior dining room. When he took it over, Jean-Pierre made the decision not to cook; instead, he supervised the kitchen and did all the buying of meat, fish, and produce, drawing on the network of suppliers he had come to know in the region. The menu was pretty much what you'd expect on the beach in Cannes: oversize salads, gargantuan slabs of beef fillet or breaded veal (the latter dwarfed by heaps of spaghetti on the side), grilled whole fish big enough to give Jonah the jitters. Every time I saw him at the place, sporting not a chef's apron but a white short-sleeve shirt with the legend "Le Chef C'Est Moi" embroidered on the pocket, Jean-Pierre looked tan and relaxed. He liked to call himself a *plagiste*—a beach proprietor.

The story still wasn't over, though. In 2012, after almost a decade at L'Ondine, Jean-Pierre, Isabelle, and Dorothée made another change: They sold the restaurant and opened a wineshop in Cannes, specializing in the wares of about fifty top Burgundy producers. It is, he says, "the best Burgundy cellar in the south of France." He is considering opening a thirty-seat restaurant next door, to serve "very simple food to a local clientele"—but, he adds, "It's easier to sell bottles than to cook meals." The life he and his family will lead, he says, will be "plus tranquille"—more peaceful. It will, he adds, be "almost normal."

Chapter 13

EL MOTEL,

Figueres, Spain (1961–)

&

ELDORADO PETIT,

Barcelona (1978–2001)

IN ALL MY TRAVELS AROUND EUROPE, I HAD NEVER been to Spain. As a good young leftie, I avoided it—and its neighbor, Portugal—because they were fascist dictatorships. I'd also developed an early affinity for Italy, and Italy and Spain, like their respective languages, seemed so different and yet so similar that I wasn't sure one could like them both. I crossed the Spanish border for the first time in 1980; by that time, as Chevy Chase used to assure us on *Saturday Night Live*, Generalísimo Francisco Franco was still dead. Leslie and I were staying in the French Basque port town of Saint-Jean-de-Luz, and we decided to go to San Sebastián, only about twenty miles away, for lunch one day. We'd done no restaurant research, so when we got there we just wandered around the Parte Vieja, the old quarter, until we found a place that looked okay—casual, big, and crowded. I don't remember the details, other than that I had cigalas a la plancha, grilled scampi, very fresh and good.

For the next few years, on our European vacations, we stuck mostly to France and Italy, with side trips to London, Brussels, and Amsterdam. In early 1985, though, as we started planning our next trip to Europe, Leslie said, "Why don't we go to Spain this year?" I agreed, and we plotted out a trip: We'd start in Paris, then drive down through western Provence and across the Pyrénées on the Mediterranean side. We'd stop in Barcelona for a few days, then move down to Valencia, Seville, and Jerez de la Frontera before swinging back up and finishing in Madrid. This time I did my homework, and one of the books I read was *The Simon and Schuster Pocket Guide to Spanish Wines* by Jan Read, which included brief restaurant recommendations for each region. In Catalonia, Read singled out, among other places, the dining room at the curiously named Motel Ampurdán in Figueres, describing it as a "highly sophisticated restaurant started by Josep Mercader, founder of the new Catalan cuisine." I hadn't even known there was an *old* Catalan cuisine, but I was intrigued, and the Motel Ampurdán was the first place we stopped, for lunch, when we entered Spain.

Walking into the dining room, I was engulfed by an attractive but exotic aroma that I couldn't quite place, earthy, sweet, and a little dark, but not in a heavy or ominous sense. I later learned that this scent, unique to Catalan cooking, comes from a combination of long-cooked onions, garlic, and tomato and a mortar-and-pestle-ground paste of nuts, garlic, chocolate, and other ingredients—the so-called sofregit and picada, respectively, with which many traditional Catalan sauced dishes are made.

We sat down at a table set with thick white napery and ate plump, mild, oily anchovy filets with little rounds of bread rubbed with tomato and drizzled with olive oil (my introduction to the quintessentially Catalan dish called pa amb tomàquet, bread with tomato), then salt cod croquettes, grilled squid, and baby eggplants stuffed with anchovies and fresh herbs. The raw materials were familiar to me, mostly from my meals in Italy, but the flavors were somehow different, and I was definitely intrigued.

Over the next few days, in Barcelona, we ate at two contemporary Catalan places, both now long gone, Farín and Montse Guillén; the good but very French Neichel; a traditionally Catalan hole-in-the-wall in the Gothic Quarter called Quatre Barres; and the elegant Via Veneto, where we sampled both international haute cuisine (sautéed goose liver with sherry cream sauce, wild mushroom gâteau) and real Catalan fare (red peppers stuffed with salt cod mousse, botifarra sausage with white beans). This was, I now realize, a curious assortment of restaurants, only intermittently representative of what the region had to offer gastronomically. Nonetheless, from this brief, imperfect sampling, I realized that Catalan cuisine could make a great story.

Back in America, I quickly sold an article on the subject to *Met Home;* it is a measure of the obscurity of the region to Americans in those days that the illustrated map the magazine used to accompany my piece labeled Catalonia as "Catalan." Before the piece was published, my literary agent took me to breakfast in Los Angeles and asked, "What's new in food?" I told her that it was probably too obscure for a whole book, but there *was* this little corner of Spain. . . . "You should write a proposal," she said. I did, and in June 1985, I signed a contract with Atheneum for my first cookbook, to be titled *Catalan Cuisine*. I was thrilled by the imprint—Atheneum published all my favorite poets, like James Merrill, Mark Strand, and Norman Dubie—and even the advance didn't seem so bad: $12,500, payable in two installments, one upon signing, one upon delivery and acceptance of the "complete and final manuscript." What I didn't realize, of course, was what the book would ultimately cost me.

IT WAS APPROPRIATE that the Motel Ampurdán, which introduced me to Catalan cuisine, would become the most important restaurant in my Catalan culinary education. In the 1960s, the Motel had been almost as revolutionary a restaurant as the legendary elBulli, fifteen miles or so to the east, was to become thirty years or so later, even though its innovations never had the international reach that elBulli's did. To understand its significance, you have to realize that until the latter half of the twentieth century, the food served in white-tablecloth restaurants in Spain was primarily French, either literally or in inspiration. Menus were often written in the language of Carême and Escoffier, and while they may have included a handful of traditional Spanish dishes, even those were often Gallicized (*"les tripes à la madrilène"*).

The dominant Spanish culinary text for much of the past hundred years or so—the Escoffier of Spain, if you will, written for professional chefs—had been *El práctico,* a compendium of about 6,500 recipes published in 1895. It certainly included Spanish specialties—empanadas, pucheros, various rice dishes, and the like—but it was mostly full of instructions for the correct production of vol-au-vents, quiche, frogs' legs, bouillabaisse, andouillettes, chateaubriand, and the other French classics that any serious chef in Spain was expected to be able to prepare.

Josep Mercader knew the classics as well as anyone, but he also saw the value in simple Spanish—and especially Catalan—home cooking, and knew how to refine it just enough to earn it a place on his tables alongside all those French specialties. He went a step further, though, and dared to tamper with tradition: Instead of just applying the techniques he knew to indigenous fare, he began re-thinking the fare itself, making it lighter, rearranging its elements, and presenting them in different form—something it apparently had never occurred to other good chefs of the era to do. This re-casting of familiar dishes into forms that recalled the original but changed their texture and composition very much anticipated the basic notion of the "deconstructions" that Ferran Adrià, who had not yet appeared on the planet when Mercader opened his estab-lishment, was to develop some decades later.

Born into a family of fishermen in the seaside village of Cada-qués, a town beloved by Picasso, Miró, Duchamp, and most of all Dalí, who built a house there, Mercader started cooking young, apprenticing at local restaurants, often under French-trained chefs. His most important mentor was Pere Granollers, who, for twenty years, had run the kitchen at the Hôtel de Paris in Monte Carlo (where Alain Ducasse now holds sway), before returning to Cat-alonia to take over the railway station restaurant in the Spanish-French border town of Portbou. This was a grander establishment than it might sound. In France, there was a tradition of fine res-taurants in railway stations, and because French and Spanish trains ran on different gauge rails, all passengers between the two coun-tries had to stop in Portbou to change carriages. As a result, there was a constant stream of customers, many of them used to the high standards of French cooking.

As Mercader worked under Granollers, he grew increasingly confident in his own skills, and began to think about creating a different kind of cuisine. With investments from local friends, he constructed a three-story hotel in a streamlined, quasi-deco style on the edge of Figueres, on the old pre-autoroute road between Barcelona and the French border. He called the place the Motel Ampurdán—"motel" because he saw the place primarily as a rest stop for automobile-borne travelers, Ampurdán because that was the Castilian Spanish form of Empordà, the name of the region in Catalan, a language whose use was forbidden by law until after the death of Franco.

Mercader never identified himself with the nouvelle cuisine movement that began redefining French cooking a few years after he opened his restaurant, but he pursued many of the same goals that chefs like Paul Bocuse, Michel Guérard, the Troisgros brothers, and Alain Chapel did. Like them, he modernized and lightened traditional dishes, simplified preparations, and brought regional fare into the formal dining room, anticipating changing tastes. He was encouraged in this pursuit by a group of cosmopolitan friends, chief among them the prominent local writer Josep Pla, and by Pla's friend Dalí, who became a faithful customer of Mercader's.

An example of Mercader's approach is his faves a la menta, literally fava beans with mint. There is a traditional Catalan dish called faves a la catalana, typically made with large, starchy favas, cooked for a long time, with blood sausage and bacon added. Mercader reconceived the dish as a salad of small, fresh favas—he only made it in the spring, when they were in season—flavored with lots of fresh mint, and, in place of rich blood sausage, he used only a few shreds of ham and bits of translucent, fat-streaked meat sliced paper-thin from a pig's foot.

Among his other innovations, Mercader turned samfaina, the Catalan ratatouille, into a rosy-hued, complexly flavored sauce for roast loin of veal; made a surprisingly delicate mousse out of escalivada—eggplant, red peppers, and onions charred in the embers of a live fire; recast straightforward roasted salt cod with allioli (the basic Catalan garlic-and-olive-oil emulsion) by topping the fish with a souffléed garlic mousseline; played off the "mar i

muntanya" (sea and mountain, or "surf-and-turf") dishes of traditional Catalan cooking by stuffing roast lamb leg with the superb
anchovies of his hometown of Cadaqués; and had the inspiration
of processing crema catalana (crème brûlée), caramelized sugar
topping and all, in an ice cream machine (this became probably
his most copied dish). Long before other Catalan chefs started ex-
perimenting with centrifuges and vaporizers, liquid nitrogen and
calcium chloride, Mercader was thinking about ways to transform
the dishes with which he'd grown up, retaining—and in some
cases clarifying and/or intensifying—their flavors while deftly
altering their forms. There's no telling what greater influence he
might have had on the cuisine of his region, and of Spain in general, if he hadn't died of a heart attack in 1979.

ONE OF THE RESTAURATEURS I had gotten to know in Los
Angeles, through various culinary events, was Jean Leon, whose
La Scala in Beverly Hills had fed movie stars and politicians for
decades. Jean's name sounded French, but he was Spanish, and it
wasn't his real name anyway. He'd been born Ceferino Carrión
in Santander, in Cantabria, and renamed himself when he'd emigrated to America. La Scala wasn't a Spanish place. When Jean set
up shop, in 1956, "Spanish" meant Mexican to Southern California
restaurant goers, so he made the quite sensible decision to serve
Italian food.

Jean loved good wine, and after he'd become successful, he
started thinking about running his own vineyard. Good California wine land was already getting expensive, but Spain was still a
bargain. In 1961, having lived in Barcelona briefly before coming to
the United States, he decided to buy a 350-acre plot of good grape-
growing real estate in the Penedès, about twenty miles west of the

city. The Penedès is Spain's capital of sparkling wine, or cava, and the principal grapes there at the time were the local white varieties on which cava was traditionally based, xarel.lo, parellada, and macabeu. Jean broke the rules, planting cabernet and merlot from Bordeaux (including grafts from Château Lafite Rothschild and Château La Lagune) and chardonnay from Burgundy. He also built his own small winery and, to the surprise of many locals, began producing excellent wine. (The Jean Leon label still exists, but is now owned by the massive Torres company.)

When I signed my contract to write a book about Catalan cuisine, Jean was one of the first people I told, and he became my real entrée into the world of Catalan food and drink. He asked his winery manager to introduce me to other local winemakers and restaurateurs when I came to Barcelona. He offered me the use of the little house he'd built for himself in his vineyards, equipped with a refrigerator full of wine and a beautiful jamón ibérico resting in a holder on the kitchen counter. Most important of all, Jean put me in touch with his Spanish attorney, a vigorous, intelligent, food-loving Catalan from the Pyrénées named Agustí Jausas. Agustí and his wife, Lluïsa, became my guides, protectors, teachers, and certainly my dining companions (and usually my hosts) for the next three years, and we have been close friends ever since. (Jean ended sadly: He was forced to close La Scala when the lease ran out, and neither the new one he opened a few blocks away nor the various outposts he launched later had the cachet of the original. He retired and, terminally ill, sailed the world alone on his yacht until his death in 1996.)

Leslie came with me at the start of my first real research trip to Catalonia, and we spent a very pleasant week or so on the Costa Brava and in Barcelona. Then she went home and I got to work. I quickly found myself immersed in a whole new culture, a whole new world. Flavors I'd never imagined became my daily bread, and a language I'd never before heard—vaguely medieval-sounding, I thought, and very different from Castilian Spanish—started singing in my head. The food seemed medieval, too, with its use of "sweet" spices like cinnamon and nutmeg in savory dishes, its combinations of fruit and meat (duck with pears, apples stuffed with ground meat), its big one-pot dishes mixing seafood and poultry and/or meat. It occurred to me that, in a way, this food was probably not dissimilar to what a lot of Europeans ate five or six hundred years earlier.

Agustí and Lluïsa introduced me to one excellent Barcelona restaurant after another: Petit París, named not for the city but for the street it was on, where a former architect and his wife served modern Catalan food with an emphasis on salt cod, a beloved ingredient in Catalonia (a version with Roquefort sauce and another one, fried, with honey, were particularly good); Els Perols de l'Empordà (the Cooking Pots of the Empordà), which served the exquisite escupinya clams of Minorca and big cauldrons of seafood rice that were as good as anything on the Costa Brava itself; the stylish Florián, where I first ate not only toro de lidia, meat from a bull killed in a local bullfight (the menu helpfully identified the beast by name and breeder and noted the place, date, and hour of his execution and the name of the matador who had dispatched him) but also bull testicles, sliced thinly, breaded, and fried in olive oil with minced garlic and parsley, and pretty delicious; Ca l'Isidre, a clubby, old-style place where the wild mushroom and wild game dishes were some of the best in town (whole cèpes, brushed with foie gras fat and roasted in parchment paper, then sliced and sprinkled with sea salt, remain one of the most memorable dishes I've ever had in Barcelona); and many more.

And they introduced me to Eldorado Petit, which was on another level altogether. The establishment occupied a large house—a villa, really—on a residential street in the Sarrià district in the northwestern corner of the city. The moment I came through the door, I knew that it was my kind of restaurant. It was something about the lighting, the sound level, the pleasant aromas, the confidence of the decor, the warmth of the welcome. Walking into Eldorado Petit for the first time, I felt the way I used to feel walking into Chasen's or Trader Vic's or Scandia—that I was in the right place, that everything was going to be fine.

The dining room was under the command of an impressively mustachioed, genial sprite of a man named Lluís Cruanyas. Since 1942 his father had run a popular tavern called Eldorado in Sant Feliu de Guíxols, a small port and tourist town, once the center of the local cork industry, about fifty miles northeast of Barcelona. It was a place where local fishermen came to play cards, drink, and eat simple fare, like espardenyes, or sea slugs, an ugly and unpopular bycatch that almost no one but they would eat. Lluís worked at Eldorado, gradually introducing some new dishes, and in 1970, at the age of twenty-three, with his father's blessing, he opened his own restaurant next door. Because it was smaller than the original, he dubbed it Eldorado Petit ("petit" is Catalan as well as French).

Lluís served an ample menu of mostly traditional dishes, focusing on rice and fideus noodle dishes and on the region's excellent fish and shellfish—the anchovies caught off Sant Feliu, legendary in Catalonia; the plump red shrimp landed in Palamós, just up the coast; tiny octopuses (popets) and squid (calamarcets) no longer than a joint on your finger; small, sweet Mediterranean sole; fearsome-looking but delicious escúrpora, or scorpion fish, which the French call *rascasse* and consider essential to bouillabaisse; and dozens of other sea creatures. The restaurant thrived, drawing travelers off the autoroute between France and Barcelona, food lovers who made the pilgrimage up from the Catalan capital for lunch, and, of course, many of the tourists who throng the Costa Brava every year.

In 1978, buoyed by his success in Sant Feliu and with the financial support of a group of his regular customers, Lluís and his wife, Lolita, opened a second Eldorado Petit, in Barcelona, taking over an existing place called La Martinica. The new restaurant wasn't the least bit starchy, but it was elegant in an understated way. The walls were a warm pink, the tables were large and set with thick white linens, the light was soft and inviting, some of it radiating from graceful floor lamps on easel-like legs by the top Barcelona designer Jaime Tresserra.

The food was imaginative, mostly Catalan in inspiration, and dazzling. There were fat Costa Brava shrimp, less than half a day out of the Mediterranean, served in what the menu called the style of Dénia, a coastal town in the Alicante region: very lightly poached in seawater, then immediately chilled between two layers of ice so that they were tepid and still partly translucent, and so full of flavor that they seemed like essence of shrimp. There was a deft elaboration on the traditional Catalan salt cod salad called "esqueixada," here a dish of paper-thin raw salt cod and white beans garnished amply with fresh angulas, the famous and pricey miniature eels from the Basque Country. There were bright red piquillo peppers, cut to look like flowerpots, with chives growing out of them, filled with scorpion fish mousse; walnut-size whole artichokes sautéed with garlic and baby shrimp; silky vichyssoise-like soup made from fava beans; four-inch-long red mullets dressed with vinegar and shallots; cabbage leaves stuffed with monkfish; black rice, full of cuttlefish; whole turbot roasted on a bed of thin-sliced potatoes, which soaked in the fish juices and caramelized on the bottom—just magic. There were also espardenyes, no longer viewed as the cheap throwaway fare of Costa Brava fishermen but as a delicacy among Catalan diners, more expensive per pound in the market than even lobster imported from northern France. Jean Luc Figueras, the restaurant's excellent chef, usually just browned them quickly in olive oil, with garlic and parsley; they were the texture of firm squid, a little squeaky when you chewed them, and tasted of earth and sea at once.

My favorite dish was fideus rossejats, "blonded" noodles. These are short, thin lengths of vermicelli-like pasta, sautéed raw in olive oil to a golden brown color, then cooked in concentrated fish stock and served with allioli negat, "drowned" allioli, which means that the emulsion is intentionally broken, yielding thickened, intensely garlicky olive oil to be stirred into the noodles. That's it. No bits of fish or seafood, no other garnish. Just medium-firm pasta soaked in flavor. I couldn't imagine any chef in France or the United States having the restraint and the confidence to serve a dish that simple, and indeed, whenever I've had a version of fideus rossejats in America, there is always seafood added.

At Eldorado Petit, more than at any other restaurant in the region, even more than at the Motel Ampurdán, I came to realize how extraordinary the raw materials were in this part of Spain and just how appealing—how varied, how (pardon the expression) "world-class"—Catalan cooking could be. Lluís generously shared many recipes with me, at least some of which ended up in my book, and answered all my questions about sources, cooking methods, and historical background. It was a special treat to go through the Boquería, Barcelona's fabled main covered market, with him, and watch his eyes light up when he came upon a rare giant Mediterranean turbot at a fish stall (he immediately bought it for the restaurant) or discovered that the first local morels of the season had come in at the famous "products of the forest" stand of Llorenç Petrás.

On one occasion, Dorothy Kalins and two other editors from *Met Home* came through Barcelona while I was there, and of course I took them to Eldorado Petit. As we sat soaked in warm light, pampered by the service, drinking bottle after bottle of good Catalan wine and eating one extraordinary dish after another, Dorothy sighed and said, "This is the best restaurant in the world." I reminded her that the late Roy Andries de Groot had once written an article for *Playboy* about Troisgros, which he titled "Is This the Best Restaurant in the World?" Well, said Dorothy, maybe Troisgros was then, but Eldorado Petit is now—so I wrote a piece about the restaurant for *Met Home* with precisely that title, in which I answered my own question affirmatively.

In 1990, hoping to take advantage of the new interest in Barcelona that had been sparked by the announcement that the 1992 Olympic Games would be held there, Lluís opened an outpost of Eldorado Petit in New York City. In the months leading up to its debut, I started getting worried. "I understand that Americans don't eat a lot of seafood," he said to me one night in Barcelona, "and that they don't like garlic very much." *What???* Another time, he confessed that he was afraid he wouldn't be able to put his magical turbot roasted on a bed of potatoes on the menu, because we didn't have the right kind of potatoes in America.

I couldn't get to his grand opening, but the morning after the event, a faxed copy of the menu arrived in my office in Santa Monica. I took one look at it, and my heart sank. It was a dumbed-down, Americanized rewrite of the Catalan original; one of the dishes listed was salmon—an insipid fish compared with what Lluís served in Spain, but one that he had been assured Americans were particularly fond of (true, alas, but still . . .)—on a bed of that old Catalan staple, arborio rice; another was filet mignon with blueberry sauce. Bryan Miller, writing in *The New York Times,* later described the food as "undistinguished Continental fare" and opined that "Eldorado Petit seemed to be taking the condescending and potentially disastrous attitude that ethnic food must be tempered for American tastes."

The restaurant improved in the coming months, but never really found its focus. Lluís returned to Catalonia, and in 1993, the restaurant closed. One afternoon in 2001, I was driving in Sarrià on my way to lunch at another restaurant, and I thought I'd swing by Eldorado Petit just to see how it was doing. I happened to pass the place in time to see two pairs of workmen carrying tables out the front door. Was Lluís remodeling? I later asked Agustí. No, he said, hadn't I heard? It was closing. Business had flagged, and when Lluís and Lolita were offered a good price for the restaurant, they sold it and retreated to Sant Feliu. It is now a private home.

As I sank deeper and deeper into my subject, I started haunting some of Barcelona's many bookshops, collecting cookbooks, works of history, essays by Josep Pla and others. I spent hours at a time in Agustí's large private library, too, poring through books in half a dozen languages. I did plenty of field research as well. The more I read and learned, the more I realized that I needed to expand the scope of my book to cover not just Catalonia itself but what the Catalans like to call "els Països Catalans," the Catalan lands—a vast, linguistically related area that includes the region of Valencia, the Balearic Islands, the Roussillon in France, the Pyrenean principality of Andorra, and even one town on the Italian island of Sardinia, Alghero, or L'Alguer, where some Catalan traditions are maintained and a bit of the language is still used. I visited all these regions more than once, bearing introductions to exactly the right people. In Majorca, it was the well-known local journalist Pablo Llull who told me, "My dear Colman, you can't possibly write that Majorcan cuisine is Catalan" (but I did anyway, and explained why). The distinguished Valencian poet and culinary historian Llorenç Millo taught me so much about real paella that I can barely eat most examples of the dish today, even in Spain. The Andorran wine merchant Jordi Marquet told me much about his tiny principality's cooking, though to my disappointment he was unable to arrange for me to eat the old local specialty of rice with squirrel. Unfortunately, he told me, it had become illegal to hunt squirrels and the dish was only made if someone "accidentally" brought one down while supposedly aiming at a bird.

But Catalonia itself remained my focus. Time after time, I'd head out of Barcelona, driving all over the region in my rental car, usually an indestructible Ford Escort, heading up into the Pyrénées to visit sausage makers and country inns, calling on winemakers in the Priorat (there were only two to speak of at the time, and their wines were unknown internationally), eating at seafood restaurants in and around the old Roman capital of Tarragona, south of Barcelona. In Valls, near Tarragona, I went to a calçotada, a feast built around oversize green onions, grilled and then eaten dipped in a sauce of ground nuts and chiles. I ate a hundred tiny snails, grilled live on black metal trays, at one sitting in Tornabous, in the region of Lleida—and then polished off my share of the grilled sausages and baby lamb chops that followed. At an isolated Lleida farmhouse, I watched a pig being slaughtered—the man who killed it, I was delighted to learn, was called a *matador*—then helped cut up the still-warm meat for sausages. And I returned again and again to the Motel Ampurdán, learning more, devouring more, on every visit.

The Motel Ampurdán didn't miss a beat after the untimely demise of Josep Mercader. His son-in-law, Jaume Subirós, was there to carry on his work. In fact, he'd been there from the beginning.

One day in 1961, just before Mercader opened the place, he stopped at a farmhouse in the village of Vilamalla, a few miles south of Figueres, to ask permission to paint a sign for the motel on a wall that faced the road—a common practice in prebillboard Spain. The man of the house said yes, on one condition: that Mercader give his young son a job. Thus, at the age of eleven, Jaume went to work for Mercader, first as a bellboy during the summer and on holidays, later as a full-time employee in the kitchen and dining room. He grew up in the business and went on to help run a second Mercader hotel, the Almadraba Park in nearby Roses. In 1974, he married Mercader's daughter, Anna María.

Mercader had been gone for half a dozen years by the time I first got to the Hotel Ampurdán—he had upgraded it to hotel status in 1968—but Jaume welcomed me graciously and went out of his way to help me. He drove me out to the Almadraba Park to see the jars of Roses anchovies he was salt-curing in the hotel's dark basement. (His car reeked of anchovies—a jar had tipped over several days before while he was driving it back to Figueres—and he was apologetic, but to me it smelled like perfume.) He introduced me to local olive oil producers and winemakers, and took me to a wine cooperative a few miles from the hotel where wine was dispensed into customers' own vessels from what looked like gasoline pumps. When I asked about the Catalan rolled cookies called "neules," he led me to a village called Tortellà, where a man named Valentí made what were reputed to be the best neules in the region. Whenever I asked about some reasonably obscure specialty of the region, Jaume would not just describe it to me but cook it or find it for me to sample—the sugar-cured pork sausage called "botifarra dulce," for instance, or the meat-stuffed baked apples called "rellenos." And of course he served me, over a two-year period, virtually everything in the hotel repertoire.

I ate whole fish, typically gilthead bream, roasted on a bed of thin-sliced potatoes and scattered with onions, green peppers, rounds of botifarra sausage, and small black olives; scorpion fish suquet, the classic Catalan fish and potato stew; veal shank braised in red wine; "platillos" of cuttlefish with mixed vegetables or goose with locally foraged wild mushrooms. Every meal began with "garum," Mercader's tribute to the fermented fish sauce favored by the ancient Romans, the best of which was said to have come from the Costa Brava, and with deep-fried anchovy spines, which are just what they sound like and are remarkable.

Sometimes, I'd have just local seafood, simply prepared—squid sautéed with garlic and parsley, red mullet on the grill, mussels steamed in white wine. Other times, I'd sample classic Mercader specialties such as his fava bean salad with mint, his salt cod gratinéed with garlic mousseline, his veal loin with samfaina cream. Probably my favorite Mercader dish was perdiu amb farcellets de col, cabbage stuffed with boneless partridge. The chef created it in honor of his friend Josep Pla, the distinguished essayist and laureate of the landscape and seascape of the Costa Brava, and also a noted gourmet who wrote a wonderful book about Catalan cooking called *El que hem menjat*, *What We Ate*. One of Pla's favorite dishes was roast partridge, traditionally served with cabbage stuffed with pork forcemeat on the side. As he got older and started losing teeth, he found it increasingly difficult to gnaw the partridge off its bones, so Mercader invented this preparation for him, melding main dish with accompaniment. It was an intensely savory dish, homey but complex in flavor and texture, and typified for me the imagination and culinary good sense that Mercader possessed, and obviously passed on to his son-in-law.

For years, habitués of the Hotel Empordà, as it was eventually renamed yet again, had called the dining room, offhandedly and affectionately, "el motel"—and in 2011, in honor of the establishment's fiftieth anniversary, Jaume officially renamed the restaurant just that. He has continued to extend the menu, recasting familiar regional ingredients and dishes into new forms just as his father-in-law did. He makes a "pepper steak" of fresh tuna, wrapped around a denuded ham bone, then braised in red wine with black peppercorns. He turns monkfish into a warm terrine, then tops it with Mercader's garlic mousseline. One afternoon, he proudly brought me one of his latest creations, combining tiny snails and the sweet meat of pigs' feet, two common ingredients in the baroque multi-ingredient stews of the region, into a rich, complexly flavored, completely original terrine. Another time, he came up with a "paella" made not with rice but with lentils, and ornamented it with minuscule, vividly fresh scampi. And his black-eyed peas with shreds of crispy pig's ear has been known to convert even picky eaters who ordinarily eat no part of the pig except pork chops and bacon. There is nowhere that I'd rather eat in Spain.

IN 1986, IN THE MIDST OF MY RESEARCH, I took time out for an interlude of sheer gastronomic indulgence, a week of pure and excessive eating and drinking with no notebook in hand but some of America's leading culinary figures in tow. I'd become something of a regular at many of Barcelona's better eating places by this time, and word was starting to get around the local culinary community that there was an American writer in town asking serious questions about the region's cooking. One day, the gruff-voiced, highly respected local restaurant critic Luís Bettónica conveyed to me an irresistible invitation: His friends at the Barcelona Restaurant Association would like to fly in half a dozen or so top American chefs for a culinary tour of the city, at the association's expense; in return, the chefs would agree to cook a dinner based on Catalan ingredients for a group of local restaurateurs and food writers. Would I be interested in choosing the chefs and bringing them along on my next visit? Of course I would. I loved the idea, because it would give me a chance both to introduce some of my American chef friends to the food I'd been going on about in recent months and to help show off to my new Catalan acquaintances some of what was going on gastronomically in my own country.

Back in California, I started assembling the cast. Alice Waters was a given; more than anyone, she had championed Mediterranean cooking in America. Jonathan Waxman, then almost midway through his tenure as chef and coproprietor of the California-inspired Jams in Manhattan, was another easy choice, partly because we had become good friends by then and he would have killed me if I'd left him out, but also because he was a natural, intuitive cook, who I knew would be able to meet with aplomb the challenge of cooking a high-profile meal in a strange city. With the two coasts taken care of, I decided that I should bring somebody to represent other parts of the country, and thought at once of Mark Miller, who had made a name for himself cooking southwestern-inspired food at the Santa Fe Bar & Grill in Berkeley and was now working on a restaurant in Santa Fe itself, to be called the Coyote Cafe. To represent the Midwest, I invited Michigan-born Bradley Ogden, an amiable young chef who—though he was then in the kitchen at Campton Place in San Francisco—had come to prominence as chef at the American Restaurant in Kansas City. Because I wanted to acknowledge New England, and because I thought we needed another woman in the group, I added someone I'd met only once, Lydia Shire, then chef at Seasons in the Bostonian Hotel in Boston, and a cook whose food was big and bold in a way that I thought might appeal to the Catalans. Finally, to the delight of the publicity-conscious restaurant association, I invited two journalists to record the proceedings: my friend and former *New West* restaurant critic Charles Perry and—how could I resist?—Ruth Reichl, who had by that time become food editor of the *Los Angeles Times*.

A problem arose our first morning in town: It quickly became apparent that our hosts had arranged a program for us that included guided tours of the city and meals at a succession of old-line restaurants—the ones at the heart of the restaurant association— most of which, frankly, were a long way from the city's best. I wanted to show the group *my* Barcelona, and let them enjoy it at their own pace. We were good guests for a few hours, going along with a very pleasant young man from the city tourist board as he walked us along the Ramblas and through the Boquería, and then, happily, led us into Boadas, a tiny triangular bar known for its excellent cocktails and its showoff bartenders. Here, out of earshot of our guide, we agreed on mutiny. From a pay phone outside the bar, I called Luís Bettónica and explained the situation; if it wouldn't put him in a difficult position, I said, we wanted to be on our own, choosing our own restaurants, and would pay for our own meals— and, of course, still cook that dinner. He gave us his blessing and promised to square things with our hosts.

For the next six days, loosed from our keepers, we consumed Barcelona. Bradley, who had been to Europe only once previously, years earlier, before he'd become a chef, was quiet but obviously wide-eyed. Mark, on the other hand, was full of energy from the start, scrappy and opinionated, ready to sample almost any foodstuff, head off down almost any alleyway. Alice walked around with a contagious sense of wonderment, eyes wide, asking what everything was, sometimes exclaiming in delighted recognition, sometimes shaking her head briskly, in that way she has that reminds you that she was once a Montessori teacher, as if to say,

"I don't care if that's something everybody eats here, it's not very good." Waxman was relaxed—he'd been here before—and seemed to be standing back from the fray a little, sipping his cocktail, popping a few more deep-fried whole baby squid into his mouth. Lydia was quiet and observant, coming to life in the market when we'd pass a butcher's stall (she was probably the only one who knew what all the animal parts were, and how to cook them) or vegetable stand where she'd spy a heap of some Central American root vegetable that only she recognized. Charlie was studious and at first a bit restrained, but he kept a list of every morsel of food we ate at every meal and in between. Ruth just seemed in her element, roaming a fascinating city with people who were mostly longtime friends, addressing every dish with her usual critical equanimity. Like most good restaurant critics, she wanted to like everything.

Our first meal after Boadas was at Can Solé, a famous seafood restaurant in Barceloneta, the city's old fishermen's quarter. An aquarium's worth of perfectly fresh, mostly local raw fish and shellfish was arrayed on beds of ice near the entrance to the place, and there was much exclamation and inquiry from the chefs as we looked it over. Once we got settled at a big table in the upstairs dining room, we ordered almost everything. We shared big dishes of cuttlefish in tomato sauce; whole giant shrimp fried golden brown in their shells; monkfish and potatoes in caramelized garlic sauce; and, of course, espardenyes.

Over the next few days, we went to Petit París and Florián and Eldorado Petit. We drank constantly, starting our days with carajillos—cups of dense black coffee spiked with anisette or Catalan brandy—around eleven every morning. We went back to Boadas more than once, and to a comfortable, old-fashioned place called Dry Martini, where we drank cava or the "cocktail del día" (every bar seemed to have one, its name scrawled on a little blackboard or carefully lettered on small cards along the counter). Siestas were popular after lunch, which meant around five or six in the afternoon, and then it would be time for an aperitif, followed by a wine-fueled dinner, followed by a nightcap or three at Tres Torres or some other soigné "design bar."

One night I took everybody to La Vie en Rose, a dark, Piaf-themed watering hole in the Barrio Chino, which isn't literally a Chinatown, as its name suggests, but an old-fashioned seedy neighborhood of little urine-soaked streets off the lower end of the Ramblas. After a round or two of sidecars accompanied by the sound of scratchy 78s playing "Non, je ne regrette rien" and, yes, "La vie en rose," we headed off down the street back toward civilization. A tall, gaudily garbed transvestite prostitute walking past us must have assumed, from our singing and laughing, that we were making fun of her (nobody was, as far as I know) and pulled a little can of pepper spray out of her purse and let us have it. Poor Alice and Lydia got it the worst. I hustled them out of the barrio and we piled into cabs that sped us to a considerably more sophisticated drinking establishment called Ideal Scotch, where Alice and Lydia repaired to the ladies' room to flush out their eyes and wash their faces. "Forget it, girls," I'm afraid I said when they came back out to join us. "It's Chinatown."

We were having a great time, but there was a cloud on the horizon: The Dinner. The event was to be held at a little restaurant called Café de l'Acadèmia on the plaça Sant Just in the Gothic Quarter. It was a nice establishment with a modest menu of Catalan specialties, but certainly not one of the city's gastronomic landmarks, and I've always wondered if this choice of venue was some sort of act of revenge by the restaurant association for my rejection of their program and our subsequent gustatory independence. Of course, my chefs didn't realize quite how small and ill-equipped the Café de l'Acadèmia was. Everybody was having too much fun eating and drinking to worry about cooking.

The day before the dinner, we took an excursion out of town, taking a van the restaurant association had provided for us, to Tarragona, for lunch at a highly regarded restaurant called Sol-Ric. It was there, over a disappointing meal of mostly overcooked seafood, that the shape of the dinner was discussed for the first time. (Alice was later to maintain that the enterprise was cursed because we had talked about it over bad food.) Each chef, reasonably enough, wanted to prepare something that had at least some connection to what he or she might make back home. Waxman, who has a traditionalist streak, thought it might be fun to make clams casino as an appetizer. Mark felt that he had to grill something over a wood fire, and hoped that the kitchen had the facilities. Bradley had brought along blue cornmeal, something he rightly assumed would be a novelty to the Catalans, and was determined to make corn bread. Alice had some kind of gorgeous fresh salad in mind, and wanted to make sorbet. Lydia, still considered the junior member of the group, said something in an uncharacteristically meek voice about calf's brains, but nobody paid her much attention.

The next morning, the day of the dinner, we mounted a raid on the Boquería. Mark had seen some quail he liked the looks of a few days before, and thought that they'd be good to grill. Alice luxuriated in the produce, gathering up bundles of long, wire-thin wild asparagus and loading baby lettuces and plump blood oranges into her sack. Waxman went looking for his clams, and came back with some fresh shrimp and tuna, too. Bradley somehow found chiles and cilantro, neither in common use in Barcelona back then, and Lydia . . . well, she found her calf's brains, along with some jars of oversize salted capers.

When the shopping was done, we took everything back to the

restaurant, and for the first time the chefs took a close look at the kitchen. And blanched. It was tiny and ill-equipped. There was no grill, of course. There was no broiler or salamander (hence no clams casino). There was no ice cream maker (hence no sorbet). There were only four little burners, and barely any pots and pans. Even metal spoons and tongs were in short supply, and would obviously have to be shared. There was only one thing to do: We went out to lunch. The restaurant was a place called Senyor Parellada, near Barcelona's Picasso Museum, where we consumed a particularly rich, traditional-style meal including canelones with a livery filling (the defining dish of Barcelona's *fondes*, or casual inns, since an influx of Italian immigrants reached the city in the nineteenth century), pigs' feet with turnips, and a fricassée of veal tongue, pork cheek, and chicken livers, with plenty of rough Priorat red to wash it all down with. Before we knew it, it was almost five. Dinner was at ten, a respectable hour for the evening meal in Spain, with the reception starting an hour earlier. Now we were really in trouble.

I have no idea how we did what we did next. Somehow we got out of Senyor Parellada and found our way to the plaça Sant Just. Somehow we shrugged off the effects of the pigs' feet and the chicken livers and the wine. Because a grill was deemed essential, some kind Catalan or other went off to borrow a backyard barbecue from somebody's terrace, while Charlie and I trudged off down a winding stone street, found an old-fashioned charcoal seller in an alcove, and lugged two bags of blackened wood back to the restaurant. It started to rain lightly. I think because they were by that time a little mad at me for having gotten them into this, the chefs elected me to stand outside in the drizzle and get the fire started. Then Charlie took over and charred red peppers on the grill.

The kitchen, meanwhile, was in tumult. The wild asparagus

Alice had been so happy to find earlier was chewy and bitter, and ended up in the trash. Waxman started shucking clams with no apparent end in mind. "Peel this garlic," Mark ordered no one in particular (I took the job). Ruth was everywhere, putting her old cook's skills to good use, rinsing, peeling, dicing, stopping periodically to scribble notes. Lydia worked quietly in one corner, cleaning her calf's brains. Bradley saved the day for dessert—and impressed the other chefs along the way—by whipping up a kind of sangria sorbet, made with red wine and blood orange juice, using a couple of stainless steel bowls, some rock salt, and some ice in place of an ice cream maker. "I didn't know you could do that," said Alice.

The restaurant filled up at the appointed hour with some of my Barcelona friends, including the Jausases and Luís Bettónica, and more than a few of the chefs and journalists who had been helping me in my researches, as well as a few civic officials and, of course, the officers of the restaurant association. Leaving the professionals to their work, I sipped cava with the crowd, which was bursting with curiosity about just what kind of "American" food they would be served. Mark scared off at least a handful of the locals with his passed appetizer of tuna tartare with lime and chiles on toast. Lydia, on the other hand, scored big with her calf's brains, which she'd deep-fried in a light, crisp batter and served with deep-fried capers and parsley.

We sat down to a first course of clams and shrimp in the form of a seafood salad, with roasted peppers, green beans, white asparagus, radicchio, and peeled favas (which occasioned much comment, as Catalans never peel the beans). The main course was Mark's grilled quail, not a great favorite of the group—Catalans apparently prefer wild quail, and this was farm-raised—with assorted vegetables and some misshapen blue-corn muffins Bradley had gamely essayed. Everybody loved the sorbet, though, served with thin-sliced blood oranges and fraises des bois moistened with moscatel. The chefs got, and deserved, a standing ovation.

At about two in the morning, we staggered out of the Café de l'Acadèmia, looking for something to eat, and ended up toasting each other with cheap wine over bad pizza at a "drugstore" on the Passeig de Gràcia, then pillaging everybody's hotel minibars and drinking in Waxman's room until the sun came up.

Chapter 14

THE WEST BEACH CAFÉ,
Venice, California (1978–1996)

&

REBECCA'S,
Venice, California (1983–1998)

A S MY BOOK ON CATALAN CUISINE TOOK SHAPE and I became obsessed with following little gastronomic and historical pathways all over the western Mediterranean, I began spending more and more time away from home. On one of those evenings abroad, I called Leslie to catch up. We talked for a few minutes about the usual things, then she broke down in tears. "I'm just so *lonely*," she said. I should have gotten on the next plane back to L.A. right then and stayed home for a while, but instead I thought, I'm a professional and this is what I do; she's a professional, too, so she'll understand. Roughly one year and four or five trips later, in 1987, Leslie wasn't there to meet me at the airport when I landed, as she usually was. She moved out the following month.

As an unofficial bachelor in the months that followed, I spent three or four evenings a week between two Venice restaurants, the West Beach Café and Rebecca's, both owned by my friend Bruce Marder and his wife, the eponymous Rebecca. Like Ports before them, they became a second home to me. I knew everybody, staff and customers alike, got a lot of free drinks, could always nab a good table. The two restaurants were just across the street from each other, a block from the beach, and I sometimes thought of them as a kind of Scylla and Charybdis, each dangerous in its own way.

The West Beach—inevitably referred to, by at least some of its habitués, as the Wet Bitch, for reasons that would have soon become obvious to any young man spending much time at the bar there—was in many ways the definitive Southern California restaurant. It occupied a rectangular white cinder-block building with windows across the front; inside, the dining room, an open rectangle, was white with industrial gray carpeting and dark gray booths and a regularly changing, informally hung exhibition of art on the walls, most of it pretty good. There was an excellent wine list; there were short little tumblers filled with an assortment of loose cigarettes on the tables (this was years before restaurant smoking bans, of course); and there were people doing cocaine and beyond in the bathrooms.

The menu was smart and contemporary: At lunchtime, there were great Caesar salads and burgers and fries, among other things; the dinner menu might offer baked mozzarella with warm radicchio and green chiles, oysters topped with California caviar, vermicelli with six kinds of mushrooms, porcini risotto with fresh thyme, grilled duck breast tacos, roast pork loin with sage and sherry vinegar, a terrific New York steak seared on a *comal*, a Mexican griddle.

If the West Beach was minimalist in style, Rebecca's was baroque, in a contemporary way. It was, in fact, spectacular, a restaurant built around art and fun. The celebrated architect Frank Gehry designed the interior, a silly, playful jumble of onyx and Naugahyde, copper and glass, Brazilian blue granite and Plexiglas. A cartoon octopus hung with thirty thousand chandelier beads hovered over one part of the dining room; two limousine-length Formica crocodiles, lit up from within, were suspended over another part; telephone pole "trees" loomed here and there; and there was a private dining room with translucent, amber-colored walls above the bar. The booths were turquoise and the windows decorated with tarantulas painted by the artist Ed Moses. There was a forty-foot-long Peter Alexander black velvet painting on one wall, and a couple of Gehry's own trademark glass fish leapt up from a low dividing wall.

The food at Rebecca's was Mexican, but hardly the usual Cal-Mex stuff. Diners dug into red snapper ceviche, grilled tuna tostadas, lobster enchiladas, crab and shrimp tamales, chiles stuffed with pork picadillo, and squash-blossom quesadillas (made the real Mexican way, from raw flour tortillas, their edges sealed around their fillings), charred flank steak asada with cascabel chile sauce, and a remarkable flan served cold so that it almost suggested a nougat glacé. The margaritas were dangerous. People went comatose from them all the time—sometimes literally falling asleep over their dinners—because they were real margaritas, potent cocktails, as strong as martinis, made with good tequila, Cointreau, and fresh lime juice, not the lightly spiked fruit punch people were used to. I usually limited myself to one, then switched to wine. I also flirted ceaselessly with all the waitresses, an unusually attractive crew, though I never quite managed to go home with any of them. I took visitors from out of town, especially New Yorkers, there all the time, and they were always dazzled by it. There was simply nothing else like it, anywhere.

LESLIE AND I had discovered the West Beach shortly after we'd gotten married and moved to Venice. We liked it and went fairly often, and I also started meeting people there for lunch while Leslie was at work, or even just going in for a midday meal by myself. A lot of people thought Bruce Marder was sort of a jerk, not so much for anything he'd done but for what he didn't do—like greet customers warmly, send out free food, ask how folks were enjoying their meals. Like smile. As I got to know him, though, I discovered that I liked him pretty well. He was quiet and sometimes oblique, but he turned out to have a deadly sense of humor, and he really knew food.

I used to joke that Bruce smoked his way into the restaurant business, and I wasn't talking about the cigarettes he gave out at the West Beach. Brought up in Los Angeles, he enrolled in the UCLA School of Dentistry, decided that he didn't like it, and went off to hitchhike around Europe for a year. He ended up in southern Spain and wanted to go to Morocco. He took the ferry to Tangier, he told me over a bottle of Provençal rosé at the West Beach one afternoon, but the immigration man took one look at his long ponytail and told him to get back on the boat. He tried again the next week, and got turned away again. Finally, he lopped off the offending hair, put it into his passport, and handed the arrangement to his nemesis. The man smiled, tossed the hair into the garbage can, and waved him through. Once in Morocco, he ended up living in a van on a communal beach campsite, lying back and getting high. Everybody had to do something around the campsite, and he volunteered to cook meals. He discovered that he liked it, and on Christmas of 1972, he would tell Ruth Reichl sixteen years later, "All of a sudden it came to me that I wanted to be a chef."

Bruce thought he should start with a grounding in traditional French cuisine but couldn't afford to go to culinary school in

France. He ended up at a small institution in Chicago called the Dumas Père School of French Cuisine, run by a classically trained caterer and food stylist named John Snowden. Bruce learned the basics there, then returned to L.A., where he got a job as a cook at the Beverly Hills Hotel, and then worked for a week at the elegant and very French L'Ermitage in West Hollywood, before getting fired for leaving some plates in the oven to crack. His next job was cooking lunches at a little bistro called Café California, on Abbot Kinney Boulevard in Venice. Lunches did all right at the place, but it was dead at dinnertime, and it soon became apparent that the restaurant wasn't going to last very long. Bruce put up $500 of his own money to become a partner, closed the restaurant's dinner service, and kept the place going. After six months, it was doing fairly well, but the principal partner and Bruce didn't get along, so she offered to buy him out for $35,000. At almost the same moment, a Moroccan restaurant at the beach end of Venice Boulevard, called Casablanca Café des Artistes, was put up for sale—for thirty thousand bucks. A month or so later, the West Beach opened its doors.

I think Bruce was one of the best natural cooks in Los Angeles in that era. He had the French grounding, but he quickly picked up techniques from other cuisines. His risotto was as good as anyone's in town; his tacos tasted like something you'd get at a really good restaurant in Puerto Vallarta or Monterrey—and he was probably the first to interleaf Mexican fare on his menu with Italian and American dishes; his steaks put a lot of steak house meat to shame. He was miserly in the way that smart chefs used to be, always looking for a way to cut out the superfluous elements, and to cut costs by intelligently using by-products that other chefs would throw away. I'm pretty sure he was the only chef in the state who rendered the fat from all his beef trimmings—and then used it to cook his superlative French fries.

Bruce's partner in the West Beach—besides his wife, Rebecca, a onetime dance instructor from the California poultry capital of Petaluma—was a refugee from Nazi Germany named Werner Scharff, who helped start the Lanz clothing company and had been buying up and restoring property around Venice since the late 1940s. Scharff owned the West Beach building and another building across the street. When he decided that he wanted to put a restaurant there, too, he asked Bruce first. Bruce hesitated, but then decided that he didn't need competition from somebody else in his front yard, and that he could use the new place to showcase the Mexican food he was increasingly enamored of. Rebecca knew Frank Gehry, and asked if he'd consider designing the new place. He must have had a lot of fun with it—but Bruce worried that the interior was so busy and unusual that people wouldn't pay enough attention to the food. I thought the food held its own very nicely.

I SPENT THE Christmas holidays in 1987 in New York, staying in a cozy and comforting room at the Algonquin, which was then my favorite New York hotel by far—it was shortly to be sold and its quirky charms neutered—reading galleys of my Catalan book. Calvin Trillin invited me to an afternoon party on Christmas Eve at his place in Greenwich Village. One of the other guests, a good-looking woman of about my age with a young daughter in tow, looked at me with envy, if not something approaching awe, when I told her what I was doing in New York. "You're reading galleys of your book in your room at the Algonquin?" she asked. "Do you have any idea how romantic that sounds?"

Later that evening, I sat alone in my room, missing Leslie, missing California, eating a room service steak with a bottle of minor Bordeaux—which at some point I knocked over, staining a corner of the bedspread—and watching an episode of a short-lived cop show called *Beverly Hills Buntz*. "Romantic" was not the first word that sprang to mind.

Back in California, finished with Catalonia and vicinity for the moment, I dove back into freelancing, traveling around the country and going off to Europe periodically for *Met Home,* and meanwhile writing a weekly "Restaurant Notebook" column of industry news bites for the *Los Angeles Times*. I didn't have much heart for going out on dates, and stayed home and cooked for myself a lot, eating things I'd grown in our backyard—mesclun salads from French seeds; fat, deep red tomatoes, which I had to pick slightly unripe before our sweet-tempered golden retriever, Walter, gobbled them off the vine—and lots of fresh fish and shellfish and grass-fed steaks, which I grilled out back. When I did go out, it was almost always to the West Beach and Rebecca's, moving back and forth between the two, depending on who was where and what I was looking for.

Then, in the spring of 1988, *Catalan Cuisine: Europe's Last Great Culinary Secret* was finally published, to modest advance sales but good reviews. I dedicated it "To Leslie, malgré tot"—despite it all. In July, I wrote to my editor at Atheneum, "I thought *writing* the book was hard. Now my life has become a seemingly endless round of Catalan food festivals, Williams-Sonoma book signings, cooking classes (which I ought to be taking rather than giving), telephone interviews from Detroit and Denver, and who knows what else. Oh well. At least people are paying attention." In August I flew back to New York to appear live on *Good Morning America,* my first network television show, nervously demonstrating several recipes from the book and trying to impart to viewers some serious historical and cultural information. I was not a great success.

My TV appearance did have an enjoyable result. The food and beverage director at the new Scottsdale Princess hotel in Arizona happened to be watching the show. He was about to open a "fine dining" restaurant at the resort and was looking for a theme. Mediterranean cooking was just starting to get big, but that seemed to mostly mean Italian, and he wanted something with a twist, something he could promote for its originality. And there I was with my "culinary secret."

In November the Princess officially launched its Marquesa dining room as a Catalan restaurant, with a Catalan Cuisine Festival starring me. Over a three-day period there I did book signings, cooking demonstrations, and radio and TV interviews, gave the kitchen staff tips on Catalan cooking, and hosted a couple of private dinners for VIP guests. The original chef at Marquesa was a Basque, and the dining room manager was from Galicia, and though the menu was written in (imperfect) Catalan, the food wasn't much like anything in my book. Cheese tortellini with sun-dried tomatoes and manchego cheese was not Catalan cuisine; shiitake mushrooms, fontina, and fennel are not staples of the Catalan kitchen; nobody in Valencia has ever put veal in his paella. Ah, but the sun was shining, the pools were inviting, all my expenses were being paid . . . and I was there with my pretty new girlfriend, Paula.

I'd met Paula at a publike restaurant in Santa Monica called the Darwin. She was a waitress; I was a guy who came in by himself and invariably ordered a cheeseburger with fries and a bottle of good red wine. Paula was pretty and antic, and we flirted casually, and then more than casually. One night, I got up the nerve to ask her out to lunch the following Sunday. I took her to the West Beach. "Tell me all about yourself," I said when we sat down. "Make it fast and make it funny." She deftly obliged.

We got married in the fall of 1989, a few months after my divorce from Leslie had become final, and bought a two-bedroom condo in Santa Monica, just over the city line from Venice. The next year, we had a daughter named Madeleine. Two years after that, my second book, a collection of reworked older pieces and new essays called *Everything on the Table: Plain Talk About Food and Wine,* was published by Bantam Books, and by then we had a second daughter on the way.

I decided that it was time to sell another book. I wondered if I could do something on contemporary Catalan cuisine, as opposed to the mostly traditional cooking I had covered in my earlier book, but nobody considered that part of Spain in those terms yet (this was some years before the emergence of Ferran Adrià and his disciples), and I knew that it would be a tough sell. Then I started thinking in broader terms and wondered if there might not be a good book in modern Spanish food in general. I would roam the country, paying close attention, of course, to the innovative chefs of Catalonia, the Basque Country, and Madrid, but finding creative food in the restaurants of other regions as well.

I wrote up a proposal and sold it to Bantam, and made two brief reconnaissance trips to Spain, looking for good contemporary food and eating through my advance. The results were disappointing. I knew where to go in Catalonia, and to a lesser extent in Madrid and the San Sebastián area, and as expected I found some terrific modern cooking in those places. But in other parts of Spain, following friends' recommendations and a handful of guidebooks, I pretty much struck out. The comparatively few restaurants purported to be up-to-date and creative in places like Valencia, the Canary Islands, Majorca, Zaragoza, Huesca, and León mostly served things like foie gras with kiwifruit or filet mignon with blueberry sauce. I was looking for something more authentic, more organic; something with regional roots, based on traditional dishes but executed with a twist—like the esqueixada with white beans and angulas at Eldorado Petit or the crema catalana ice cream at the Hotel Ampurdán.

I decided to try once more. Jonathan Waxman came with me this time, and our trip turned out to be the most sustained, extravagant eating expedition of my life. We met in Paris and drove down toward Spain, polishing off snails in pastry, baby rabbit with sautéed cabbage, roast guinea fowl with new potatoes, truffled foie gras, and duck confit at various stops along the way. We ate well at Zuberoa in Oiartzun, near San Sebastián—lobster and asparagus salad with truffle vinaigrette, oyster and cauliflower soup, cuttlefish tartlets, and cod cheeks in green sauce.

We sat down to dinner the same night at the superlative three-star Arzak, in San Sebastián itself, but after more cod cheeks, this time with clams, and a truffle-stuffed roasted new potato, I found myself unable to eat another bite. Then Juan Mari Arzak himself proudly brought out our next course, roasted ortolans, those tiny, fabled birds, whose sale had long since been banned in France, that are eaten in a single bite, bones and all. I'd always wanted to taste one, but the way I felt, I couldn't even look at the things, and once the chef had returned to his kitchen, Jonathan looked at me and said, "I'm going to have to do this, aren't I?" "Yep," I replied. (He still regularly evokes the memory of this selfless act as proof that I owe him some vague cosmic debt.)

By the next morning, I had revived. Pushing on to Madrid, we had a leisurely, elegant lunch of fava bean salad, sea bass with fried seaweed, and oxtail with thyme sauce at Zalacaín, which had been the first three-star restaurant in Spain (it has long since been demoted to a single star). For dinner, we had a meal of a very different sort, at Iñaki Izaguirre's unconventional Jaun de Alzate, where the magnificently mustachioed chef-proprietor brought us cream of white bean soup with "sushis" of chorizo and blood sausage (the meats were not raw, but they were embedded in sushi rice, with spinach taking the place of nori); smoked eel in a potato basket with a salad of mangoes, apples, and red chiles; a salad garnished with grilled foie gras with balsamic vinegar; "hamburgers" of chopped hake with ratatouillelike pisto manchego; fried hake with piquillo peppers; and loin of wild boar stuffed with goat cheese. The meal was a lot of fun, and mostly pretty good, but I was concerned. This was some of the most imaginative "new" food I had encountered in Spain, outside of Catalonia at least, but there was something a little gimmicky about it, and I wasn't at all sure that American home cooks would want to reproduce any of it.

I got even more worried when we traveled south. The best new-style restaurant in Seville at that time was supposed to be Egaña-Oriza, partly owned by Izaguirre, and while we had a decent meal there—grilled langoustines, duck-breast ham with foie gras, stewed red partridge, wild boar ragout with dried cherries, and crispy al-mond crêpes with caramel ice cream—I ate nothing that demanded to be taken home. Driving back up Spain's Mediterranean coast, we found no intimations of the contemporary at all, though we did have some good traditional food, including a very satisfying arroz en costra—saffron rice with sausages beneath a crust that resem-bled a very dry omelette (the kind I will eat) loaded with bits of crispy pork.

In Catalonia, home territory for me, we ate extremely well, as expected, for a couple of days. Eldorado Petit lived up to my ex-pectations, as did Azulete, where Eldorado's former chef, Jean Luc Figueras, was now cooking. He made us angulas with langoustine "carpaccio," shrimp and sea snail salad, lobster with cabbage and artichokes in herb vinaigrette, sausage and potato ravioli with white beans, gilthead bream with tomatoes and confit garlic, goat cutlets with truffles, and fresh white cheese with pear compote. Driving back up to France, we had a knockout meal at Santi Santamaria's always dazzling El Racó de Can Fabes in Sant Celoni: mousse of wild mushrooms and sausage with truffles, whole truffles in pastry, savory custard with truffles, turbot on a bed of thinly sliced calf's head with sauce ravigote, and a couple of chocolate desserts. That was it for Spain.

When I appeared at the door of our condo in Santa Monica the night I got back, Paula took one look at me, shook her head, and said, "You've got Euro-bloat." She was undoubtedly correct. But I also had a bigger problem than that. My meals in Spain this time had confirmed what my repasts on earlier trips had suggested: There frankly wasn't enough good contemporary cooking in Spain in that era, especially outside the Basque Country and Catalonia, to justify a book. It had become pretty clear to me that I had sold a project about a nonexistent subject. (My problem, of course, was that I was a decade or so ahead of the times.)

I wrote my editor at Bantam a long letter explaining the problem, confessing that I had been premature in announcing the existence of viable contemporary Spanish cooking, and asked her to let me do something entirely different. That something was a book I'd had in the back of my mind for some time, a *Catalan Cuisine*–style treatment of the cooking of Liguria and its culinary cognate, the region of Nice. Not very happily, I thought, my editor agreed and rewrote the contract. "I'm going to have to start all over again," I told Paula. "I'm going to be gone a lot." Okay, she said, without a lot of enthusiasm. For the next two years, as other work—and finances—permitted, I'd go off to Nice or Genoa, prowl pretty little seaside towns, head up into the backcountry (the *arrière-pays* or the *entroterra*, depending on which country I was in), visit wineries and olive oil producers, and just generally immerse myself in the culture of the Italian Riviera and its Niçois counterpart.

In the fall of 1990, after our first daughter, Madeleine, was born, my friend and editorial mentor and boss at *Met Home,* Dorothy Kalins, sent me a fax, responding to the itinerary I'd forwarded to her for an upcoming trip of mine. "It seems to the casual observer," she wrote "that you have a certain propensity for movement . . . eating and running. . . . Why, aside from a *vacance en famille,* you are never any one place more than a single night at a time. Do you not see a certain capriciousness, a Peter-Pan-penchant-for-the-peripatetic, that seems at the very least unseemly for a *père de famille* such as your own self?" She certainly had a point.

In 1993 MET HOME changed hands, and Dorothy resigned. She spent a few months considering her possibilities, as they say, while I started trying to develop new freelance markets. Then one day in the fall of the year, Dorothy called me at my office in Santa Monica and said, "I've found us a magazine!" She'd met a couple of media entrepreneurs who had formed a partnership to buy and retool existing publications and develop new ones. The high-profile member of the pair was S. Christopher Meigher III (known jocularly by some of his former colleagues as Chris Three-Sticks), a diminutive, nattily attired, perpetually tanned twenty-four-year veteran of Time Inc. A. Douglas Peabody, his partner, had been an investor in *Hippocrates* and *Health* magazines and was a supposedly new-media-savvy member of the AOL board of directors.

The partnership's first acquisition was *Garden Design,* the Washington, D.C.–based organ of the American Society of Landscape Architects, which they planned to remake into an upscale garden-centered lifestyle magazine. Their second wasn't exactly an acquisition, but they licensed the name of, and made an agreement to reuse content from, a successful French food magazine called *Saveurs,* envisioning an elegantly turned-out American equivalent, to be called *Saveur,* singular.

In January 1994 I flew to Manhattan for an extended stay. While the hot young graphic designer Michael Grossman (late of *Entertainment Weekly*) crafted the look of *Saveur,* Dorothy and I sat with our friend Christopher Hirsheimer, who had been the *Met Home* food editor, in a conference room on Park Avenue and just made the damn thing up. Christopher was a marvel, tall and blond, smart and kind, born in California, raised in Australia and Hawaii, connected by personal history to Iowa, now domiciled in Pennsylvania with her big, quiet antiques dealer husband, Jim. She'd been a caterer and a restaurant owner and a cook, and had tested and written all the recipes for *Met Home,* becoming, like me, something of an honorary staff member.

By the time we started talking about *Saveur,* Dorothy, Christopher, and I had known one another for at least ten years. We had worked together, gone out to countless meals together, traveled together, and cooked together, mostly at Dorothy's apartment on East Fifty-Sixth Street or at the house she rented every summer for many years on Three Mile Harbor in East Hampton. We had different styles in the kitchen: Dorothy was meticulous and well organized and often seemed to be pursuing some platonic culinary ideal; I was on the rough-and-tumble, intuitive side, trying things that worked well about half the time; Christopher would let us scuffle, and then just quietly set about making little masterpieces with a "This old thing?" modesty. (One of her pet phrases, and not just about cooking, was "I know how to do this," and damned if she almost always didn't.)

As we sat endlessly in that conference room and talked, we realized that none of us, as much as we loved food, regularly read any of the existing food magazines; they just didn't seem to have any relevance to the way we thought and felt about the subject, or the way we cooked and ate. And it quickly became apparent that, however varied some of our culinary philosophies might seem, we agreed on the important things, on what our new magazine should and shouldn't do and why: We would not be trend spotters or lionize celebrity chefs but would cover restaurants only when they had some real significance, some larger meaning; we would assess wines and food products, but we would not assign numerical ratings to them; we would not offer readers yet another "new products" page full of jams and flavored olive oils and spatulas; and we would not publish, as I liked to say, "twenty-five recipes for quick-and-easy, low-fat, low-cal, boneless, skinless Tuscan chicken breast."

Instead, we talked a lot about the notion of food in context, about the stories behind food and the people who made it and the places in which it was made. We talked about how, in an increasingly complicated and fragmented world, traditional cooking could help people reconnect with their roots, with their families, with their world. And we talked about authenticity. Our standing reference point was "low-fat cassoulet," a recipe for which had recently appeared in *The New York Times*. You can make a dish of beans and turkey sausage cooked with olive oil instead of duck fat, I said, and if you're a good cook, you can probably make it taste okay. *But don't call it cassoulet.* If everybody publishes recipes for low-fat cassoulet—or for Tex-Mex cassoulet, fusion cassoulet, quick-and-easy, low-fat, low-cal, boneless, skinless Tuscan chicken breast cassoulet, whatever—then at some point real cassoulet is going to get forgotten. And that would be a shame not just because real cassoulet is a wonderful dish but also because it's a tradition, a cultural icon, a complex construction whose every element has historical and social implications. Let's give people the recipe for *authentic* cassoulet, we decided, full of sausage and duck confit and fat, as close to what you'd have in Toulouse or Carcassonne or Castelnaudary as possible. Let's give people the real thing.

THE FIRST ISSUE OF *SAVEUR*, dated Summer 1994, came out in April, and people seemed to love it. I wrote a feature story about Santa Barbara County wines and, under a pseudonym, a piece on Belgian beer for the issue. Much of the rest of the material in that and the following issues was supposed to be repurposed from *Saveurs*. We figured out pretty quickly, though, that our Gallic counterpart actually had very little to offer for our purposes. We translated and rewrote a few features, and in the early days bought rights to some of the photography, but, well, frankly their standards were not up to ours. Our name aside, we were soon completely independent of *Saveurs,* and creating a whole new kind of food magazine.

At first I worked from a distance, in my Santa Monica office, flying back to New York as often as I could, especially during closes. Inevitably, though, there came a day when Dorothy said, "I want you to start helping to manage the staff, which means you have to move east." I was hesitant. Although I'd spent a lot of time in New York, had probably as many friends there as I did in California, and knew the city fairly well, I hadn't lived outside my native state since brief stays in Atlanta and Cambridge thirty years before. On the other hand, the opportunity to edit a magazine we all knew was going to be significant, and to collect a regular and generous salary, was impossible to resist. Paula, who had lived in Manhattan for ten years before we met, getting a degree in acting from Juilliard, was all for it, too.

A few days before the end of the year, then, we packed up our condo (we'd decided to keep it and rent it out, just in case), and a moving van came and took away our California lives. The four of us—our second daughter, Isabelle, had been born in 1993— went to stay in a hotel in Marina del Rey while the truck began its transcontinental trip. Besides Chasen's, where I'd wanted to go one last time for a Christmas meal, I'd also wanted to have one more dinner at Rebecca's. This wasn't just because I was pretty sure it would be a long time before I had any decent Mexican food again, but also because I realized that the restaurant had come to symbolize a lot of what I loved about Venice and Santa Monica— the pretty girls, sure, but also the beach, the art, the easygoing social intercourse, the color and spice. In the end, we didn't have the time or, really, the money for either place.

On December 30, with Paula's cat cowering in a carrier under the seat, we flew to an icy New York City, then drove straight up to Connecticut to a hotel in Stamford, where we spent three nights waiting for our things to arrive. A few days into 1995, we moved into a two-story rental house in Old Greenwich with a fireplace, a semifinished basement, and a big, sloping backyard, which I later learned exploded into blossom in the spring.

WITH THE WEST BEACH and Rebecca's thriving, Bruce went on to open DC-3 at the Santa Monica Airport (christened after the legendary workhorse plane of the same name, some examples of which were produced in Santa Monica), with a bar-and-grill menu and an interior designed by the artist Chuck Arnoldi, and then Broadway Deli, in partnership with the great French chef Michel Richard. As these and other projects took more and more of his time, and he realized that he wanted to cook more upscale food,

Bruce decided to sell the West Beach. In 1996 it was taken over by James Evans, former general manager at the nearby 72 Market Street, and renamed James' Beach. Rebecca's lasted two more years, then Evans made an offer on it, too. The remarkable interior was mostly demolished, and the place was converted into a bistro and sushi bar called Canal Club.

Chapter Fifteen

ELEVEN MADISON PARK,
New York City (1998–)

W HEN ELEVEN MADISON PARK OPENED, IN 1998, at the southern end of Madison Avenue in Manhattan, I was working daily at the *Saveur* office in SoHo, not quite two miles to the south, and going straight to Grand Central Terminal after work every evening to take the train back to Connecticut. The restaurant was too far from *Saveur* to make it practical for lunch, and I almost never stayed in the city for dinner, so for the first year and a half or so of its existence, I remained ignorant of its charms.

When I did finally manage to get there, for dinner one night, my experience was something of a disaster, though not through any fault of the restaurant's. Dorothy had been to the place several times and become a great fan, and she contrived one evening to invite Emeril Lagasse and his wife to dinner at Eleven Madison with Christopher and myself, in the hopes of convincing him to contribute to the magazine. I'm sure we had a lovely meal that evening, perfectly served, but for whatever reasons, I was in a particularly gabby mood and monopolized the conversation, apparently alienating Emeril, with the result that we never heard from him again and Dorothy didn't speak to me for days. It was an inauspicious introduction to a restaurant that was to become such an important part of my life for the next half dozen years.

PAULA AND I SETTLED into our new lives on the East Coast. I became a commuter, with something I'd never really had before: a rigid daily routine. I'd wake up around five-thirty in the morning (the cat made sure of that), make coffee, and then descend into the basement, where I had set up my computer, and work for an hour and a half or so trying to finish my book about the cooking of Liguria and Nice, which I'd titled *Flavors of the Riviera.* The basement was damp and cold, with a big hole in one wall leading into the dirt-banked crawl space under the house, but there was no other place in the house where I could write without disturbing the family, or being disturbed by them. Reemerging upstairs, I'd quickly shower and dress, make breakfast and school lunches for the girls, say good-bye to everybody, and walk about a quarter of a mile to the Old Greenwich train station, where I'd catch the eight-eighteen to Grand Central.

At the office, I'd work all day, usually buying lunch from the halal cart on the sidewalk outside the office, then head back up to Grand Central and get on the six-thirty-seven back to Connecticut. I'd arrive home around eight, bathe the girls and put them to bed—Paula, worn out from caring for the kids all day, would by this time already be in bed, watching TV—and then make myself dinner, often just a can of soup. Then I'd go back down to the basement and work for another couple of hours. I'd get to sleep around eleven-thirty and then, as Jackson Browne once said, "Get up and do it again, amen."

I finally finished *Flavors of the Riviera,* and for a few months at least got a little more sleep. Things got better financially in 1996, when a well-known cookbook editor hired me to work on the new edition of *The Joy of Cooking*. The original *Joy*, written by a St. Louis housewife named Irma Rombauer, was full of personality and style. So were the numerous subsequent editions, in which Rombauer's daughter, Marion Becker, at first collaborated with her mother and then took over from her. This new *Joy*, though it would bear the byline of Marion's son, Ethan, was to be the work of literally scores of notable food writers, and it was to be not the vaguely folksy dictionary of home cooking that earlier editions had been but a veritable encyclopedia of recipes and techniques, comprehensive and international.

Just because it was to be comprehensive, I didn't think it had to be soulless. Working with photocopies of all the previous editions of *Joy*, I tutored myself in the Rombauer-Becker style, alternately chatty, authoritative, and witty, and always accessible. As one dauntingly long chapter after another for the new edition came my way, supplied by an A-list of well-known food writers (some of whom actually knew how to use the English language and some of whom hadn't a clue), I tried to shape the text in a way that would showcase their expertise but at the same time capture some of the feeling of the older volumes—and that would, above all, read with a certain consistency from one page to the next. I also rewrote headnotes, added or corrected historical information, and fine-tuned recipe instructions for clarity. Every word turned in by the large roster of contributors went through my computer. Each time I'd turn in my edit on a chapter, I'd add detailed notes and queries for the cookbook editor ("Do fajitas really belong in the sandwich chapter?" "On the subject of Foie Gras, here I would argue that we really should tell people how to devein it, and should give a recipe for terrine of foie gras." "I removed teff as a separate entry—I sort of worry about people who know too much about teff, unless they're Ethiopian—and placed it under millet, because though it is not botanically related, it is often grouped with millets in reference books.")

Ethan Becker seemed to like what I was doing and on two occasions, in appreciation of my work on specific chapters, had cases of expensive wine shipped to me. The cookbook editor's reactions, on the other hand, were unpredictable. She'd send me encouraging notes of the "I couldn't do this without you" variety one day and terse, scolding screeds about computer formats or excessive annotations the next. At one point, she informed me, rather belatedly, that she didn't want any "recycled old *Joy* material" after all, and the editors she hired subsequently (one of whom apparently got paid twice what I did) stripped out any intimation of "voice." I soldiered on, slogging through hundreds of thousands of words, practically falling asleep over some sections (six small-print pages on making a wedding cake?). For more than a year, I spent almost every morning and every night on *Joy*, and all day on the weekends, too. I didn't go to the beach the entire summer of 1997; I barely saw the sunlight. I barely saw Paula or the girls. But I finally finished the project, and the money I earned got us out of debt. Ultimately, when I saw what all the work I'd put into the project had become, I asked that my name be removed from the book's lengthy list of credits. Kim Severson, in *The New York Times,* later called it "the New Coke of cookbooks." I just thought it was a book in which the cooking far overshadowed the joy.

SAVEUR, MEANWHILE, HAD BECOME a hot property. *Adweek* called it "perhaps the ultimate food magazine." Readers loved it.

People discovered us quickly, the right kinds of people, people who understood what we were trying to do and liked the way we did it. I was out and about on *Saveur*'s behalf a lot, being interviewed, giving talks or chairing seminars, teaching cooking classes, and everywhere I went, people practically genuflected at mention of the magazine's name.

One of the best things about working at *Saveur* was that, with Dorothy at the helm, I could still sneak away and travel and come back with good, big stories. And since I was now in effect my own editor, I could give myself almost any assignments I wanted. I wrote articles on Haute-Provence and Margaret River, on Swiss wine and Islay whisky. I wrote about La Boqueria in Barcelona and about Claude and the restaurants we used to frequent in Paris. I wrote about cooking meat with the bone in, and cast-iron pans, and the glories of melted cheese (for which I won my first James Beard honor, the M. F. K. Fisher Award for "distinguished writing," no less).

Christopher had emerged as a first-rate photographer—she created what was to become a much-imitated style of food photography, naturalistic and sensual, and turned into what I called the magazine's visual conscience—and she and I became a team, flying off all over the place at short notice and bringing back stories. She was the perfect partner: She shot fast and smart and, quite beyond her photographic skills, knew food inside out; we'd spend hours in the car or over meals talking about what we'd just experienced, analyzing and synthesizing, which made my job as a writer all that much easier.

Our best trips were the long ones, for special sections. For one on California, our mutual native territory, Christopher and I drove the length of the state, literally from border to border (and down a few miles into Mexico), eating, interviewing, shooting, and talking. For a multipart celebration of Venice (the one in Italy), Dorothy joined Christopher and me, and we spent weeks, in various configurations, in that mythic city, even renting an apartment briefly at one point so that we could cook food straight from the markets. For a special issue on Burgundy, we traveled around that region for weeks, starting with an elegant lunch at the Hostellerie des Clos in Chablis, including escargots with confit garlic and pike perch with Chablis butter, and finishing with a remarkable meal cooked for us by the great chef Marc Meneau at the home of his friend Gérard Oberlé: tourte de groin de porc (a tall, round construction of golden brown puff pastry enclosing alternating layers of smooth, waxy potato and sweet, moist shards of meat from the snout of a well-fed Burgundian pig) and a real coq au vin, made with a real rooster, Oberlé assured us, "one that has crowed and screwed and had children and grandchildren!" "So much of what we eat in America is just arranging food on plates," Dorothy observed at one point, "but food like this is *cooking.*" Paula, meanwhile, was at home with Maddy and Isabelle.

IN 2000 THE *SAVEUR* OFFICES moved up to the corner of Park Avenue and Twenty-Third Street and, I soon figured out, into the culinary orbit of Danny Meyer. When I first met Danny, I didn't know anything about him, other than that he was a slender young fellow with a well-cut suit and a smile that looked more genuine than was often the case among practitioners of his métier. I found out later that he was brought up in St. Louis, where his father ran a travel business; worked summers as a guide for his father in Rome, and studied international politics there; graduated from Trinity College in Hartford with a political science degree and worked on the Illinois congressman John Anderson's failed independent presidential campaign in 1980; studied cooking in France; took his first food service job in 1984, as assistant manager at the now-vanished Pesca in Manhattan; liked the business and opened Union Square Cafe the following year.

The rest I learned gradually. To help Union Square Cafe stand out, Danny tried to parse the customer experience and trained his staff to offer the best possible service, in every sense—a refinement that was often forgotten in the vigorous Manhattan restaurant scene of the era, alternately cynically commercial and obstreperously creative. His efforts helped Union Square to flourish, and in 1994 he opened a second restaurant, Gramercy Tavern, nearby, in partnership with Tom Colicchio. I loved the place. Before he became a TV celebrity and built a restaurant empire, Colicchio was merely a terrific chef, his food confident, technically perfect, full of big flavors, and I particularly appreciated the fact that you could have fare like this in a restaurant that had a lived-in, almost rustic feeling to it.

In 1998 Danny opened two more restaurants, sharing the ground floor of an art deco skyscraper across the street from Madison Square Park. The original plan had been to install just one large restaurant in the 22,000-square-foot space, but it was bisected by a load-bearing wall, so Danny would have ended up with two dining rooms connected by a door. That didn't make sense to him, so instead he created two separate places: a stunningly beautiful modern American one in the larger portion of the space, and what was almost certainly the country's first serious Indian fusion restaurant on the other side of the wall. The Indian restaurant, with the talented Indian-born Floyd Cardoz in the kitchen, was called Tabla. The showplace was Eleven Madison Park.

The designers, Bentel & Bentel, had a lot to work with: The

ceilings were twenty-five feet high, the walls and floors were pristine marble, and one whole side of the dining room was inset with broad, twenty-foot-high paned windows looking out onto the park. Bentel & Bentel raised the bar area and half the dining room slightly to improve sight lines and transected the lower portion of the space with a long two-sided banquette. Handrails and trim were made of nickel bronze, commonly used for accents in the deco era but rare today (the metal was imported from Australia). Room dividers were lustrous blond English sycamore inset with geometric tracery and pale green images of leaves. In three places around the room, immense black-and-white oils by the artist Stephen Hannock depicted scenes of Madison Square Park, based on photographs from the early twentieth century. All this added up to a brilliant job of evoking the past without descending into caricatured nostalgia. It was also purely and unmistakably a *New York* restaurant, full of energy and majesty and a subtle conjuration of the glamour of an earlier era. I thought it was a vivid expression of the style and spirit of the city as much as, though in a different way than, the legendary Four Seasons was. There was a kind of Gothamite grandeur to both.

FOR MY FIRST FEW YEARS AT *SAVEUR*, I remained blissfully ignorant of larger management and financial issues at the magazine, mostly because Dorothy shielded me (and Christopher) from such concerns so that, she later told us, we could concentrate on our work. I began learning more about the internal workings of the company when Chris Meigher instituted monthly department head meetings, in which I was included. These were basically state-of-the-business sessions, with progress reports from the publishers and circulation people. To my initial surprise, the news was rarely good, and the editorial side was continually asked to cut costs, reduce staff, and keep manuscript and photography fees low (they were already substandard). I used to be quite vocal in my opposition to cost-cutting attempts, pointing out that we were already putting out a champagne product on a beer budget, and that saving money in the short term could undermine our value over time. After one of the meetings, at which I had directed my ire directly at Chris, I ended up at the urinal next to him in the men's room. "Are you going to piss on me, too?" he asked.

The situation had degenerated seriously by 1999. Chris and Doug were fighting. Our investors were unhappy. *Saveur* and *Garden Design* hadn't started making money yet, and a society magazine cum real estate throwaway Chris had bought, called *Quest*, was apparently draining capital from the company. So was Doug's pet project, a doomed web portal he called (not very imaginatively) Europe Online, which ended up costing Meigher Communications a large write-down. In January 2000, Chris and Doug sold *Saveur* and *Garden Design* to a Florida-based publisher of water sports and game fishing magazines. The sale was a good thing: The company was pretty much dead by that time anyway, and if Chris and Doug hadn't found a buyer, the magazines would have disappeared. But it was also, we found out soon enough, a bad thing—sort of like being rescued from a sinking ocean liner, then discovering that you're on a lifeboat manned by cannibals.

For some time, it was business as usual. Our new owner and his wife—I'll call them Dick and Bambi—took an apartment in New York and tried to develop a social life in the city. But while Bambi flourished in the downtown party scene, Dick seemed ill at ease, intimidated, suspicious of New York and the way people lived there. There was speculation that Dick had bought *Saveur* in the first place as a plaything for Bambi—who had been to culinary school (and who asked me, wide-eyed and with no sense of irony, the first time I met her, "Are you a foodie?")—and she would periodically show up at our office looking for something to do, staying for a day or a week or occasionally a month until she got bored.

Dick was a weird bird, with a slightly nasal, slightly whiny voice and a clammy handshake, and an almost pathological aversion to confrontation. He seemed incapable of expressing himself in a group without the aid of PowerPoint, and was a micromanager who never seemed to be reachable when some micromatter needed to be managed. And he couldn't keep a publisher: We had six in the first five years of Dick's ownership.

It became apparent pretty quickly that Dick didn't have the slightest idea what made *Saveur* work, or what made it special. He wanted it to run like his other magazines. He thought we were "arrogant" because we cared so much about accuracy, good grammar, and production values. ("Nobody cares if there are mistakes in the magazine," he once said. "Everybody makes mistakes.") He also thought guidelines governing the interface of editorial material and advertising were for suckers. I told him once that I thought he was like a guy who had built a chain of successful coffee shops in Florida and then, for some reason, bought Daniel or Jean-Georges in New York City, expecting it to work the same way. I pictured him, I said, casting a jaundiced eye on his new holding and saying, "My chefs in Florida don't wander around the dining room"; "My chefs in Florida don't run food costs that high"; "My chefs in Florida don't change the menu every day." . . .

Dorothy saw where things were going and left in 2002 to take a job as executive editor of *Newsweek*. Christopher followed Dorothy out the door a month or so later, taking a short-lived post at Rodale Press, then going off to freelance as a photographer, shooting books for what seemed like every famous chef in America and continuing to work on stories for us. (Today, she and Melissa Hamilton, who had run the *Saveur* test kitchen for some years, create and publish the wonderful Canal House series of periodical cookbooks.)

Dorothy's good advice to me when she left was that I should just keep doing what I was doing for as long as I could. We had a solid editorial team—I always said I would have put them up against any editorial staff in the country—and we kept trying to put out the best magazine possible. Sometimes the obstacles we faced were almost comical. One day Dick called a meeting of the magazine's top editorial, sales, marketing, and circulation people. When I walked into the conference room, there was Bambi, sitting up straight, with a notepad in front of her and her eyes sparkling expectantly, as if it were her first day of secretarial school. I had no idea what she was doing there. As it turned out, her main contribution to the proceedings came when we were discussing an upcoming article—one of our trademark authoritative pieces, narrow and deep, on the subject of octopus, by the respected Greek-American writer Diane Kochilas. "Are the recipes just going to be for octopus?" she asked. That was the idea, I said. "Well . . . ," she asked, "what if you added some recipes for things people eat *with* octopus?"

I don't think like this—really—but that day I went back to my office, sat down at my desk, and said to myself, Ferran Adrià keeps my Catalan cookbook in the kitchen at elBulli, Alice Waters came all the way to Budapest a few months ago to help me celebrate my birthday, I just got a note from Michel Guérard apologizing for not having been able to spend more time with me on my recent visit to Eugénie-les-Bains, and that contraption propped up on the cabinet is a wood-frame chitarra for making pasta that Marcella Hazan went to some trouble to order for me as a gift—and I have to listen to Bambi telling me how to edit an article?

AS THINGS WERE GOING DOWNHILL at *Saveur,* first under Chris and Doug and then with Dick in charge, I started having trouble at home, too. Paula had turned forty in 1996, and was beginning to question what she'd done with her life, where she'd ended up, where she was going. My long absences—not just all my travel around the country and to Europe but the simple fact that, as Paula pointed out, I went to work every morning in a different state—had again taken their toll, and what must have once seemed like the pleasures of being married to a guy who went to restaurants for a living and talked about food and wine all the time had turned into annoyances. When Maddy and Isabelle both got old enough to spend much of the day in school, Paula had started working out at a nearby health club and found kindred spirits there, people whose idea of a good time was a twenty-mile bike ride, not a four-hour meal. She got a job selling memberships at the club and began teaching Spinning classes and yoga there, and the club, and its habitués, became the focus of her days.

We had a rough couple of years and talked about separating, but kept putting it off. Finally, in June 1999, the day after the girls had gotten out of school for the summer, we sat them down before lunch—they had been promised a trip to McDonald's—and told them that I would not be living with them anymore. There were a few moments of silence. Then Isabelle asked her mother, in what I remember as a very small voice, "Will Daddy ever come live with us again?" "Nobody can predict the future," Paula answered, "but probably not." There was another pause. Then Isabelle asked, "Can we still go to McDonald's?" I thought that was about the saddest thing I'd ever heard.

THE NEW *SAVEUR* OFFICES were only two blocks from Eleven Madison Park. I'd been back a few times by then, and the gorgeous interior and good food had pretty much erased any memories of my disastrous first meal there. The chef was a tall, soft-spoken, Pennsylvania-born Irish-American named Kerry Heffernan, who'd cooked under David Bouley and, at Mondrian, under Tom Colicchio. Kerry was a solid technician who seemed equally at home making grilled sandwiches of chicken, bacon, and Saint-André cheese or English pea flan with morels or lobster with lemongrass velouté. The service was vintage Danny Meyer, which is to say intelligent and efficient, and the interior settled a kind of calm on me, transporting me into a world far from my daily concerns.

Eleven Madison became my canteen, my after-work hangout, my preferred venue for business lunches. I made almost everybody come to me there. I'll buy lunch, or drinks, I'd say, but I'd like to go to Eleven Madison. Nobody ever turned me down. Sometimes I'd have a serious meal at the place, maybe roasted root vegetables with a truffled chèvre parfait or twice-baked fingerling potatoes with truffles, followed by roasted capon or some beautifully presented, very fresh fish of some kind. (Kerry was an avid fisherman who knew his seafood.) Other times I'd have what I called my "diet lunch"—half a dozen oysters followed by Kerry's oxtail and foie gras terrine. The restaurant's plateau de fruits de mer was one of the most spectacular in the city, sparkling fresh and full of variety, and the oysters in particular were always superb. One day I took Johnny Apple, who had written some pieces for *Saveur*, to lunch at Eleven

Madison. There were Martha's Vineyard oysters that day, and we ordered a dozen to share. They were so good that we ordered a second dozen. And then a third. I don't remember what we had as main courses.

It is a measure of how much at home I felt at Eleven Madison that when I looked around the office on the afternoon of September 11, 2001, and realized that there were still ten or twelve of the editorial staff at their desks—whether they couldn't get home or just didn't have anybody to go home to, I didn't know—I spontaneously invited them to lunch with me at the restaurant. There were only a handful of people sitting at scattered tables, talking in hushed tones, and an appropriately dark mood suffused the interior. Richard Coraine, one of Danny's partners, welcomed us. I explained that we'd been working, and needed some comfort before figuring out what to do next. He brought us food, he brought us pricey wines on the house—Château Rayas, Château Lafite Rothschild—and he brought us updates. We all talked, nervously at first, more confidently as the wine took hold; we relaxed; as a staff, we had always been reasonably close, but I thought we somehow drew still closer together over our well-laden table. After lunch, we all went our own ways, by no means immunized against the day's horrible events, but somehow at least a little bit restored. That's the kind of place Eleven Madison had become for me.

WITHIN THE FIRST SIX MONTHS Dick owned *Saveur* and *Garden Design,* every single member of the sales and marketing staff for both magazines, publishers included, had either quit or been fired. He quickly restaffed, mostly with junior people who would work for a lot less money than the experienced crew he had inherited, and a sea of new faces appeared around the place. One of these was a young woman named Erin Walker, many years my junior. She'd been hired as the publisher's assistant, and then almost immediately, with no sales experience, was thrust into a job selling the magazine's wine and spirits advertising.

I didn't notice her at first, and then I did. She was petite but buxom, with gray-green eyes and hair that she seemed to change in style and color every six weeks or so. She walked around as if she knew a bunch of secrets. There was something mysterious and alluring about her—something sexy in what may or may not have been an unwitting way. Since 1998, estranged from Paula even though we still shared a house, I'd had an on-again, off-again long-distance relationship with a strawberry-blond PR woman from Texas named Pam, great fun and a good excuse for me to spend time in a state that I'd always found particularly appealing for many reasons (food, music, landscapes, people)—but now I started flirting casually with Erin, too.

When my Texan and I broke up for the last time, I started wondering if I should ask Erin out. I'd bought tickets to see an Austin-based honky-tonk band called the Derailers, intending to take my friend Carolynn, a sometime *Saveur* contributor, but she went out of town at the last minute. I'd learned by then that Erin liked music, country and otherwise, and sent her an email offering her the tickets. Or, I added, if you just want to go see the band and don't have anyone else to go with, we could just go together. She chose option B. The Derailers were terrific. Erin later told me that when I got up to go to the men's room, one of the people we were sharing a table with said, "I think it's so nice that your dad takes you out to hear music." A few months after our first evening out, we had become a couple, though we made sure that nobody at the office knew.

Erin and I both had expense accounts, and we started using them frequently to take each other out to lunch. At least once a week, and sometimes more, we'd have that lunch at Eleven Madison Park. Though it was only two blocks from our office, it simply wasn't the kind of place Dick and his people would dream of going. It was too expensive, and too urbane. On only one occasion did we ever encounter somebody related to *Saveur* there—not an actual employee but an old-school magazine consultant widely known as Old Walrus-Butt, whom Dick considered his mentor—and we feigned a serious business strategy conversation until he left.

The restaurant was our escape. Whatever the stresses or frustrations of our jobs, they were always temporarily alleviated by the warm calm of the place, and the pampering we inevitably enjoyed there. Even Kerry played the game: Chefs who know or recognize me commonly send out extra dishes when I'm sitting in their restaurants, and surprisingly often these are contrary to the spirit of the dishes I've chosen myself, or repeat ingredients that I've already ordered enough of (if I've asked for the grilled asparagus, I probably don't need the asparagus soup, too); their largesse is inevitably presented with the announcement that "the chef wanted you to try this." (I always think, but never say, "But what about what *I* want?") If Kerry had something he thought Erin and I might enjoy, on the other hand, he'd send a waiter out to ask whether we were in a hurry that day or settled in for a leisurely lunch. If the former, he'd just let us eat what we'd ordered; if the latter, he'd send out a small portion of some new dish or something based on an ingredient that had just come in, just enough for us to try and always chosen to work in harmony with the rest of our meals. We appreciated his thoughtfulness far more than we appreciated some other chef's extra offering of sautéed foie gras or wild mushroom risotto.

Erin quit *Saveur* in 2003, in part because she was having trouble working with the current publisher, but also because she thought it would be better for our relationship. We continued to have lunch and drinks at Eleven Madison, though—I guess you could say it was where we courted—and even chose it as the place to meet on the icy, windy evening when we agreed that things weren't working out and we should go our separate ways. A week later, we were back at the restaurant having lunch, and a couple of years after that, we met Eleven Madison's special events director there to investigate the possibility of getting married in the restaurant.

In October 2004, *Saveur* celebrated its tenth anniversary with a special issue featuring a roundtable discussion about how food in America had changed over the ten years of our life thus far. Ten of us—including Dorothy Kalins, Mario Batali, Deborah Madison, Zarela Martínez, Chuck Williams, Rich Melman, Marion Nestle, Mimi Sheraton, Robert Schueller (of Melissa's Produce), and I—sat down for lunch at Barbuto, Jonathan Waxman's restaurant, and a couple of hours of vigorous conversation. The anniversary issue itself introduced a slightly redesigned cover and some new departments. It seemed like an appropriate time to freshen up *Saveur*, to enliven and update it without losing our basic identity.

Dick had other plans for us, though. When people used to ask me what it was like to work for him, I'd always grimace, but say, "At least he doesn't touch editorial." And then he did. He flew up from Florida one day to meet with me privately, one-on-one—remarkable in itself—and to announce that "we're making some changes in *Saveur*." He was moving the positions of managing editor, art director, photo editor, and production manager to the

Florida office, he said, and I needed to give the people currently occupying those posts in New York three weeks' notice. He had also had the magazine redesigned by his most talented art director, a graduate of the Ringling College of Art & Design in Sarasota, who up till then had performed design duties for *Sport Diver*, another of his publications. I'd get to see the new look shortly, but it wasn't open to negotiation. I was welcome to stay on, he added, as long as I could work within the new framework.

I needed the job—I was paying alimony and child support to Paula by this time—so I axed four talented, hardworking colleagues, gritted my teeth, and tried to keep the magazine going on the highest level that I could. The letters and emails that poured in when the first "new" issue hit the stands were heartbreaking: "After all your hard work your new format belittles the quality you so strove to achieve," wrote one correspondent. Another said, "Please see to it that the subscription to this address is canceled. I can't bear to watch this magazine be dragged down like this." More than one correspondent suggested that our new cover resembled that of *Better Homes and Gardens* (one said *Woman's Day*). One of the hardest things I've ever had to do professionally was to read these comments and know that I couldn't respond to them, because I agreed with them absolutely and couldn't say so without losing my job.

I looked around the office one day, early in 2006, and realized that *Saveur* wasn't fun anymore. I felt that our name had been cheapened by the tacky redesign, and by inferior spinoff projects under the *Saveur* name, over which we had no control (an embarrassing "advertorial" publication called *Saveur's Wine Country*; one-shot recipe compilations coedited by, lord help us, Bambi). Our very watchword, "authenticity," had become commonplace, a marketing cliché. "Why can't you do an article on twelve authentic chefs?" asked our associate publisher one day.

That crack staff we'd once had was almost all gone. The ones I hadn't been forced to fire left either for personal reasons (a new baby, a spousal transfer to another city) or just because they had grown disheartened. There were some talented, if comparatively inexperienced, new people at the editorial desks, and we were still somehow managing to put good words and images on the pages; readers still regularly praised our stories; but the process of producing those stories, at least with the same standards we'd always maintained, had become agonizing, and the results, however good they might sometimes have looked, had grown empty at heart.

In the spring of 2006, the Swedish publishing giant Bonnier bought a forty-nine percent interest in *Saveur*'s parent company— the original *Saveurs*, ironically, was published by the French branch of the Bonnier family—and Dick told me that Jonas Bonnier, the executive vice president of the company, had specifically demanded further reductions in our magazine's budget. For starters, he was cutting my salary in half. I probably should have left *Saveur* a couple of years earlier, but now there was no way I could stay on. Late in July, I packed up almost thirteen years' worth of books, papers, artifacts, and memories and moved out of my office, ready for the next course.

DANNY MEYER KNEW that Eleven Madison Park was a gem of a restaurant, a unique space with a crack service staff, and at some point he began thinking that the food was too casual, too brasserielike. An establishment as unique and elegant as Eleven Madison, he reasoned, should offer sophisticated fare to match—

food as good as that served by the top French restaurants in the city. Shortly before I quit *Saveur*, he asked Kerry to move over to Hudson Yards, his new catering operation, and, in pursuit of his culinary goal, brought in a Swiss-born chef named Daniel Humm, who had worked at Pont de Brent, Gérard Rabaey's three-star restaurant in Montreux, and then won accolades as the chef at Campton Place in San Francisco.

Humm banished such plebeian fare as seafood platters and grilled cheese sandwiches from the menu, and the restaurant became less and less the kind of place you could stop by for a casual lunch. He introduced sea urchin "cappuccino" with cauliflower mousse, peekytoe crab salad, and sea urchin roe; slow-poached egg with brown butter hollandaise, asparagus, Parmesan foam, and a Parmesan tuile; and poached lobster with curried granola to the menu. Frank Bruni gave Humm four stars in *The New York Times* and declared that his cooking "bridges the classically saucy decadence of the past and the progressive derring-do of a new generation." The restaurant soared so high that it left Danny's orbit. In 2011 Humm and his general manager, Will Guidara, who had worked at Spago in Beverly Hills and then run the restaurants at the Museum of Modern Art, bought the place and took it in their own direction.

There are no à la carte offerings at Eleven Madison these days, only a fifteen-course prix fixe menu at $195 per person. That menu has a New York theme; the diner will enjoy sophisticated reimaginings of a bagel with smoked sturgeon, an egg cream, and a black-and-white cookie (actually served twice, first in savory, then in sweet form), among other things, in addition to such dishes as seared scallops with pear gelée and caviar and roast duck crusted with Sichuan peppercorns and served with sweet cabbage and foie gras. Eleven Madison is now surely one of the half dozen best restaurants in New York City, a place with a lot of stiff competition—which is, frankly, not something that could have been said about it in the old days. But it is the chef's restaurant, not the customer's.

Chapter 16

COUNTRY CHOICE,

Nenagh, Ireland (1982–)

&

ELBULLI,

Cala Montjoi (Roses), Spain (1961–2011)

IN THE FIRST DECADE OF THE TWENTY-FIRST CEN-
tury, the two most important restaurants in my life, after Eleven
Madison Park, were a modest café and food shop in the Irish ag-
ricultural town of Nenagh, in County Tipperary, that served soda
bread with farmhouse butter, artisanal cheeses, and beef and Guin-
ness pie, and an avant-garde Catalan temple of gastronomy on an
isolated piece of rugged coastline eighty miles northeast of Barcelona, hailed as the best restaurant in the world, where the menu was
more likely to offer spherified Parmesan gnocchi and sea anemone
with rabbit brains and oysters. Both places made me feel at home
and fed me frequently and well, though with particulars so different
as to seem from different planets, and both inspired books that, in
their turn, consumed me.

I MADE MY FIRST TRIP to Ireland late in my traveling career, in 2002, to participate in an International Specialty Food Symposium in the town of Kinsale, in County Cork. The symposium, held at a local hotel, was frankly not the most exciting I'd ever been to. I did my part, speaking on the importance of recognizing and nourishing regional food traditions, and participating in panels with the legendary Myrtle Allen of Ballymaloe House and Paul Rankin, the chef who'd brought Northern Ireland its first Michelin star. But when various government ministers and academicians started talking about subsidies and export schemes, I slipped out and found my way to the hotel bar, in which a closed-circuit monitor had helpfully been installed, so that it was possible to have a glass or two and still be apprised of the conference proceedings. Here I fell into conversation with the proprietor of a seafood restaurant near Dublin, and for half an hour or so helped him deplete a bottle of Jameson.

Then something coming from the TV screen got my attention—an unmistakable change in tenor. My ears perked up. A casually dressed young man with slightly unruly hair, clearly no government minister, had taken the microphone and was orating with great passion about the wondrous simple pleasures of the basic Irish diet—about the richness of the milk, the opulence of the butter, the homey flavors of the fresh-baked bread. Ireland was blessed with some of the finest raw materials in all creation, he proclaimed, and honest Irish home cooking was part of the nation's cultural heritage. His punch line, widely quoted in the days to follow in the Irish press, was something to the effect of "When we invite visitors here from England or America and give them imported food from a German-owned supermarket, it ought to be considered an act of treason!"

This was a man I had to meet. When the conference recessed

for the afternoon, I found him talking with some cheese producers and went over and introduced myself. His name was Peter Ward, he said, and he owned a little grocery shop and café called Country Choice in the Tipperary town of Nenagh. I asked if I could come visit him on a future trip to Ireland and get to know some of that wonderful Irish food he had enthused about so vividly. He'd be delighted, he said. A few months later, with Christopher in tow, I returned to Ireland to spend time in Nenagh and concoct a story for *Saveur*. We had a wonderful time with Peter and his wife, Mary, a delightful diminutive blonde with a sunny smile and a no-nonsense core. Country Choice turned out to be a small place on Nenagh's main street, with a lacquered dark magenta façade bearing the words "Country Choice Delicatessen Coffee Bar P. & M. Ward." From one end of the storefront hangs a sign reading "Rogha na Tuaithe An Rogha Nádúrtha"—Irish for "Country Choice the Natural Choice" (Peter is an Irish speaker and champion of the language), below a picture of a pig with an expression that suggested he'd be delighted to become your bacon.

Inside, there was a short glass display case on the left, full of cheeses and cold meats plus a few plucked pheasants and some fresh eggs from a nearby chicken coop, and a long shelf on the right stocked with everything from Irish apple balsamic vinegar and dried seaweed to Italian olive oil and cans of Spanish peppers. Farther back in the shop, past a few baskets full of inexpensive but well-chosen wines, was a scattering of bare tables with a miscellany of chairs. (There were more tables in a small room upstairs.) Behind an L-shaped counter in one corner, a couple of women brewed pots of tea and pulled shots of espresso, heated up homemade scones (served with one of Mary's preserves or marmalades), sliced wedges of quiche made with various Irish cheeses, and at lunchtime fried hamburgers made with beef from local grass-fed

Herefords or ladled up Cashel Blue and broccoli soup and other similarly homey fare.

We hung out at Country Choice for days, meeting the neighbors (the old man who grew vegetables for Peter in a tiny strip of land in a courtyard across the street; the nun from a few blocks away who'd arrive at the shop every morning in summer with baskets full of greens from the convent garden), learning at Peter's side how to make three kinds of Irish bread, tasting the preserves Mary had just put up. We drove with Peter out to a farm a few miles from town where a young woman produced exquisite butter every day by hand. We ate dinner at home with the Wards while Peter filled us full of Irish history and lore, and of lamb's liver in whiskey sauce and heaps of colcannon, the Irish staple of potatoes mashed with butter, cream, and shredded kale.

Peter told us stories bemusedly (about, for instance, the high-tone woman who wanted to know why he couldn't ask his farmers to grow all their asparagus to the same length in order to make preparing it easier), disdained various politicians and bureaucrats who he thought were squandering Ireland's culinary heritage through dim-witted laws or erratically enforced regulations, excoriated the big supermarket chains selling imported meats and produce of inferior quality in competition with the necessarily more expensive locally grown alternatives, and often suddenly remembered yet another Irish product or artisan producer that we simply had to get to know. As we sat there with him, sipping coffee and sometimes wine, nibbling dense bread with rich butter and good cheese or plowing into something heartier, we gradually came to realize that Peter knew almost everyone concerned with food in any part of Ireland—and that little Country Choice, in a town not many people outside Ireland had even heard of, was in a way the focal point of all that was exciting and delicious in Irish food today.

Our piece appeared the following March as a *Saveur* cover story. Peter was very pleased. So were we. Christopher has pointed out that when we travel someplace to do an article based around somebody's shop or restaurant or home, we become part of their lives for two or three days, often almost part of their family—and then, when our work is done, despite the proclamations of eternal friendship that accompany the good-bye hugs, we usually never see them again. But we stayed in touch with Peter and Mary, exchanging letters and emails, and in 2004, with their encouragement, we flew back to Ireland to research another Irish story.

At first we were going to concentrate on a retired chef named Gerry Galvin, one of the pioneers of modern Irish cooking, who now wrote about food from his home near Galway. He agreed to cook a meal for us in the borrowed catering kitchen above Sheridans, the Galway cheese shop that was considered Ireland's best. Galvin was a charmer and obviously a natural good cook, and the day went well. Peter had suggested that, as long as we were in Galway, we should drive a short distance to the north to a town called Oughterard, to visit a young small-town butcher, trained in Germany, named James McGeough, who made pig-shaped salami flavored with local heather and cured Connemara lamb shoulders like prosciutto. We took his advice, and liked McGeough and his inventive but somehow very Irish-seeming products, and at some point, driving back to Dublin to meet Peter and Mary for a farewell dinner, Christopher and I decided that what we really ought to do about Ireland wasn't just another story but a whole special issue of the magazine.

We made four trips back to the island in the months that followed, driving all over the country, covering thousands of miles up and down and around the Republic and into Northern Ireland. We spent much more time at Country Choice and at home with

Peter and Mary, but we also went to Hare Island off the West Cork coast, where a reclusive French-trained Irish chef, who'd once cooked at Taillevent, prepared fixed-price dinners nightly for a handful of diners. We prowled the eerily beautiful glaciated limestone reaches of the Burren in County Clare, and ate immense pink Clare lobsters at a hotel there called Gregans Castle. We visited half a dozen cheese producers and three artisanal salmon smokers, each with a different philosophy of smoke. We ate in country house hotels and small-town pubs, and were invited into private homes not just to dine but to watch how dinner was made. We spent time at the consistently influential and inspiring Ballymaloe House country hotel and restaurant and the nearby Ballymaloe Cookery School. We dined with pleasure at Chapter One, the most Irish of Dublin's top restaurants, and interviewed its suppliers of beef, fish, vegetables, and cheese.

Almost everywhere we went—even in the north, so lately riven by sectarian violence—we found good things happening: rural entrepreneurs building little businesses around artisanal food production and distribution; restaurants revising their menus to take better advantage of the native bounty, or new ones opening with a sense of Irish-based innovation and adventure; writers delving seriously into the history and culture of Irish food, sometimes finding greater refinement than they had expected or discovering the virtues of the rough foods of their rural ancestors.

Our special issue, which appeared in March 2006, made quite a splash in Ireland. A major American epicurean magazine had praised the quality of Irish food! Tourism Ireland in New York bought up every copy they could find for distribution. Artisan producers and shopowners in Ireland, who often complain of excessive regulation, took copies along to meetings with Irish government and European Community officials as a way of saying, "Look how important what we're doing is." The Irish issue was the last big project Christopher and I did for *Saveur*.

INSTEAD OF HAVING a big New York wedding at Eleven Madison Park, as we'd once considered, Erin and I contrived another plan. One April weekend in 2006, we got married by a county clerk in Naples, Florida—where her mother and stepfather live—and the following month had our wedding blessed in a formal ceremony (Erin wore a wedding dress, and had a maid of honor) at the quirky little Anglican church of St. Mary Woolnoth, in the City of London. My daughters came, as did friends like Dorothy Kalins, Christopher Hirsheimer, the Jausases, Peter and Mary Ward, Jonathan Waxman, Tim Johnston, and Carl Doumani (at whose Napa Valley winery I'd gotten married the first time), and, of course, lots of Erin's family and their close friends. Our Texas singer-songwriter friend Kimmie Rhodes sang "Amazing Grace" as we walked out of the church—which was apposite, as the hymn's lyrics were written by the abolitionist cleric John Newton, rector of St. Mary Woolnoth from 1780 to 1807.

Then we repaired to my old friend Terence Conran's Blueprint Café, overlooking the Thames on the top floor of the Design Museum. We sat at two long tables, set not with flowers but with sprawls of artichokes, asparagus, and other fresh spring vegetables, and the chef, Jeremy Lee, served us a knockout banquet of Scottish langoustines with homemade mayonnaise, pâté de campagne and Middle White pork rillettes, roasted rump of Belted Galloway beef with pickled walnuts, English peas with mint, and Jersey Royal new potatoes, and, in place of a wedding cake—neither Erin nor I is a great lover of dessert—an entire wheel of Mrs. Montgomery's cheddar, topped with several sets of vintage wedding figures, with chocolate truffles on the side for those who needed something sweet.

WHEN I LEFT *SAVEUR* a few months after our London ceremony, I signed a contract to write ten long restaurant pieces a year for my old friend Ruth Reichl at *Gourmet*—not reviews, exactly, but appreciations of individual establishments, chefs, regional food scenes, or culinary genres. It was a perfect job for me, with a generous monthly retainer that paid me more than I would have made if I'd stayed on at *Saveur*. Again, I had a wonderful time, traveling around America and Western Europe, writing stories that were not unlike the big pieces I'd been doing for a dozen years at *Saveur*. I went to Gambero Rosso, in the Tuscan coastal town of San Vincenzo, where Fulvio Pierangelini was cooking some of the best food in Italy. I did pieces on the food and wine of the Valle de Guadalupe in Baja California; on the innovative, vegetable-loving chef Jean-Luc Rabanel in Arles; on the River Café in London and its alumni; on the surprising Mexican food scene in Durham, North Carolina. I ordered and compared the same multicourse dinner at the Guy Savoy restaurants in Paris and Las Vegas (they came out roughly even). I wrote about Jitlada and other wonderful Thai restaurants in Los Angeles and Richard Melman's restaurant empire in Chicago, and revisited my old friends Jaume Subirós at the Hotel Empordà and Jean-Pierre Silva at his beachside L'Ondine in Cannes.

I traveled for other reasons, too. In early 2007, Peter Ward asked me if I'd come back to Nenagh on St. Patrick's Day and help cook a dinner he had planned for the Tipperary Slow Food Convivium. I said sure. Then I started wondering if I'd lost my mind. I love to cook, but I usually do it just for myself and Erin and sometimes my daughters. The last time I'd worked on a restaurant line was eight or nine years earlier, when I'd gone into the kitchen at Chez Panisse one night to assist in the production of a dinner from *Saveur Cooks Authentic Italian*. (No one was dazzled by my technique.) Now Peter had put me in charge of the main course for sixty-five paying customers, and I'd be working in the kitchen with a couple of practiced professionals. What was I thinking? Peter had said that there'd be whole lamb shoulders, and I wasn't even sure what to do with those; the only bone-in lamb I'd ever cooked had been legs or chops (or racks). Before I left for Nenagh, I called up Jonathan Waxman and asked him what a real cook would do with lamb shoulders. "Roast them in a hot oven for about an hour," he said, "then lower the heat and let them cook for about three more hours." Okay, I figured, that didn't sound too hard.

My fellow cooks were two people I'd gotten to know on earlier trips around Ireland: a pretty young blond chef, cookbook writer, and TV personality from West Cork named Clodagh McKenna, and an amiable chef-fisherman from the Aran Islands named Enda Conneely. I arrived from New York around lunchtime the day of the dinner, and we consulted on the menu over coffee and scones. The first course was going to be simple, a salad of local organic greens with a few slices of jamón serrano that one of Peter's Slow Food buddies in Spain had sent him. Enda had arrived with a burlap sack full of Galway Bay mussels and a box of wrasse— scrawny little fish with not much commercial value, generally kept by fishermen for their own consumption—that he'd salt-cured himself in the traditional manner. He planned to steam the mussels and flavor them with herb butter, and to make his version of an ancient Irish fishermen's dish of chopped-up wrasse mixed with onions in a floury white sauce, served with boiled potatoes. "Irish brandade," I suggested. "Except that there's no garlic," he replied.

"Isn't that what makes it Irish?" I asked. Dessert would be Clodagh's rhubarb crumble and also a bombe of crumbled meringues mixed with whipped cream and rhubarb, followed by a selection of Tipperary cheeses.

I went into the kitchen to have a look at the lamb, which came from a nearby organic farm. The meat was in the form of half a dozen pretty little shoulders, with collarbones attached, weighing no more than five or six pounds each. There wasn't a fresh herb in the kitchen except for some little branches of green bay leaves, but there was a big waxed-paper-lined cardboard box full of lovely, sticky Irish butter. I massaged the shoulders with it and splashed on some olive oil and some lemon juice (from a bottle), then seasoned the meat with abandon with Maldon salt and ground black pepper. Then I put the shoulders into baking pans and slid them into Peter's three-tiered convection oven at the equivalent of 475 degrees Fahrenheit for about an hour to get them nice and brown. Next, I lowered the heat to about 375, added some water to the pans, put some chopped-up onions and peeled, crushed garlic cloves around the sides of the meat, and threw in some of those bay leaves.

I'd brought along a pound of very smoky pepper bacon that I'd gotten shipped up from Velma Willett's Lazy H Smoke House in Kirbyville, Texas, shortly before I left New York, and I cooked this crisp, to be crumbled, later, over the colcannon that Enda was going to make. I set the bacon grease aside in a little earthenware bowl, intending to mix it in with the root vegetables—parsnips, carrots, and celeriac—that I was going to roast, attaching a note to the bowl reading, "Do Not Touch—Valuable East Texas Bacon Grease." Then I went off to check in to my hotel and take a nap, leaving the lamb to roast, with Enda and Clodagh agreeing to baste it for me.

About three hours later, I pulled the lamb out of the oven, set it aside to rest, and put all the pan juices, along with the onions and garlic and bay leaves and some middling Valpolicella that was sitting around, into a big pot. I brought the mixture to a boil, then reduced it to a steady simmer and let it cook down while Enda worked on his wrasse, Clodagh helped clean the mussels, and I started chopping up the root vegetables and tossed them with olive oil and butter and plenty of salt, throwing in some chopped-up baby leeks. I put the vegetables into the convection oven to roast, sadly without the Texas bacon grease. The dishwasher, like so many people in the service economy in Ireland, was Polish, and apparently didn't or couldn't read my note; when I got back to the kitchen after my nap, the bowl was empty and clean.

As the guests gathered in the shop, Enda made his colcannon in a big industrial mixer. Then he and I pulled the lamb off the bones with our hands, in big shards, and put it back in the roasting pans to reheat briefly in the oven. When it came time to serve, Enda and Clodagh and I start filling big oval serving bowls—a mound of meat at one end, with the sauce ladled over it, a big mass of colcannon in the middle, and heaps of the root vegetables on the other end. Out the food went. Almost immediately, the empty bowls started coming back to the kitchen—more please! We sent out the rest, leaned back for a few minutes and drank some wine, and then started plating Clodagh's desserts. When those, too, had been consumed, we ventured out into the dining areas. People applauded. They smiled, they called out, they wanted to talk. We circulated, answered questions, accepted compliments.

Then we perched in the front of the shop with a bottle of Jameson. Sweat was soaking my shirt beneath my apron, and I'd nicked the tip of my left index finger trimming baby leeks and burned a spot the size of a quarter on the back of my right hand on the roof of the convection oven, but it occurred to me as I sat there that I hadn't felt so good in months. It also occurred to me that I wasn't done with Ireland yet, that the surprise of Irish cooking—how good it could be, how varied it was—would make a book as unexpected, in its way, as *Catalan Cuisine* had been.

That fall, I had drinks with my agent and Bill LeBlond, the cookbook editor from Chronicle Books. Chronicle had recently published an attractive tome, with about 250 recipes and many gorgeous photographs, called *The Country Cooking of France*, by the esteemed director of the La Varenne cooking schools, Anne Willan. Chronicle wanted to extend the franchise, and Bill asked if I'd be interested in tackling *The Country Cooking of Italy*. Well, okay, I said, but what I'd really like to do is a book about Irish food. To his credit, he didn't fall off his barstool laughing. In fact, once I'd explained a little about what I'd found in Ireland and sent him a copy of the Irish issue of *Saveur*, he offered me a two-book deal: first something on Ireland, then, once that was out of the way, the Italian book. I figured that he meant a modest little volume in the first case, but it turned out that he'd decided I should give Ireland the Country Cooking treatment, too.

Over the next year, I made half a dozen more trips to Ireland, spending probably two more months there, cumulatively, meeting more people, visiting more corners of the island, eating more good (and sometimes not so good) food. I logged many hours in the National Library in Dublin going through handwritten recipe books and folders of loose-leaf recipes in the estate papers from eighteenth- and nineteenth-century English and Anglo-Irish manor houses all over Ireland. I spoke with an archaeologist, a baker, several butchers, even an orchardist who was trying to grow French wine grapes a few miles from the Dublin airport. And, of course, I spent many more hours at Country Choice and at home with Peter and Mary. In between trips, I worked on the book at home, and gradually shaped it into something I could be proud of. Christopher had a good-size inventory of outtakes from our earlier travels to Ireland, and she and her colleague, Melissa Hamilton, made a long trip back to fill in the holes. They also helped test the recipes, especially the surprisingly elaborate and refined ones I had discovered in those old collections from grand estates.

The Country Cooking of Ireland was published in late 2009. Peter threw me a splendid party at Country Choice, and I did countless interviews in Ireland and America both. More than one interviewer asked me how a putative expert on the cooking of Catalonia and other Mediterranean regions like myself could be so passionate about Irish food. "Good food is good food," I'd reply.

The book won James Beard Awards in 2010 as Best International Cookbook and Cookbook of the Year, and the 2011 Best International Cookbook prize from the International Association of Culinary Professionals. By that time, I had finished the project Chronicle had originally wanted me to do, too, and *The Country Cooking of Italy* came out in the fall of 2011. It was a very different kind of book from its predecessor, not so much an account of culinary discovery as a record of the food I'd eaten over more than forty years of visits to Italy. Maybe partly for that reason, though it was well reviewed and got nominated for several awards, it has never sold as well as the Irish book—which, as Chuck Berry once observed in another context, goes to show you never can tell.

MY AGENT HAD CLEVERLY MANAGED to get me working on two parallel tracks as an author: My contract for the Country Cooking books specified that I could work simultaneously on other projects that were narrative in nature, as opposed to cookbooks, and that Chronicle's option on my next work, whatever that might be, applied only to books built around recipes. Once I'd signed up to write about Ireland and Italy, I took a look at the respective deadlines for the two and realized that I might be able to sneak another book in between them.

For a couple of years, I'd been thinking about Ferran Adrià, the then newly ascendant Catalan chef whose elBulli, on a small cove called Cala Montjoi, near the Costa Brava town of Roses, was starting to get called the best restaurant in the world. His new celebrity aside, I knew enough about him at that point to know that he, like elBulli itself, had an interesting story, and I wondered if there might not be a market for a biography of the man, interwoven with a history of the place.

I've recounted at length elsewhere how I met Ferran and gradually got to know him, and how eventually—with the help of our mutual friend José Andrés—I convinced him to let me write a book about him. I finished my Irish book in early 2009, then was able to focus on what was to become *Ferran: The Inside Story of El Bulli and the Man Who Reinvented Food* for more than a year before addressing *The Country Cooking of Italy*. I learned the history of elBulli—how it began life in 1961 as a mini–golf course built by a German doctor and his Slovakian wife, evolved into a beach bar, then a grillroom, then a restaurant serving sophisticated French-style nouvelle cuisine. I followed Ferran's story from his childhood in L'Hospitalet de Llobregat, just next to Barcelona, to his first cooking jobs, which he took for beer and disco money, to his days as a cook in the Spanish navy, which in turn led to an apprenticeship at elBulli. I heard, from Ferran and many of his former colleagues, what life was like at this isolated place, unloved by the old-school Spanish critics, before it started to earn international acclaim, and I followed Ferran's path as he discovered his own cooking style and eventually, as one longtime friend put it to me, "left the planet."

And of course I spent a lot of time at elBulli. Ferran opened the restaurant to me, inviting me to come anytime, go anywhere, ask anybody anything, observe and make notes on whatever I wanted. For days at a time, on one trip after another, I'd arrive at Cala Montjoi in the afternoon, park myself with my laptop at Ferran's big worktable in the kitchen, and record everything I saw and heard. Sometimes Ferran would be in a talkative mood. He would sit with me and gab, interspersing bits of professional philosophy with anecdotes about his and the restaurant's past. And he'd make jokes. One night, as I was sharing in the "family meal," the always savory but unfailingly traditional repast he served his staff every evening, he exclaimed, "Colman! Tonight you're eating at elBulli!" "I'm waiting for the next thirty courses," I replied.

In fact, I did eat at elBulli, in the dining room, maybe half a dozen times while I was working on the book, and I came to see the restaurant as a magical place. Behind the scenes, the kitchen was comparatively quiet and very regimented. There was lots of repetitive prep work early in the workday, especially for the *stagiaires* (unpaid apprentices)—hours spent hunched over long stainless steel tables peeling pine nuts, meticulously shelling miniature fava beans, cleaving rabbit skulls in two and scooping out the brains. During the service, all the chefs and cooks and stagiaires moved through the room with what Micaela Livingston of Ports used to call the ant patterns, an interweaving flow of purposeful movement, fast and efficient and without collision. There was no open flame, no pyrotechnics literal or otherwise—the cooking was done with induction coils, circulating water baths, and sometimes liquid nitrogen (if that counts as cooking)—and the aromas of anything that smelled like food were rare. All this restrained precision, however, exploded into the dining room in a vivid display of unexpected flavors, textures, and, yes, aromas; the machinery behind the curtain somehow produced a spectacular, jazzy culinary show.

The building that housed the restaurant sometimes surprised people. Old mixed with new. You entered past an oxidized iron stele bearing the restaurant's name, through an iron-slat gate. You approached the front door through a parking area that suggested a Zen rock garden, then walked up broad concrete-slab steps, from which you could see into the cool, calm, modern kitchen through a huge bay window. Through the door, next to a piece of painted stone inset into the wall that depicted a French bulldog (a *bulli*), you found yourself walking past a pretty, partly covered terrace giving onto the cove. It looked like the kind of place where you could have sat and ordered a pizza and a bottle of rosé.

The dining room had whitewashed walls, dark wood-beam ceilings, and floors inset with decorative Catalan tiles. The tables were large and draped in white; the red-cushioned wood-frame chairs in one room resembled those you might find in any mid-range Spanish restaurant, those in the other were more formal, with tall backs, upholstered with floral faux tapestry. A miscellany of bric-a-brac, old prints, and small paintings decorated the room. In short, there was nothing avant-garde, nothing surrealistic, nothing high-design about it. It seemed comfortable, lived-in, and organic, which it was. I know that the dining room developed this way over the years, and that at one point Ferran and his partner in the restaurant, Juli Soler, made a conscious decision not to remodel or redecorate the place. I always wondered, though, if leaving the place the way it had become was a subliminal expression on Ferran's part of his belief that his revolutionary cooking was somehow intimately connected with the tradition it seemed to have left far behind.

I was enamored of elBulli, in any case. I know that I was in an extraordinary position: The restaurant so many other food lovers could only dream about, or at most would be likely to visit once in their (and its) life—the restaurant that first earned Spain its reputation as a gastronomic capital, and that influenced and inspired chefs all over the world—was open to me anytime, especially if I was willing to sit in the kitchen. And the dining experience that must have intimidated so many customers, at least at first, was never anything but a great pleasure to me—even when I didn't like some of the individual courses, as often happened. But there was something so warm and right and confident about elBulli to me, that the moment I stepped through the door, I always felt immediately at home, in the same way that I had at Chasen's, Scandia, and Eldorado Petit.

I had my last meal as a customer at elBulli about eight months before it closed. Though the restaurant was generally open only for dinner (and open at all only for about half the year, at that), it would occasionally serve lunch instead—usually when Ferran had other obligations in the evening. I'd invited my old friend Jonathan Waxman to elBulli as a birthday present, and we ended up there one crisp, bright autumn day. As usual, the meal was dazzling, challenging, occasionally maddening; Jonathan might be best known for his straightforward American and Italian cooking (roast chicken is his signature dish), but he absolutely got what Ferran was up to. "People who've never been here and who criticize Ferran's food just don't understand what he's doing," he said. After lunch, we repaired to the terrace to sip Armagnac and smoke cigars. Juli, who was upstairs in his office, noticed us and started hooting and waving. Then he came down and joined us, and we sat and talked and drank and smoked until the light faded.

I'd long since finished my book about Ferran by the time el-Bulli served its last meal, and I hadn't been back since that afternoon with Jonathan, but I was at the party in the restaurant parking lot after dinner service on the last night of its existence as a restaurant (the site is being transmogrified, with the help of an avant-garde Catalan architect, into a foundation for gastronomic studies, and Ferran regularly insists, for that reason, that "elBulli is not closed!"). Ferran had assembled a large crowd of journalists, suppliers, faithful customers, and colleagues, including an A-list of chefs who had worked in his kitchen over the years—among them José Andrés, Grant Achatz, René Redzepi, Massimo Bottura, Joan Roca, Andoni Aduriz, and Carles Abellan, all of them now culinary stars themselves. The Rolling Stones—Juli's favorites—were playing over the sound system set up in the parking lot, and there were two bars with free-flowing wine and liquor, and stands dispensing Joselito ham, smoked salmon, lightly cooked shrimp and crayfish, and other snacks. Ferran looked tired, his eyes glazed, his brow sweaty, but he joined in the festivities enthusiastically. "How do you feel?" I asked him. "I'm very happy," he said, and I believed him. I wandered back into the now quiet restaurant for the last time, not quite believing that it wouldn't fill up again the next night with quiet, focused chefs and dazzled diners, not quite believing that the magic was gone. I was glad that Ferran was very happy. I was very sad.

Envoi

I'M NOT AT THE AGE YET WHEN ALL I CAN DO IS SIT on the front porch and daydream about the good times past, but I do seem to spend more time than I used to reflecting on my life. One thing I think about a lot is how lucky I am. I've been able to travel all over Europe and America and beyond, eating and drinking well, meeting wonderful people, learning all manner of things (and not just about food and wine)—and to do all this under circumstances that barely still obtain today. The magazine budgets that paid for so many of my adventures are largely a thing of the past, as magazines themselves have grown stingy or been replaced by tightfisted "new media" (I doubt very much that anybody goes to Guy Savoy on Arianna Huffington's dime). Book advances are now typically split into three or four parts, meaning less up-front capital to pay for research trips, and thus such trips become fewer and shorter.

More than that, in a sense there's less reason to travel: the rare culinary treats I used to trek thousands of miles to seek out in Alicante or Saint-Rémy, Casablanca or Camogli, are now available on Amazon or even at the A & P, and the most famous chefs of Europe and beyond will be cooking at your local food festival this Saturday night. The popular food-based travel shows these days seem mostly dedicated to the consumption of live insects or monkey organs—connoisseurship as fraternity initiation ritual. I may have been less adventurous, but I can't help feeling that I got the better deal in my pursuit of the perfect trenette al pesto or the ultimate jamón ibérico.

Did my culinary travels ultimately cost me a couple of marriages? Probably. Mire me in debt and thicken my waistline? Sure. Did writing all those articles and books based on my explorations keep me at my typewriter and then my computer when I should have been relaxing, exercising, spending time with my family? I'm afraid so. But while I can't flippantly just say, "Oh, it was worth it," I can certainly maintain that once I realized that these wonderful opportunities were open to me, I couldn't possibly have ignored them.

I STILL TRAVEL A LOT, though my trips now rarely last longer than four or five days (and Erin often comes with me, which helps with that travel-vs.-marriage issue). One thing that has changed in my life, though, is that, quite possibly for the first time since my parents started taking me to Chasen's all those years ago, there is no one restaurant at the center of my life. I have favorite restaurants in various cities, of course, but there is no single place I go to regularly, no single establishment that seems to define this period of my existence. This is an unfamiliar situation for me, but one that has come about for reasons both practical and geographical: I'm working a full-time desk job again, running The Daily Meal, a big food and drink website in Manhattan, and its demands are such that I almost never have time to go out for lunch the way I did at *Saveur.* After work, Erin and I like to get on the first train we can back to Connecticut, and, frankly, there is not an abundance of interesting restaurants around where we live. These days, we usually prefer to cook and eat at home anyway, especially in warm weather, when I can grill out on our terrace, surrounded by a small forest of tomato and chile plants and assorted herbs, a glass of good red wine at hand.

I can't imagine never having a restaurant at the heart of things again, though. I miss the promise of dependable good food, the warm welcome, the sense of contentment that floods over me when I walk into the right place, *knowing* that it's the right place. As I've reported in the preceding pages, many of the restaurants that once afforded all this to me are gone, or have changed too much with time. The handful that remain, in something resembling the form in which I first knew them, are far from where I now live and work.

I haven't given up restaurants, by any means—Erin and I dine out at least once or twice a week, and we build our travel around anticipated meals, just as I've always done—but my usual table these days isn't in a restaurant at all: It's the big white farmhouse one in our dining room, in front of a window that looks out on a thicket of fir trees and a patch of sky. I'm sure I'll find another restaurant home one of these days, but for now, in my real home, my usual table suits me fine.

INDEX